Tributes
Volume 45

Mathematical Foundations of
Software Engineering
Essays in Honour of Tom Maibaum on the
Occasion of his 70th Birthday and Retirement

Volume 35
Language, Evolution and Mind. Essays in Honour of Anne Reboul
Pierre Saint-Germier, ed.

Volume 36
Logic, Philosophy of Mathematics and their History.
Essays in Honor of W. W. Tait
Erich H. Reck, ed.

Volume 37
Argumentation-based Proofs of Endearment. Essays in Honor of Guillermo R. Sima
on the Occasion of his 70th Birthday
Carlos I. Chesñevar, Marcelo A. Falappa, Eduardo Fermé, Alejandro J. García, Ana
G. Maguitman, Diego C. Martínez, Maria Vanina Martinez, Ricardo O. Rodríguez, a
Gerardo I. Simari, eds.

Volume 38
Logic, Intelligence and Artifices. Tributes to Tarcísio H. C. Pequeno
Jean-Yves Béziau, Francicleber Ferreira, Ana Teresa Martins and
Marcelino Pequeno, eds.

Volume 39
Word Recognition, Morphology and Lexical Reading. Essays in Honour of
Cristina Burani
Simone Sulpizio, Laura Barca, Silvia Primativo and Lisa S. Arduino, eds

Volume 40
Natural Arguments. A Tribute to John Woods
Dov Gabbay, Lorenzo Magnani, Woosuk Park and Ahti-Veikko Pietarinen, eds.

Volume 41
On Kreisel's Interests. On the Foundations of Logic and Mathematics
Paul Weingartner and Hans-Peter Leeb, eds.

Volume 42
Abstract Consequence and Logics. Essays in Honor of Edelcio G. de Souza
Alexandre Costa-Liete, ed.

Volume 43
Judgements and Truth. Essays in Honour of Jan Woleński
Andrew Schumann, ed.

Volume 44
A Question is More Illuminating than the Answer: A Festschrift for Paulo A.S.
Veloso
Edward Hermann Haeusler, Luiz Carlos Pinheiro Dias Pereira and Jorge
Petrucio Viana, eds.

Volume 45
Mathematical Foundations of Software Engineering. Essays in Honour of Tom
Maibaum on the Occasion of his 70th Birthday and Retirement
Nazareno Aguirre, Valentin Cassano, Pablo Castro and Ramiro Demasi, eds.

Tributes Series Editor
Dov Gabbay   dov.gabbay@kcl.ac.uk

Mathematical Foundations of Software Engineering

Essays in Honour of Tom Maibaum on the Occasion of his 70th Birthday and Retirement

edited by

Nazareno Aguirre

Valentin Cassano

Pablo Castro

Ramiro Demasi

ISBN 978-1-84890-399-9

College Publications
Scientific Director: Dov Gabbay
Managing Director: Jane Spurr

http://www.collegepublications.co.uk

Cover design by Laraine Welch

Contents

Preface

Describing in just a few pages the impact and long lasting effect that Tom has had on our careers, on the Department of Computing at the University of Río Cuarto, and on the many colleagues who have had the chance to meet him and work with him is not an easy task. Nevertheless, the story needs someone to write it, we will give it a try.

Tom's strong ties with Argentina started in the mid 80s. The initial connection was due to Armando Haeberer. Tom and Armando's relationship began in Brazil, where they both coincided for a long period of time. Armando was a distinguished Argentinian computer scientist who was, at the time, working with Paulo Veloso at Pontifícia Universidade Católica do Rio de Janeiro (PUC). How Tom made it to Brazil is part of a larger story between the Universities of Toronto, Waterloo –Tom's place of work at the time– and PUC –where Tom was traveling regularly as a Visiting Professor. Long story short, Tom and Armando became very close friends and research collaborators. They worked together on various different subjects, including formal approaches to software specification and epistemological principles of software engineering (Tom and Armando's joint journey and academic endeavors are wonderfully recollected by Tom himself in [1]). The collaboration between Tom, Armando and Paulo Veloso on relational approaches to software specification led to their joint work on Fork Algebras. This work also involved other Argentinian researchers, in particular Gabriel Baum and Marcelo Frias, two important figures in the connections between Tom and Argentina.

The relationship between Tom and Río Cuarto also involves Jorge Aguirre. This is where it all becomes intertwined. Jorge was the designer of the Computer Science degrees at the University of Río Cuarto (UNRC) and a close friend and colleague of Armando's; Gabriel Baum was a Visiting Professor at UNRC, and had a key role in the development of the Computer Science Department; and Marcelo Frias, who in the late 90s finished his PhD under Armando's supervision, had returned to Argentina and initiated a research group to work on relational methods in Computer Science.

It was actually Marcelo who suggested that Nazareno Aguirre, then an undergraduate student finishing his Licenciatura at UNRC (under Gabriel's supervision, on Fork Algebras), should approach Tom to do his PhD. Tom was very kind to offer Nazareno to do a PhD in London in 1999, under really attractive conditions. Tom was at the time moving from Imperial College to King's College London. The move would give Tom more time to do research after a decade as Head of the Department of Computing at Imperial. Tom suggested as a PhD topic the design of a logic for reasoning about reconfigurable component-based systems. This seemed very exciting to Nazareno. Moreover, funding for covering a PhD scholarship was taken care by one of Tom's research

1

projects. This sealed the deal. Nazareno went to do his PhD under Tom's supervision. By 2004, Nazareno finished his PhD, returned to UNRC, and the work with Tom very quickly shaped a significant part of the research carried out in the Department of Computing at UNRC.

The next PhD student from Río Cuarto that Tom supervised was Pablo Castro. It was 2005, and Tom had just moved to McMaster University, in Canada, hired to cover the place left by David Parnas, who had recently moved to the University of Limerick. Pablo was also supervised by Gabriel Baum in his undergraduate degree thesis, and had shown during his Licenciatura a special inclination to formal aspects of software engineering, including epistemological aspects of software development. Pablo worked under Tom's supervision on fault tolerance, more precisely on the development of deontic logics for reasoning about fault-tolerant software. This was a subject that Tom found very interesting since the early 90s, and it was a great opportunity to develop it with Pablo, a mathematically oriented student. Pablo finished his PhD in 2009, and decided to return to UNRC, broadening the research areas of the Department of Computing.

Tom visited the University of Rio Cuarto on a couple of occasions. One of those was in 2008 during a Summer School on Computing –Rio 2008– organized by the Department of Computing. The Rio 2008 School had Tom as one of its invited lecturers, and was the place where he met Ramiro Demasi and Valentin Cassano, his two final Argentinian PhD students. Tom's course at Rio 2008 was entitled 'The Methodology of Formal Specification'. At that time Ramiro and Valentin were finishing their Licenciatura degrees under the supervision of Nazareno. In particular, Ramiro was working on the parallelization of a model-checking tool based on relational algebra. In turn, Valentin was working on proving temporal properties of CommUnity designs. The work involved adding temporal properties to the CommUnity language and verifying, using a model checker, whether these properties were true of programs written in this language. The Rio 2008 School gave Ramiro and Valentin the opportunity to meet Tom and to establish a connection that ultimately led to both of them pursuing a PhD under his supervision, at McMaster University in Canada. Studying under Tom's supervision was attractive not only at an academic level, but also at a personal one. On the personal side, it provided Ramiro and Valentin the opportunity to get to travel and study abroad, learning not only a new culture, but also a new way of "doing things". On the academic side, Tom was not only not short of interesting topics to explore, but also very willing to offer his students the academic freedom to investigate new areas. This breadth of topics and academic freedom is reflected rather succinctly in Ramiro's and Valentin's PhD theses. Ramiro's PhD thesis focused on the problem of automatically synthesizing fault-tolerant systems from logical specifications, provided in a branching-time temporal logic equipped with further deontic modalities. In turn, Valentin's PhD thesis involved an analysis of the logical foundations of Default Reasoning (a non-monotonic logic originally developed in the field of Artificial Intelligence) and its presentation in the setting of entailment systems, with some applications to Software Engineering. It goes without saying that the years studying under Tom's advice were also full of great opportunities: traveling to conferences across the world, enjoying good food, and many great anecdotes.

At some point in time, the majority of the PhDs in the Department of Computing at UNRC had either been supervised by Tom, or worked in close collaboration with Tom. This gave the Department of Computing at UNRC a new perspective on research in Formal Methods and Software Engineering. This had a profound impact in the growth of the Department.

Of course, Tom's ties to Argentina are not restricted to the Department of Computing at UNRC. They are much larger, and were recognized through the 'Dr. Luis Federico Leloir Prize', that Tom was awarded in 2013. This prize was installed in 2010 by Argentina's Ministry of Science and Technology. It is named after Dr. Luis Federico Leloir, to pay tribute to one of Argentina's most prominent scientists, who received the Nobel Prize in 1970. The awarded scientists are selected via a consultation to leading scientific and academic figures from Argentina and abroad. The prize recognizes those scientists who significantly contributed to strengthening international cooperation with Argentina in science, technology and innovation. Tom is one of the first recipients of the prize, and one of the very few who have received the prize in the field of Computing.

It is obvious from the lines above the enormous appreciation that we have for Tom. Nevertheless, this Festschrift would be incomplete without recognizing, at least in a very short form, Tom's academic achievements. Tom has worked extensively and for a very long period of time on the theory of specification and its applications in various contexts. These ventures started at the Pontifícia Universidade Católica do Rio de Janeiro – where Tom has been an Honorary Professor since 1992 – with Armando Haeberer, Paulo Veloso, Roberto Lins de Carvalho, and Carlos José Pereira de Lucena. This work has mainly revolved around a syntactical First Order Logic approaches to software specification, and dealt with a wide range of specification issues, including parameterization, refinement, and, eventually, modularity. As already mentioned, Tom has also worked on a foundation for software engineering based on the epistemological principles advocated by Carnap. More recently, Tom has been involved in the areas of software and system certification and model driven engineering. He has worked closely with Mark Lawford and Alan Wassyng on establishing the Software Certification Consortium with the aim of promoting awareness of safety issues for safety-critical systems, and to act as a coordinator for research on this topic.

To pay tribute to Tom in 2019, we organized in the Department of Computing at UNRC an 'International Symposium on the Mathematical Foundations of Software Engineering'. The Symposium took place from February 16 to February 17, at UNRC, in Río Cuarto, Córdoba, Argentina. The choice of the place was not without thought. It is our workplace and home, and is deeply influenced by Tom's research and view on academia. It is worth noticing that

3

all of us who studied under Tom's supervision stayed in academia, and returned to our alma matter. Moreover, Argentina is also a place that Tom has greatly enjoyed each and every time he visited (in particular, the countless asados and great wines).

The Symposium got together various researchers from Argentina and abroad and included technical presentations on formal aspects of Computing and Software Engineering, as well as social gatherings. The contributions to this Festschrift stem from this Symposium, and tell yet another part of Tom's story: the influence that he has had on the development of formal methods for software development. We wish to thank all contributors for their work, and the patience they had with us while we were putting this volume together. So, without further ado, let us provide a brief description of each contribution:

In *"Living" and Often Laughing with Tom Maibaum,* Alan Wassyng and Mark Lawford describe their collaboration with Tom in McMaster University. They discuss in particular their success in developing a research group on formal methods in Canada, and interesting projects applying formal methods to automotive software. This article provides a detailed depiction of the time Tom spent at McMaster University.

In *Exotic Logics, Specifications, Operas and Much Much More,* Axel van Lamsweerde looks back on delightful anecdotes with Tom, while at the same time detailing their mutual interest in using logical formalisms to express software requirements.

In *My Three Shared Values with Tom Maibaum,* Carlo Ghezzi expresses some academic and personal shared values with Tom Maibaum, in particular the formal vision on software development, and the shared love for classical music and opera.

In *Integrating Deduction and Model Finding in a Language Independent Setting,* Carlos López Pombo and Agustín Martínez Suñé discuss a categorical formalization of proof systems, that can be used to prove the existence of models. This work is inspired by Tom's categorical view on software engineering.

In *A Rely-Guarantee Specification of Mixed-Criticality Scheduling,* Cliff Jones and Alan Burns present a formal approach for reasoning about mixed scheduling. The paper shows the usefulness of formal methods for reasoning about interesting practical problems in Computing, a view shared by Tom and Cliff.

In *On Refining Choreographies,* Emilio Tuosto, Hernán Melgratti, and Ugo de'Liguoro investigate the use of categories for formalizing choreographies (components communicating via message exchange). This work shows the power of categories for capturing the dynamic structure of software systems.

In *πPML: A Product-Centred Formal Language for Business Processes,* Germán Regis and Marcelo Frias define and formalize πPML, a π-calculus based adaptation of Tom's PPML (Product/Process Modelling Lan-

4

guage), a language for business process modeling with support for product property specification with support for product property specification.

In *Logic and Formal Methods in Model-Driven Engineering*, Kevin Lano introduces and illustrates the use of formal methods in Model-Driven Engineering. Kevin and Tom have had a fruitful interaction on this topic, from their common years at Imperial College and King's College.

In *A Personal Perspective on Logic and Category Theory in the Foundations of Software Engineering*, Paulo Alencar presents a personal account of how Tom has influenced his research through Tom's contributions to logic and category theory, in the context of the foundations of software engineering.

In *Assurance of Assurance, Bridging the Great Assurance Divide with Modus Ponens and Cartesian Closed Categories*, Zinovy Diskin describes the use of Cartesian Closed Categories for reasoning about software assurance. Zinovy describes the advantages of having at hand the abstract machinery of categories. This work is deeply influenced by Tom's works on software assurance.

In *Effectiveness and Programmability*, Javier Blanco and Pío García present an intentional account of computation that distinguishes between effectiveness and programmability, as two essential aspects of Computing.

Nazareno, Pablo, Ramiro and Valentin.

References

[1] T. S. E. Maibaum. In memoriam armando martín haeberer: 4 january 1947 - 11 february 2003. In *Formal Methods at the Crossroads (From Panacea to Foundational Support), Revised Papers from the 10th Anniversary Colloquium of the International Institute for Software Technology of The United Nations University (UNU/IIST)*, volume 2757 of *LNCS*, pages 1–25. Springer, 2002.

This page is intentionally left in blank.

"Living" and Often Laughing with Tom Maibaum

Alan Wassyng

McMaster Centre for Software Certification, Department of Computing and Software
McMaster University, Canada
wassyng@mcmaster.ca

Mark Lawford

McMaster Centre for Software Certification, Department of Computing and Software
McMaster University, Canada
lawford@mcmaster.ca

Abstract

This is a blow-by-blow account of about 14 years working with Tom Maibaum at Mc-Master University. It serves as a record of what our group lived through and achieved, thanks in large part to Tom joining us in 2004. We had some tough times, but lots of fun and successes. We hope that we helped to provide a strong foundation for our Department (Computing and Software) and the Centre we co-founded (McMaster Centre for Software Certification).

1 Early Days

Tom Maibaum was already an extremely successful academic when he came to join us at McMaster University in 2004. He was an acknowledged leader in the formal methods community, and had served as Head of Department of Computing at Imperial College and of Computer Science at Kings College! Since Tom grew up in the Toronto area, returning to Canada had significant attraction – and some of his immediate family still lived in Toronto. The Faculty of Engineering and the Department of Computing and Software (CAS) also held out the promise of supporting an application for a Canada Research Chair (Tier I) in the Foundations of Software Engineering. Of course, the most important attraction was to work with us!

2 Finding Our Way

Once Tom arrived at McMaster he was off to a quick start. His Canada Research Chair (CRC) was approved and funded, and he was soon at the centre of research activities in the Department. He was keen to start a Formal Methods group with other researchers at neighbouring universities, and there began a series of meetings to explore funding opportunities. When Dave Parnas was at McMaster, he formed a research group called the Software Quality Research Laboratory (SQRL), and when Dave left, Alan took over as Acting Director of SQRL. After some discussion, we decided to focus our research activity on *Software Certification*, i.e., the certification of software intensive systems. We used SQRL to spearhead funding initiatives targeted at software certification – primarily safety certification. In those early years, 2004/2005, safety certification was not yet a priority for many of the potential industry partners we contacted. We also seemed to have a strange power. Companies that were receptive to starting funded projects suddenly got merged, taken over, moved their R&D out of Canada and went bankrupt. It was not really Tom's fault! It got to be a talking point in our Department, and there was a situation when we were exploring a project with GM, and our Administrator in CAS, Laurie LeBlanc, noted that at least we could not force GM into bankruptcy. This was shortly before the financial crisis in 2008 that forced GM into creditor protection and a bailout from the Canadian and American governments. Ha!

By 2006 we had a few small successes that were encouraging. One was a grant from IBM that included an IBM BladeCenter QS20, to study the use of multi-core processors onboard cars. The other was a Canadian Foundation for Innovation (CFI) grant to develop a large, high resolution, multi-screen display. This was a project with our colleague William Farmer. However, we were still experiencing some setbacks in attracting large funding.

In 2007 life changed. There was much more interest in safety certification of software intensive systems, and we were involved in what became known as *The Pacemaker Grand Challenge*. Through Dave Parnas, we had met a colleague, Brian Larson, at Guidant Corporation. The company manufactures cardiac pacemakers, and Brian invited us to visit Guidant as a start to a possible collaboration on rigorous approaches to safety for pacemakers. We never did get to collaborate on a project. Boston Scientific took over Guidant, and Brian managed to organize the release of a slightly modified requirements document of a (then) 10 year old pacemaker. This was as close to a real industrial requirements specification as it is possible to get into the public domain. It was released under the condition that its usage for research was to be undertaken by SQRL at McMaster, and that SQRL would be responsible for dealing with questions from interested academics etc.

As useful as The Pacemaker Challenge proved to be, there was even better to come. Brian also challenged us with the idea of starting a consortium that would discuss formal, rigorous approaches to the certification of software intensive systems. We loved the idea, and a few of us started planning what was to become *The Software Certification Consortium* (SCC). We held the first meeting of the SCC in 2007, in the offices of the Software Engineering Institute (SEI) in Arlington, USA. SEI made available the space, and our VP Research at McMaster, Mo Elbestawi, provided funding for lunches and refreshments for the two-day meeting, and for travel and hotel expenses for Alan, Mark & Tom. About 20 people attended that meeting. From the start, the idea was to

8

involve government agencies, industry and academia. SCC proved to be more successful than we could have hoped for. We held our 20th meeting in May 2019!

3 First Major Funding Success

With some proof that interest in certification was growing, we set off with renewed energy to see if we could convince industry partners to join with us in an application to the Ontario Research Fund - for Research Excellence Funding (ORF-RE). This time we managed to avoid bankrupting our industry partners. In 2008 we submitted an ambitious proposal for a 5 year project entitled "Certification of Safety-Critical Software-Intensive Systems", with 8 industrial partners (Biosign Technologies, Legacy Systems International, Ontario Power Generation, Atomic Energy Canada Ltd, Systemware Innovation, AMD, QNX and the Center for Integration of Medicine and Innovative Technology). In addition to McMaster colleagues, we also included colleagues from University of Waterloo and York University. The funding request was $7,440,200.00, and the Principal Investigator (PI) was ... Tom Maibaum. The Pacemaker Challenge and support for SCC were included in the proposal. Many months later, we got exciting news. Our project was to be funded at about $7.1M! This marked a turning point in the visibility of our research group, and completely changed the dynamics of our research. We now had enough funding to set up research groups with enough "mass" to tackle the ambitious goals we had developed with our industry partners. The funding success raised the profile of our Department and suddenly researchers and administration on campus had some idea of who we were and what we were doing. Our PI basked in the glory but was also generous about always including his co-PIs. Sometimes we felt like the Three Stooges, but luckily others on campus referred to us as the Three Amigos. McMaster suddenly even wanted photos of us. See below.

Fig. 1. The Three (Happy) Amigos – Alan, Tom, Mark

As part of the proposal to ORF-RE, we included plans for a new McMaster Institute housed in the Faculty of Engineering. In the proposal it was called the "Centre for Software Certification". With the success of the ORF-RE, this Centre became a reality, and in 2010 (these things take time) the *McMaster Centre for Software Certification* (McSCert) was approved by the McMaster University Senate. Our logo followed soon after – designed by a friend of Tom's.

Fig. 2. The McSCert Logo

4 Success = Way Too Busy

The ORF was advertised by McMaster as a $21M project. That was a little misleading. The way ORF worked was that $\frac{1}{3}$ of the funding came from the government agency – that was real cash. $\frac{1}{3}$ of the $21M came from industry collaborators – and that was a mixture of half cash and half in-kind support. Finally, $\frac{1}{3}$ of the funding was through university support – and that resulted in zero cash available to the project. So, really, the project had a limit of $10,500,000 over 5 years. Not satisfied with $10.5M, Tom was interested in spearheading more projects! He was approached to be the Principal Investigator on a Canada-wide project to investigate the application of Model-Driven Engineering to the development of software in the automotive industry. This was another $10.5M 5 year project, funded by Automotive Partnership Canada, involving General Motors, IBM, Malina Software, 7 universities (British Columbia, McGill, McMaster, Queen's, Toronto, Waterloo and Victoria) and the Centre de Recherche Informatique de Montréal. The project was run out of McSCert at McMaster and the title was *"Network for the Engineering of Complex Software-Intensive Systems for automotive systems"* - commonly known as *NECSIS*. The topic was Model-Driven Engineering for software systems in automotive vehicles.

Tom was now the PI on two major funded projects. Nice! But difficult to contend with. His heart was really in the NECSIS project, and Mark & Alan teased him about it – often. So, we made plans. Mark & Alan were not heavily involved in NECSIS anyway, so Alan concentrated on the ORF-RE project, with Mark's help, Tom focused on NECSIS, and Mark concentrated on another proposal for lab equipment funded by CFI. The proposal was successful and funded $1.7M for equipment to be used in model-driven automotive software

10

research. At that time McMaster welcomed a star researcher in the automotive field, Ali Emadi. We started collaborating with Ali very soon after he joined McMaster, and Ali led the development of a large collaborative proposal with Chrysler. Mark was the obvious one of us to spearhead our contribution to this proposal, and we were included as one of 5 "thrusts" in Ali's proposal to Chrysler and Automotive Partnerships Canada. The project was called *"Leadership in Automotive Powertrain"* (LEAP).

In the same way that the ORF funding facilitated the creation of McSCert, the success of NECSIS and our involvement in LEAP in the automotive domain helped to get us awarded space in the new (at that time) *McMaster Automotive Resource Centre* (MARC), spearheaded by Ali Emadi.

Fig. 3. The McMaster Automotive Resource Centre

About a 15 minute walk off-campus, MARC was designed to provide dedicated space for McMaster Engineering groups conducting advanced automotive R&D. McSCert was allocated space for two very large labs, plus offices, student carrels, meeting areas, a secure lab for work on confidential projects, and a dedicated computer machine room. To Tom's delight, the Faculty of Engineering named this entire area as "Tom Maibaum's Software Lab" – until Mark & Alan got it changed to something far more suitable.

Mark was also the PI on another proposal for lab equipment funded by ORF-RI this time (RI = Research Infrastructure) This proposal was successful and resulted in important acquisitions for our facilities at MARC. The project with Chrysler, now Fiat Chrysler Automobiles (FCA), proved to be more successful than we could ever have imagined. It has resulted in detailed software engineering methods and tools that are truly effective in large industrial scale systems. On top of the research, FCA supports McSCert students as FCA interns, so that we are deeply involved in FCA R&D.

One of the lessons we learned throughout all of this, is that success like this brings responsibilities. The funding treadmill is important if you build an enterprise of any size. We now had a small staff to help run McSCert, as well as researchers and graduate students all dependent on continued funding. Over the years our McSCert managers (Chris George, Deepa Mathews, Paul Joannou and Lynda Bruce) as well as our administrative assistant (Magda Sztajnmec), and part-time technician Derek Lipiec, have transformed our centre into a professional organization, ably backed up by Research Associates (Vera Pantelic & Zinovy Diskin). Luckily, the large projects provided a base, and we managed to attract new funding for projects with IBM, Toyota InfoTech Center, and GM. Tom will be delighted with recent advances in McSCert. Again, he had some impact even in these. Through Tom, the Three Amigos learned that Richard Paige was interested in returning to Canada, and McMaster in particular. We very subtly encouraged Richard, and in January 2020 he joined the Department of Computing and Software (CAS). His arrival has ushered in a splendid revival of energy, reputation and early success. He is now the Director of McSCert, having taken over from Mark who is currently Chair of CAS, who took over from Alan who was the inaugural Director of McSCert. Richard has already spearheaded a successful ORF-RE proposal on automating processes for developing mobile health devices, and a contract to collaborate on safety of medical devices with a local company, Arrayus, who are bringing to market a focused ultrasound machine for non-invasive surgery.

5 Day-to-Day Life with Tom

The previous sections focused on funding. Without the funding we would not have been able to do things that have made our academic lives interesting, fun, and useful. So, what were we able to do?

Students, Post-doctoral Fellows and Research Engineers:

The ORF funding had a huge impact on the number of graduate students we could fund. Mark & Alan already had been co-supervising graduate students, with each other and with colleagues in CAS. Now Tom, bolstered also by funding from his CRC, started co-supervising graduate students while still supervising many on his own. For the first time ever, our group could afford to fund post-doctoral fellows, and this marked a dramatic increase in our ability to produce project deliverables as well as publications. It was exciting to fill a good-sized room for "scrum-type" meetings in order to get progress reports from all the students and faculty involved in McSCert focused research. To date, with the help of many of our faculty colleagues in CAS, McSCert has supported 20 Research Engineers, 20 post-docs, 52 PhD students and 89 Master's students. Having Tom join us attracted excellent students from new locations such as South America. Tom had great contacts in South America, and we were fortunate that some of them recommended a few excellent students come and work with Tom. Contact with at least one of those students

12

still exists! We also routinely employed undergraduate summer research assistants. We still do. Many of them later join us as graduate students. Students are the driving force behind any successful academic unit, and we have been fortunate in attracting excellent students.

Our graduate students have also been in high-demand! They routinely find good positions at leading engineering companies. GM and Fiat Chrysler Automobiles clearly appreciate the capabilities of our students. The long-term funded projects with these companies, starting with NECSIS, has resulted in a steady stream of McSCert graduates being hired. Sometimes even post-docs go that route. So, Tom may have been wise to spend all that effort on NECSIS.

Research:

McSCert is primarily a research and development centre. We focus on how to effectively certify software intensive systems, and how to build such systems to facilitate certification. One question to ask is how did we use the funding and the expertise of our industrial partners to further this research? The answer is "wisely" – but not "brilliantly". Most of the funding, as expected, went to support people. Summer students, graduate students, post-docs, research engineers, research associates, administration assistants, a part-time technician, managers, and visitors. Most of those people also needed computers and software. Over the years we have hosted a steady stream of visitors. Visitors from all over the world, and many of them because of Tom's previous life. As mentioned previously, Tom had long standing connections with South America, primarily Brazil and Argentina. We had a steady stream of talented researchers – Marcelo Frias, Nazareno Aguirre, Carlos Gustavo Lopez Pombo, and Valentin Cassano who first came to our notice as Tom's PhD student. We also spent a lot on travel. An essential component of building a reputation is to be visible. For many of our years together, the Three Amigos travelled in a pack. It would have saved money if we had split attendance at conferences and other meetings between us, but it would not have achieved the same result as telling the world we were a team. It also would not have been as much fun!

What can we look back on in terms of research expertise and contributions?

- Expertise in, and methods for safety assurance of safety critical software intensive systems:
  - Rigorous foundations for assurance cases;
  - Model management for safety assurance;
  - Product focused assurance;
  - Confidence in argumentation in assurance cases;
  - Incremental safety assurance;
  - Assuring safety for systems that use machine learning components
- Expertise in safety analysis of software intensive systems, such as hazard analyses;
- Application of formal methods to practical problems in industry:

13

- ○ Verification techniques;
- ○ Formal specifications;
- ○ Effective use of tabular expressions
- Using separation of concerns to deal with complexity;
- Safety of automotive vehicles;
- Safety of medical devices;
- Safety of nuclear power plants.

Visibility & Reputation:

Our relationships with people we work with; mentoring of students; impact on research – these are the typical outcomes we strive towards. We were lucky! Most of the people we worked with are people we would choose to work with. They still are. It was/is fun sharing with them. Our students are the primary point of our academic lives, and we have interacted with excellent students who were also wonderful people. That was a definite plus. Still is for Mark & Alan. We are proud of our impact in our research areas. It is not easy or even possible to say what would have happened if Tom had not joined us at McMaster. However, there are clear reasons to think that things would have been markedly different. Tom opened doors that may eventually have opened, but not nearly as quickly.

Three obvious successes that affected our subsequent visibility were The Pacemaker Challenge, The Software Certification Consortium, and NECSIS. The Pacemaker Challenge reached formal methods researchers all over the world, and demonstrated to them that formal methods was alive and well at McMaster. It even had a small role in bringing Formal Methods 2006 to Canada, organized by our colleague Emil Sekerinski and others. In 2014 there was a Dagstuhl Seminar (14062) dedicated to the Pacemaker Challenge. The SCC introduced us to a vibrant community dedicated to assuring safety and security of software intensive systems. It also introduced that community to McSCert. Meetings have been running regularly since 2007, sometimes more than once a year. Since 2011 SCC meetings have been co-located with the High Confidence in Software Systems Conference in Annapolis. The 20th meeting of the SCC was held in 2019. Participants in these two-day meetings have included world recognized researchers from government agencies/regulators, industry and academia. And then there was NECSIS. NECSIS started off quite inauspiciously. Mark & Alan were dismayed that at the first of the annual NECSIS meetings, a popular refrain from presenters was "well, this does not have anything to do with automotive, but it could have!" NECSIS recovered from that, and went on to demonstrate to our industry partners, especially GM, that Canada has a wealth of talent and expertise in software engineering.

Traveling with Tom:

We have to say a little more about traveling with Tom. We did that a lot. For most of our years together, we participated in conferences and meetings as a group. Sometimes we traveled separately, but once at the location we spent a

14

lot of time together. Tom knew a lot of people at these conferences, and so conversation was interesting and plentiful. All three of us enjoy good food, and good wine and beer. When you are with Tom, good is not always good enough. Better to go for excellent. The most expensive meal that Alan has ever eaten was in Tom's company. It was a strange day. The three of us (and others from CAS) were participating in FM 2005. Alan arrived in Newcastle first, Mark was due to arrive the next day, and at about midday Tom arrived at the hotel looking agitated. He had left his insulin in London. Well, it was good that Tom knew the health system in the UK. Tom & Alan set off in a taxi to track down insulin. It took hours to achieve. At the end of this a visibly tired Tom announced that we should end the day with a good dinner. He asked the taxi driver for a recommendation and was told that there were two top restaurants in the area. Tom chose one of them. It really was excellent. Except for the bill. The cost for each of Tom & Alan was more than it would normally have cost for all three of us to have a good meal! When we travelled, we also wanted espresso to start the day. (We wanted that even when we did not travel.) Mark solved that problem for us on a number of occasions. He brought his travel espresso pump with him. And pods.

And then there was the actual travel. We have shared many flights, taxis, car rides with Tom. Most of the time they have been just fine. Every now and again there has been a little bit of a hiccup. The problem with the hiccups is that Tom seems to think that they single him out on purpose. The most famous of these was that same trip as the lost insulin. Tom & Alan were flying from Heathrow to Toronto together. When Tom flew from Toronto to London it was just days before the bombings in London. One reaction to that incident was that airlines changed the size of carry-on luggage that could be used. The airlines had been giving out plastic bags for people to transfer their luggage into and then they had to check the carry-on bag. Since Tom had arrived before the bombing, his carry-on was just a little too large. It also had quite sturdy wheels, so it was definitely not squeezable. This is Alan's recollection of what happened at the airport. Tom tried to squeeze his bag into the new-sized frame. It was not even close. After considerable time spent in trying to defy physics, Tom gave up. He approached the agent at the desk and explained what the problem was. The agent then informed him that he would need a plastic bag and they would check his bag for him. So Tom asked for a bag. The agent then informed Tom that they no longer gave out plastic bags and he would have to go and buy one. At this stage there was a sudden transformation in Tom's demeanour. His face went red. Very red. He dropped all the items he had removed from the case ready to put into a plastic bag. He dropped then on the desk with an almighty bang. The agent stepped back hurriedly and looked upset. Tom looked at her and explained that he was not angry with her, just angry at the situation. Too late. She had already called security. There followed a few minutes of discussion, and Tom was then allowed to check in at another station. Alan does not remember how a plastic bag had now appeared. Tom & Alan then joined a very long line of people waiting to get through security. Tom's face had not resumed its normal colour. Eventually Tom was at the front of queue, Alan right behind him. Everything went smoothly and Tom's plastic bag and contents passed inspection. And then Alan's world went dark. He saw Tom take his syringe from his pocket, wave it under the security agent's nose, and say "You did not find this!" The world stopped for only a second, and then the agent said "It's ok. It's for medical use, sir. Go ahead please."

6   Lasting Impressions

After 14 years of working very closely together, what comes to mind immediately when we think of all those years with Tom?

- Tom watching football on his laptop during meetings;
- Tom agitated, making derogatory comments about *'Spurs*, watching football on his laptop during meetings;
- Gratitude to Jan for enabling all these years with Tom to be such a positive experience – for us;
- Traveling all over the world with Tom:
  - Enjoying technical meetings and discussions;
  - Enjoying great food and wine, usually selected by ... Tom;
  - Enjoying searching out espressos;
  - Enjoying limited but fascinating sight-seeing;
  - Not always enjoying the actual travel – as described above, he is not a patient traveler and seems to invite *trouble*!
- Enjoying lunch and a beer (or wine) at the University Club;
- Tom enjoying being lauded at many consecutive dinners hosted by the VP Research to honour McMaster Faculty who had achieved noteworthy success in that year;
- Tom laughing and complaining about Alan's pronunciation of *Templits*;
- Tom searching for esoteric words to use in our papers – or it may have come naturally to him;
- Tom, red in the face, angry about a perceived injustice;
- Watching Tom make technical connections and potential breakthrough strategies on the fly when presented with a problem;
- Holding our breath when Tom says "I wrote an email to ..."

7   Thanks Tom

Tom, we have had tremendous fun with you! Most of the time. Almost all the time! You were the heart of a team that transformed the funding situation in CAS for the better. You undoubtedly helped to raise the research profile and visibility of CAS and McSCert. Our work on rigour in software engineering and safety has built a reputation that we can be proud of, and it would not have happened without you (and without us). We have complemented each other's skills and knowledge while building on common interests. You are a great friend and we miss notre Grand Fromage very much. We do aim to find ways to continue our collaboration! You just may have to learn how to use GIT, and LaTex, and find a software app that prevents you sending emails to the wrong Mark.

Exotic Logics, Specifications, Operas
and Much Much More

Axel van Lamsweerde

ICTEAM Research Institute & Unité d'Informatique
Université Catholique de Louvain, Belgium
`axel.vanlamsweerde@uclouvain.be`

This short, non-technical note aims at outlining the influence and fun brought all along my career by a strong personality and active researcher on the foundations of Software Engineering.

I'd like first to briefly mention a few ways in which Tom Maibaum influenced my research work –ways he might probably be unaware of. At the good old time of the FOREST project [2], Tom through discussions made me discover the elegance of some exotic logics together with their relevance to software requirements formalization, particularly deontic logics [3] –in my case, for the specification of capabilities, responsibilities, permissions and obligations of agents in a software system. Beyond that, there were a few books Tom co-authored at that time that I considered as bibles for fruitful bedtime reading; in particular, his handbook on logic for computer science [1] and a technically deep thinking on the mathematical nature and role of specifications in reasoning about programs and their construction [8].

A little bit later, I invited Tom to deliver a keynote address at IWSSD'93, one of those lively workshops considered as key meetings in software specification research. Tom's main point, as I recall it, was a plea for hiding formal methods under some layer so that the software engineer does not need to know about all the undelying mathematical machinery –much the same way as in other engineering disciplines [5]. This point haunted me for years and influenced the content and organization of my book [9]; the core chapters there allow requirements engineers to use linear temporal logic without really knowing it.

I further enjoyed multiple inspiring discussions with Tom on the need for multi-formalism specifications [6] and the really complex problem of semantic interconnection among multiple formalisms [4] –in my opinion, a fundamental problem in requirements engineering research that I tried to address in my work as well [9]. I have to admit though that the papers by Fiadeiro & Maibaum reflecting all their work on category theory for software engineering were much harder for me to digest and apply than the recipes their authors gave me while cooking together during our sabbatical time in Palo Alto (CA).

This brings me up to the more anecdotal part of this short note. I was happy enough to join a group of colleagues in software engineering research who became good friends, partly due to a common determination to never talk about technical matters during the infinitely many dinners following tiring, jet-lagged sessions of technical conferences and workshops. This was not the only trick though. Shopping together in huge US malls after meetings, with a few other close colleagues, became a tradition. I remember once we had the delicate mission of finding a very special belt for Tom's daughter. We were instructed by a sketch Tom drew on a piece of paper for each of us. We were desperately looking through a large Macy's store until I heard one of us yelling through the store: "I got it". (It was Anthony Finkelstein if I remember well). Mission accomplished. Frantically shopping for classical music CDs in Tower Records stores became a post-meeting sport we regularly practiced together as well. Operas were another real passion shared with Tom and a few other colleagues. Beyond lively discussions about our favored ones and their best interpretations, I can't resist mentioning another anecdote. Tom was program co-chair of ICSE'96 in Berlin [7]. As everyone in our community knows, ICSE is the premier conference series in software engineering; co-chairing one of these is supposed to require a lot of involvement during the conference, including attendance of organizational meetings at night, other business meetings, banquets, get-together drinks, and so forth. Instead of all these duties, the program co-chair attended wonderful operas, one different every night, together with a very few other colleagues who knowed that Berlin is the opera capital worldwide.

Let me finish with a climax memory. Our respective sabbatical time at Stanford Research Institute (SRI, Palo Alto, CA) overlapped in the summer 1998. The 1998 football world cup took place right at that time. Being myself Dutch (although neither nationalist nor football fan), I felt morally obliged not to miss the semi-final early July, Brazil vs. Netherlands, which was displayed in real time on a large screen in a dedicated room on the Stanford University campus. The color of the audience was approximately 90% orange, all Dutch people wearing the same T-shirt "As a final touch God created the DUTCH". There were very few Brazil supporters in the room; I remember, however, that there was one with a green-and-yellow T-shirt. The game went fairly well for the Dutch supporters, who were yelling vehemently on every occasion, until a final Brazilian penalty shoot-out allowed our green-and-yellow supporter to reveal his enthusiasm for the Brasilian victory. The victory was clearly anticipated by this supporter; I was kindly invited with my wife at his place right after for a grandiose celebration meal where all dishes were green, yellow, or a combination of both. This green-and-yellow supporter was among those colleagues and friends who made my job so enjoyable. Thank you so much Prof. Dr. Thomas Stephen Edward Maibaum!

References

[1] S. Abramsky, D. Gabbay, and T. Maibaum. *Handbook of Logic in Computer Science.* Clarendon Press, 1992.
[2] R. Cunningham, A. Finkelstein, Goldsack. S., T. Maibaum, and C. Potts. Formal requirements specification — the FOREST project. In *3rd International Workshop on*

Software Specification & Design (IWSSD'85), pages 1–2. IEEE Computer Society, 1985.

[3] J. Fiadeiro and T. Maibaum. Temporal reasoning over deontic specifications. *Journal of Logic and Computation*, 1(3):357–395, 1991.

[4] J. Fiadeiro and T. Maibaum. Interconnecting formalisms: Supporting modularity, reuse and incrementality. In *3rd ACM Symposium on Foundations of Software Engineering (SIGSOFT'95)*, pages 72–80. ACM, 1995.

[5] T. Maibaum. Taking more of the soft out of software engineering. In *7th International Workshop on Software Specification and Design (IWSSD'93)*, pages 2–9. IEEE Computer Society, 1993.

[6] C. Niskier, T. Maibaum, and D. Schwabe. A pluralistic knowledge-based approach to software specification. In *2nd European Software Engineering Conference (ESEC'89)*, volume 387 of *LNCS*, pages 411–423. Springer, 1989.

[7] H. Rombach, T. Maibaum, and M. Zelkowitz, editors. *18th International Conference on Software Engineering (ICSE'96')*. IEEE Computer Society, 1996.

[8] W. Turski and T. Maibaum. *Specification of Computer Programs*. Addison-Wesley, 1987.

[9] A. van Lamsweerde. *Requirements Engineering: From System Goals to UML Models to Software Specifications*. Wiley, 2009.

My Three Shared Values with Tom Maibaum

Carlo Ghezzi

Politecnico di Milano, Italy
`carlo.ghezzi@polimi.it`

It has been a great honor to participate in the Symposium on the Mathematical Foundations of Software Engineering, held in February 2019 at the University of Rio Cuarto (Argentina), to honor Tom Maibaum on the occasion of his retirement.

I have met Tom for the first time in 1985, when the International Conference on Software Engineering (ICSE) was held London, and since we met again many times while he was at Imperial and later when he moved back to Canada. Tom and I never worked together, and even our research avenues never really intersected, although we were both interested in software engineering. However, Tom has been a colleague in research with whom I shared both important values and great memories.

Among the great gifts of a being a researcher are the opportunities one finds to meet with peers from all over the world and establish relations that have no boundaries and range from merely scientific to personal.

With Tom I share three important values: we both have a long history of attachment to Argentina; we both believe that mathematics, and logic in particular, are pillars on which the science and engineering of software should rely; and we both love classical music (and opera in particular).

I visited Argentina for the first time in 1986, and gave a talk at the national conference JAIIO. My visit to Argentina was organized under the auspices of an Argentinian expatriate (Norma Lijtmaer), who was a researcher at the Italian Research Council (CNR) in Pisa. Norma has been an unforgettable research colleague and close friend, who gave tremendous contributions to the Argentinian Computer Science research. At the time, Argentina was resurrecting after the long tragic and dark time of dictatorship. In particular, Norma gave her enthusiastic contribution to creating ESLAI (Escuela Latino Americana de Informatica) and bringing to Argentina scientists from all over Europe to help create a new generation of world-class graduates, who could then guide the developments in the field. I had the privilege of being in this group and I still remember the excitement of the (alas short) ESLAI experience. Digging further into this will bring us too far from Tom's celebration. However, I would like to mention that at ESLAI I worked and developed a friendly personal relation with two influential Argentinian scientists –Jorge Aguirre and Armando Haeberer. Jorge pioneered Computer Science at the University of Rio Cuarto, and indirectly linked to Tom through the great students the department nurtured, which he then supervised for their PhD in Canada. Armando had a life-long research collaboration with Tom since, until his premature death.

As for my connection with Tom in research, since the early 1980s he pioneered the studies on the fundamental notion of software specification (as complementary to implementation). His approach was based on formal logic. Over the years, his research contributions continued to shed new light on the fundamentals of software engineering. I can certainly say that Tom's ideas were very influential on my own research approach, which also recognized the need for basing software development on rigorous, mathematical foundations. In my own work, I also explored the use of logic, in conjunction with operational models, to specify and verify certain classes of software systems (time-dependent, space-dependent, adaptive).

Another value I share with Tom is passion for classical music and opera. I vividly remember two excellent productions we enjoyed together, by two of my favorite composers: Haendel's Ariodante, in London at ENO; and Wagner's Rheingold, in Berlin at Staatsoper Unter den Linden. The latter still stands in my long operatic experience as a memorable production, mainly ascribable to Daniel Baremboim's inspired baton. I wish we could have shared more opera expeditions. For the future, I wish I could sometime invite Tom to attend an opera performance in the Milano opera house (La Scala).

Integrating Deduction and Model Finding in a Language Independent Setting

Carlos G. Lopez Pombo

CONICET-UBA. Instituto de Investigación en Ciencias de la Computación (ICC).
Department of Computing, FCEyN.
Universidad de Buenos Aires, Argentina
`clpombo@dc.uba.ar`

Agustín Eloy Martinez Suñé

CONICET-UBA. Instituto de Investigación en Ciencias de la Computación (ICC).
Department of Computing, FCEyN.
Universidad de Buenos Aires, Argentina
`aemartinez@dc.uba.ar`

Abstract

Software artifacts are ubiquitous in our lives being an essential part of home appliances, cars, cel phones, and even in more critical activities like aeronautics and health
sciences. In this context software failures may produce enormous losses, either economical or, in the extreme, in human lives. Software analysis is an area in software
engineering concerned on the application of different techniques in order to prove the
(relative) absence of errors in software artifacts.

In many cases these methods of analysis are applied by following certain methodological directives that ensure better results. In a previous work we presented the notion
of satisfiability calculus as a model theoretical counterpart of Meseguer's proof calculus, providing a formal foundation for a variety of tools that are based on model
construction.

The present work shows how effective satisfiability sub-calculi, a special type of satisfiability calculi, can be combined with proof calculi, in order to provide foundations to
certain methodological approaches to software analysis by relating the construction
of finite counterexamples and the absence of proofs, in an abstract categorical setting.

1 Introduction and motivation

Software artifacts are ubiquitous in our lives being an essential part of home
appliances, cars, cel phones, and even in more critical activities like aeronautics
and health sciences. In this context software failures may produce enormous
losses, either economical or, in the extreme, in human lives. In the latter
context, compliance with certain quality standards might be mandatory. Software analysis is an area in software engineering concerned on the application

23

of different techniques in order to prove the (relative) absence of errors in software artifacts. Software analysis, usually (if not always) requires that a formal description of the behaviour of the system, known as its specification, must be available. Then, it is possible to check wether a given property of interest follows from it.

Logics have often been used as formal systems suitable for the specification of software artifacts. Moreover, logical specifications, due to its formal nature, have contributed towards the application of sound verification techniques. Several formalisms have been developed to cope with these aspects and most of them are effective in describing some particular characteristics of software systems. Among many examples, one can mention:

- linear-time temporal logics, both propositional [1,2] and first-order [3], for describing properties about single executions,
- branching-time temporal logics [4], for describing properties of the class of potential executions from a given state of the system,
- CTL* [5] as a compromise sitting in between linear-time and branching-time logics,
- the many versions of dynamic logics [6,7], formalising properties of (imperative) sequential programs,
- dynamic linear temporal logic [8], for embedding the dynamic characterisation of programs within the temporal operators linear temporal logics,
- higher-order logics [9] for capturing several notions like higher-order functions,
- equational logic [10] for capturing abstract data types [11], and the list continues.

The usefulness of logic in software design and development has always been some form of universal, and well-documented, truth in computer science. From Turing's initial observations, already in [12], stating that "the state of progress of a computation" is completely determined by a single expression, referred to as "state formulae"; through Hoare's "Axiomatic Basis for Computer Programming" [13], Burstall's "Proving Properties of Programs by Structural Induction" [14] and Floyd's "Assigning meaning to programs" [15], in the 60's; to Parnas' "A Technique for Software Module Specification with Examples" [16] and Dijkstra's "Guarded Commands, Nondeterminacy and Formal derivation of Programs" [17], in the 70's; just to start with.

Formalising a software artefact by resorting to a logical language requires people involved in the development process to agree on how such descriptions are to be interpreted and understood, so that the systems can be built in accordance to its description and, therefore, have the expected behaviour. Semantics plays a central role in this endeavour as it is a way of substituting the perhaps drier and more esoteric forms provided by syntactic descriptions, by the more intuitive modes of understanding appealing to some naive form of set theory, but the metalogical relation between these two inherent aspects of logical languages, syntax and semantics, might reveal certain discordance with significant impact regarding the appropriateness of the use of one or the other.

Back in the second half of the 70's, when formal software specification was booming due to the appearance of Abstract Data Types [18] as the main driver in programming, logic ended up in a privileged position in computer science. Tom Maibaum, and a group of Brazilian logicians leaded by Paulo Veloso, realised that the use abstract semantics for interpreting data types specifications, and thinking about their representations, was not appropriate. In such a setting, either implicit or explicit in many different approaches at that time [19,20,21,22,23,24,25,26], not every model is reachable (i.e., those built from objects that cannot be named by syntactic terms) and, even among those that are, there are some that are not minimal in the sense that they might satisfy properties other than those provable from the axioms. They also observed that such minimality was a direct consequence from requiring models to be initial, as the ADJ group, leaded by Joseph Goguen, was pushing forward for algebraic specification languages [11,27].

Maibaum's commitment with this view on semantics in computer science is best understood in his words:

"It cannot be emphasized enough that it is this concept of initiality which gives rise to the power of the method. Once the requirement of initiality is relaxed, many of the results and proof methods associated with the concept disappear."

Such a strong standpoint motivated him, and his colleagues, to pursue a research program [28] [1] aiming at producing a theory of initiality for first order predicate logic, thus, reproducing ADJ's results about equational logic, but for a logical language expressive enough to capture the behaviour of complex data structures and, therefore, more suitable to software systems specification.

In [30] Maibaum cites [31], a seminal paper by Hans-Dieter Ehrich, as an important source for the motivations behind the foundational notions of the approach, outstandingly summarised by the former as:

"Why did correct implementations not compose correctly in all cases? What were the engineering assumptions on which the technical developments were based? What results were dependent on the formalism used (some variant of equational logic or FOL [2] or whatever) and which were 'universal'?"

---

[1] A shorter version was published later in [29].

[2] As usual, FOL refers to the fisrt order predicate calculus, or first order logic.

Such questions reveal that Maibaum was committed with the provision of a tool for practical software development, and not just the capricious definition of a well-founded theory of software specification. Truth be said, while Ehrich and Maibaum had the same motivations, the work of the former was still focussed on the equational axiomatisation of abstract data types, while the latter's program was moving further to a more expressive logical framework, first order predicate calculus. Much of the progress was documented as technical reports of the institutions to which the authors were affiliated at the time [32,33,34] and later published in [35,36]. While the main objectives were preserved, the specification language adopted was $L_{\omega_1,\omega}$ [37, Sec. 11.4] (i.e., first-order predicate logic with equality, admitting conjunctions and disjunctions of denumerable sets of formulae), due to the technical need of what the authors call "namability axioms" (i.e., formulae of the shape $(\forall x : T)(\bigvee_{n \in \mathrm{Name}(T)} x =_T n)$, for each sort T) for ensuring that any model, from the traditional model theoretic perspective, is reachable.

Also in the mid 80's, Goguen and Burstall introduced *Institutions* [38] as a categorical framework aiming at providing a formal framework for defining the notion of logical system, from a model-theoretic perspective. Thanks to its categorical presentation, Institutions were key in revealing more elaborate views on software specifications (see, for example, those focussed on compositional specifications [39,40,41], software development by refinement of specifications [42,43] and heterogenous specifications [44,45,46,47,48,49], among many others) and elegantly supporting many features pursued in Maibaum's endeavour, like well-behaved composition mechanisms, semantically consistent parameterisation procedures, etc. What for some researchers, like the authors of this work, was interpreted as a source of mathematical beauty, by enabling a flexible way of formalising the notion of satisfaction associated to an arbitrary class of models of interest, for Maibaum was a deal breaker, Goguen's departure from mandatory initial semantics ended the tactical alliance forever.

The theory of Institutions evolved in many directions being *General logics* [50] of specific interest to this work. In it, Meseguer, complemented the definition of a logical system from a semantical point of view, provided by institutions, with a categorical characterisation for the notions of entailment system (also referred to as π-institutions by Fiadeiro and Maibaum [51]). Such a syntactical view of a logical system allowed for a more balanced definition of the notion of *Logic*, integrating both formalisations. Thereafter, the author sharply observes that there might be "a reasonable objection" regarding the abstractness of the notion of entailment as it hides out the internal structure the entailment relation (i.e., the mere notion of proofs). Such an abstract view of the notion of entailment might be considered more a virtue that a defect, as it enables the possibility of defining many plausible proof systems, for a single

entailment relation (for example, the same abstract entailment relation between sets of formulae and formulae can be defined as a Hilbert-style calculus,
a natural deduction calculus or by other means). Then, Meseguer completes
his view on logics by proposing categorical characterisations of the notions of
Proof calculus, *Proof subcalculus* (the restriction of a proof calculus obtained
from identifying the subcategory of theories and the subset of conclusions that
can be drawn from that theory), and *Effective proof subcalculi* (a proof subcalculus whose proving method is guaranteed to be effective by requiring sentences,
axioms, conclusions and proofs to be structured in a space [52]).

The reader may have noticed that Meseguer's viewpoint induced a new,
and further, imbalance towards syntax leaving the semantic aspects of a logical
system too abstract with respect to the syntactic ones.

Model theoretic-based reasoning techniques constitute an important stream
of research in logic; in particular, these methods play an important role in automated software validation and verification. The origin of this type of logical
reasoning tools can be traced back to the works of Beth [53,54], Herbrand
[55] and Gentzen [56]; Beth's ideas were used by Smullyan to formulate the
tableau method for first-order predicate logic [57]. Herbrandt's and Gentzen's
work inspired the formulation of resolution systems presented by Robinson [58].
Methods like those based on resolution and tableaux are strongly related to the
semantics of a logic; therefore, they can often be used as the mechanics behind
the construction of models. Such a use is not possible in *pure* deductive methods, such as natural deduction or Hilbert systems, as formalized by Meseguer.

In [59], Lopez Pombo and some colleagues, forced Maibaum into stretching
his views trying to reach common ground. This was done by introducing a
framework, analogous to Meseguer's mechanisation of the notion of proof,
but serving the purpose of formalising how models are constructed from the
sentences they have to satisfy, and how these "canonically" defined structures
relate to the abstract notion of satisfaction formalised by the institution for
which the calculus is being defined. The formalisation of such a constructive
view of model theory received the name of *Satisfiability calculus* and was
later extended, in analogy to Meseguer's presentation of proof systems, to
Satisfiability subcalculus and *Effective satisfiability subcalculus*.

Formal methods are usually divided into two categories: heavyweight and
lightweight. These names refer to the amount of mathematical expertise needed
during the process of proving a given property. For many specification languages a lower degree of involvement equates to a higher degree of automation
and, consequently, to less certainty regarding the satisfaction of the property.
Thus lightweight formal methods, like Alloy [60], cannot usually be entirely
trusted when dealing with models of mission critical systems. An alternative
is the use of heavyweight formal methods, as for instance semi-automatic theo-

rem provers [61,62,63]. Theorem provers also exhibit limitations, for instance, they usually require a high level of expertise and strong mathematical skills, that many times discourages their use. More modern analysis methodologies departed from the idea that either heavyweight or lightweight formal methods are applied, disregarding the relation between these tools. Our claim is that formally enforcing certain methodological directives as part of the process of software analysis produces better results in practice. An example of this is Dynamite [64]. Dynamite is a theorem prover for Alloy in which the critical parts of the proof are assisted by the Alloy Analyzer with the aim of reducing both the workload and the error proneness introduced by the human interaction with the tool. Another use of model theoretic tools in relation to the use of theorem provers is the fact that they provide an efficient method for: a) gaining confidence in the hypothesis brought into a proof, b) the elimination of superfluous formulae appearing in a sequent, c) the removal of minor modelling errors, and even d) the suggestion of potential witnesses for existential quantifiers.

Another example of the synergy between deduction and model finding is Nitpick [65], an automatic counterexample finder for Isabelle [63], implemented using Kodkod [66]. The integration between Nitpick and Isabelle provides the command `nitpick` [67] that, when it is applied, first translates the current sequent to a Kodkod problem consisting of: 1) the type declarations (including bounds for the amount of atoms to be considered for each one), and 2) a first-order relational logic [68] formula equivalent to the conjunction of the hypothesis and the negation of the thesis; and then invoques the latter in order to find a model of such a formula.

Nitpick also provides an automatic mode in which the command is applied every time the user inputs a rule in Isabelle's command prompt.

In this work we aim at providing a formal link supporting the methodological interaction between bounded model checkers and theorem provers by connecting the concrete structures over which models and proofs are represented in their formalisation as effective satisfiability sub-calculi and proof calculi, respectively.

The paper is organized as follows. In Sec. 2 we present the definitions and results we will use throughout this paper. In Sec. 3 we present a categorical formalization of satisfiability sub-calculus and prove relevant results underpinning the definitions leading to the formalisation of a methodology for software analysis. In Sec. 4 we present examples in enough detail to exemplify the ideas. Finally, in Sec. 5, we present some conclusions drawn from the contribution and propose a direction in which this research can be continued.

2 General logics: the category-theoretic formalisation of logical systems

From now on, we assume the reader has a nodding acquaintance with basic concepts from category theory [69,70]. We mainly follow the notation introduced in [50].

An *entailment system* is defined by identifying a family of *syntactic* consequence relations indexed by the elements of a category assumed to be the category of signatures. As usual, entailment relations are required to satisfy reflexivity, monotonicity[3] and transitivity.

Definition 2.1 [Entailment system [50]] A structure $\langle \mathbf{Sign}, \mathbf{Sen}, \{\vdash^{\Sigma}\}_{\Sigma \in |\mathbf{Sign}|} \rangle$ is said to be an *entailment system* if it satisfies the following conditions:

- $\mathbf{Sign}$ is a category of signatures,
- $\mathbf{Sen} : \mathbf{Sign} \to \mathbf{Set}$ is a functor. Let $\Sigma \in |\mathbf{Sign}|$; then $\mathbf{Sen}(\Sigma)$ returns the set of Σ-sentences, and
- $\{\vdash^{\Sigma}\}_{\Sigma \in |\mathbf{Sign}|}$, where $\vdash^{\Sigma} \subseteq 2^{\mathbf{Sen}(\Sigma)} \times \mathbf{Sen}(\Sigma)$, is a family of binary relations such that for any $\Sigma, \Sigma' \in |\mathbf{Sign}|$, $\{\phi\} \cup \{\phi_i\}_{i \in \mathcal{I}} \subseteq \mathbf{Sen}(\Sigma)$, $\Gamma, \Gamma' \subseteq \mathbf{Sen}(\Sigma)$, the following conditions are satisfied:
  - · reflexivity: $\{\phi\} \vdash^{\Sigma} \phi$,
  - · monotonicity: if $\Gamma \vdash^{\Sigma} \phi$ and $\Gamma \subseteq \Gamma'$, then $\Gamma' \vdash^{\Sigma} \phi$,
  - · transitivity: if $\Gamma \vdash^{\Sigma} \phi_i$ for all $i \in \mathcal{I}$ and $\{\phi_i\}_{i \in \mathcal{I}} \vdash^{\Sigma} \phi$, then $\Gamma \vdash^{\Sigma} \phi$, and
  - · $\vdash$-translation: if $\Gamma \vdash^{\Sigma} \phi$, then for any morphism $\sigma : \Sigma \to \Sigma'$ in $\mathbf{Sign}$, $\mathbf{Sen}(\sigma)(\Gamma) \vdash^{\Sigma'} \mathbf{Sen}(\sigma)(\phi)$.

Definition 2.2 [Theory presentations [50]] Let $\langle \mathbf{Sign}, \mathbf{Sen}, \{\vdash^{\Sigma}\}_{\Sigma \in |\mathbf{Sign}|} \rangle$ be an entailment system. Its category of theory presentations is $\mathsf{Th} = \langle \mathcal{O}, \mathcal{A} \rangle$ such that:

- $\mathcal{O} = \{ \langle \Sigma, \Gamma \rangle \mid \Sigma \in |\mathbf{Sign}| \text{ and } \Gamma \subseteq \mathbf{Sen}(\Sigma) \}$, and
- $\mathcal{A} = \left\{ \sigma : \langle \Sigma, \Gamma \rangle \to \langle \Sigma', \Gamma' \rangle \;\middle|\; \begin{array}{l} \langle \Sigma, \Gamma \rangle, \langle \Sigma', \Gamma' \rangle \in \mathcal{O}, \sigma : \Sigma \to \Sigma' \in \|\mathbf{Sign}\|, \\ \text{for all } \gamma \in \Gamma, \Gamma' \vdash^{\Sigma'} \mathbf{Sen}(\sigma)(\gamma). \end{array} \right\}$

In addition, if a morphism $\sigma : \langle \Sigma, \Gamma \rangle \to \langle \Sigma', \Gamma' \rangle$ satisfies $\mathbf{Sen}(\sigma)(\Gamma) \subseteq \Gamma'$, it is called *axiom preserving*. By retaining those morphisms of Th that are axiom preserving, we obtain the subcategory Th_0.

Note that, in the previous definition, the objects of Th are determined by a signature and a set of axioms, which are not necessarily closed under entailment.

---

[3] The theory of institutions and general logics focus on monotonic logical systems. The interested reader is referred to [71] for a presentation of entailment systems for default logic, a well-known non-monotonic logical system introduced by Reiter in [72] aiming at the formalisation of defeasible logical reasoning.

A theory is obtained from a theory presentations by requiring: 1) the former to satisfy all the axioms appearing in the latter, and 2) to be closed under entailment.

Definition 2.3 [Closure under entailment] Let $\langle \mathsf{Sign}, \mathsf{Sen}, \{\vdash^\Sigma\}_{\Sigma \in |\mathsf{Sign}|} \rangle$ be an entailment system and $\langle \Sigma, \Gamma \rangle \in |\mathsf{Th}|$. We define $\bullet : 2^{\mathbf{Sen}(\Sigma)} \to 2^{\mathbf{Sen}(\Sigma)}$ as follows: $\Gamma^\bullet = \{ \gamma \mid \Gamma \vdash^\Sigma \gamma \}$. This function is extended to elements of Th, by defining it as follows: $\langle \Sigma, \Gamma \rangle^\bullet = \langle \Sigma, \Gamma^\bullet \rangle$. $\Gamma^\bullet$ is called the theory generated by Γ.

Roughly speaking, an institution is an abstract formalisation of the model theory of a logic in such a way that the existing relations between signatures, sentences over a signature and models for a signature are made explicit. These aspects are reflected by introducing the category of signatures, defining two functors capturing the sets of sentences and the classes of models, the first one going from this category to the category Set and the second one going from this category to Cat, and by requiring the satisfiability relation to remain invariant under signature change.

Definition 2.4 [Institution [38]] A structure $\langle \mathsf{Sign}, \mathsf{Sen}, \mathsf{Mod}, \{\models^\Sigma\}_{\Sigma \in |\mathsf{Sign}|} \rangle$ is said to be an *institution* if it satisfies the following conditions:

- Sign is a category of signatures,
- $\mathbf{Sen} : \mathsf{Sign} \to \mathsf{Set}$ is a functor. Let $\Sigma \in |\mathsf{Sign}|$, then $\mathbf{Sen}(\Sigma)$ is its corresponding set of Σ-sentences,
- $\mathbf{Mod} : \mathsf{Sign}^{\mathsf{op}} \to \mathsf{Cat}$ is a functor. Let $\Sigma \in |\mathsf{Sign}|$, then $\mathbf{Mod}(\Sigma)$ is its corresponding category of Σ-models,
- $\{\models^\Sigma\}_{\Sigma \in |\mathsf{Sign}|}$ is a family of binary relations $\models^\Sigma \subseteq |\mathbf{Mod}(\Sigma)| \times \mathbf{Sen}(\Sigma)$, for all $\Sigma \in |\mathsf{Sign}|$

such that for all $\sigma : \Sigma \to \Sigma' \in ||\mathsf{Sign}||$, $\phi \in \mathbf{Sen}(\Sigma)$ and $\mathcal{M}' \in |\mathbf{Mod}(\Sigma')|$, the following $\models$-invariance condition holds:

$$\mathcal{M}' \models^{\Sigma'} \mathbf{Sen}(\sigma)(\phi) \quad \text{iff} \quad \mathbf{Mod}(\sigma^{\mathsf{op}})(\mathcal{M}') \models^\Sigma \phi .$$

Intuitively, the last condition of the previous definition says that *truth is invariant with respect to notation change*. Given $\langle \Sigma, \Gamma \rangle \in |\mathsf{Th}|$, $\mathbf{Mod} : \mathsf{Th}^{\mathsf{op}} \to \mathsf{Cat}$ is the extension of the functor $\mathbf{Mod} : \mathsf{Sign}^{\mathsf{op}} \to \mathsf{Cat}$ such that $\mathbf{Mod}(\langle \Sigma, \Gamma \rangle)$ denotes the full subcategory of $\mathbf{Mod}(\Sigma)$ determined by those models $\mathcal{M} \in |\mathbf{Mod}(\Sigma)|$ such that $\mathcal{M} \models^\Sigma \gamma$, for all $\gamma \in \Gamma$. The relation $\models^\Sigma$ between sets of formulae and formulae is defined in the following way: given $\Sigma \in |\mathsf{Sign}|$, $\Gamma \subseteq \mathbf{Sen}(\Sigma)$ and $\alpha \in \mathbf{Sen}(\Sigma)$,

$$\Gamma \models^\Sigma \alpha \quad \text{if and only if} \quad \mathcal{M} \models^\Sigma \alpha, \text{ for all } \mathcal{M} \in |\mathbf{Mod}(\langle \Sigma, \Gamma \rangle)|.$$

Now, from Defs. 2.1 and 2.4, it is possible to give a definition of *logic* by relating both its model-theoretic and proof-theoretic characterisations. In this respect, coherence between the semantic and syntactic entailment relations is required, reflecting the standard concepts of soundness and completeness of logical systems.

Definition 2.5 [Logic [50]]
A structure $\langle \mathsf{Sign}, \mathbf{Sen}, \mathbf{Mod}, \{\vdash^\Sigma\}_{\Sigma \in |\mathsf{Sign}|}, \{\models^\Sigma\}_{\Sigma \in |\mathsf{Sign}|} \rangle$ is said to be a *logic* if it satisfies the following conditions:

- $\langle \mathsf{Sign}, \mathbf{Sen}, \{\vdash^\Sigma\}_{\Sigma \in |\mathsf{Sign}|} \rangle$ is an entailment system,
- $\langle \mathsf{Sign}, \mathbf{Sen}, \mathbf{Mod}, \{\models^\Sigma\}_{\Sigma \in |\mathsf{Sign}|} \rangle$ is an institution, and
- the following *soundness* condition is satisfied: for any $\Sigma \in |\mathsf{Sign}|$, $\phi \in \mathbf{Sen}(\Sigma)$, $\Gamma \subseteq \mathbf{Sen}(\Sigma)$:

$$\Gamma \vdash^\Sigma \phi \quad \text{implies} \quad \Gamma \models^\Sigma \phi .$$

In addition, a logic is *complete* if the following condition is satisfied: for any $\Sigma \in |\mathsf{Sign}|$, $\phi \in \mathbf{Sen}(\Sigma)$, $\Gamma \subseteq \mathbf{Sen}(\Sigma)$:

$$\Gamma \models^\Sigma \phi \quad \text{implies} \quad \Gamma \vdash^\Sigma \phi.$$

Definition 2.1 associates deductive relations to signatures. As already discussed, it is important to analyse how these relations are obtained. The next definition formalises the notion of proof calculus by associating a proof-theoretic structure to the deductive relations introduced by the definitions of entailment systems.

Definition 2.6 [Proof calculus [50]]
A structure $\langle \mathsf{Sign}, \mathbf{Sen}, \{\vdash^\Sigma\}_{\Sigma \in |\mathsf{Sign}|}, \mathbf{P}, \mathbf{Pr}, \pi \rangle$ is said to be a *proof calculus* if it satisfies the following conditions:

- $\langle \mathsf{Sign}, \mathbf{Sen}, \{\vdash^\Sigma\}_{\Sigma \in |\mathsf{Sign}|} \rangle$ is an entailment system,
- $\mathbf{P} : \mathsf{Th}_0 \to \mathsf{Struct}_{PC}$ is a functor. Let $T \in |\mathsf{Th}_0|$, then $\mathbf{P}(T) \in |\mathsf{Struct}_{PC}|$ is the proof-theoretical structure of T [4],
- $\mathbf{Pr} : \mathsf{Struct}_{PC} \to \mathsf{Set}$ is a functor. Let $T \in |\mathsf{Th}_0|$, then $\mathbf{Pr}(\mathbf{P}(T))$ is the set of proofs of T; the composite functor $\mathbf{Pr} \circ \mathbf{P} : \mathsf{Th}_0 \to \mathsf{Set}$ will be denoted by **proofs**, and
- $\pi : \mathbf{proofs} \Rightarrow \mathbf{Sen}$ is a natural transformation such that for each $T = \langle \Sigma, \Gamma \rangle \in |\mathsf{Th}_0|$ the image of $\pi_T : \mathbf{proofs}(T) \to \mathbf{Sen}(T)$ is the set $\Gamma^\bullet$. The map π_T is called the *projection from proofs to theorems* for the theory T.

---

[4] The reader should note that Struct_{PC} strongly depends on the structure needed to formalise the concept of proof for a specific proof calculus. For example, while in [50, Ex. 11] the formalisation of natural deduction for first-order logic requires the use of multicategories [50, Def. 10], in [73, §3] the formalisation of the proof calculus for ω-closure fork algebras with urelements [74, Def. 7] (a variant of fork algebras [75,76] with a reflexive and transitive closure operator) requires the use of strict monoidal categories [69, Ch. VII, §1] whose monoid of objects is given by the (not necessarily finite) subsets of the corresponding class of equations.

The use of the category Th_0 for indexing proof structures responds to a technical need. Whenever we relate two theories with a morphism, say $\sigma : \langle \Sigma, \Gamma \rangle \rightarrow \langle \Sigma', \Gamma' \rangle$, the previous definition imposes a need for extending that relation to proofs of the form $\pi : \emptyset \rightarrow \alpha \in |\mathbf{proofs}(\langle \Sigma, \Gamma \rangle)|$. If theories are taken from Th, we know that there exists $\pi' : \emptyset \rightarrow \mathbf{Sen}(\sigma)(\alpha) \in |\mathbf{proofs}'(\langle \Sigma', \Gamma' \rangle)|$, but there is no obvious way to obtain it from π. If theories are taken from Th_0, this problem no longer exists as the proof π' is obtained by applying exactly the same proof rules, obtaining the same proof structure (recall the inclusion $\mathbf{Sen}(\sigma)(\Gamma) \subseteq \Gamma'$ in the definition of Th_0).

Meseguer's categorical formulation of a proof calculus is a means of providing structure for the abstract relation of entailment defined in an entailment system. The next definition provides a categorical formalisation of a satisfiability calculus as it was presented in [77]. A satisfiability calculus is the formal characterization of a method for constructing models of a given theory, thus providing the semantic counterpart of that proof calculus. In the same way Meseguer proceeded in order to define a proof calculus, the definition of a satisfiability calculus relies on the possibility of assigning, to each theory presentation, a structure capable of expressing how its models are constructed.

Definition 2.7 [Satisfiability calculus [59]]
A structure $\langle \mathsf{Sign}, \mathbf{Sen}, \mathbf{Mod}, \{\models^\Sigma\}_{\Sigma \in |\mathsf{Sign}|}, \mathbf{M}, \mathbf{Mods}, \mu \rangle$ is said to be a *satisfiability calculus* if it satisfies the following conditions:

- $\langle \mathsf{Sign}, \mathbf{Sen}, \mathbf{Mod}, \{\models^\Sigma\}_{\Sigma \in |\mathsf{Sign}|} \rangle$ is an institution,
- $\mathbf{M} : \mathsf{Th}^{\mathsf{op}} \rightarrow \mathsf{Struct}_{SC}$ is a functor. Let $T \in |\mathsf{Th}^{\mathsf{op}}|$, then $\mathbf{M}(T) \in |\mathsf{Struct}_{SC}|$ is the model structure of T,
- $\mathbf{Mods} : \mathsf{Struct}_{SC} \rightarrow \mathsf{Cat}$ is a functor. Let $T \in |\mathsf{Th}^{\mathsf{op}}|$, then $\mathbf{Mods}(\mathbf{M}(T))$ is the set of canonical models of T; the composite functor $\mathbf{Mods} \circ \mathbf{M} : \mathsf{Th}^{\mathsf{op}} \rightarrow \mathsf{Cat}$ will be denoted by $\mathbf{models}$, and
- $\mu : \mathbf{models} \Rightarrow \mathscr{P} \circ \mathbf{Mod}$ is a natural transformation such that, for each $T = \langle \Sigma, \Gamma \rangle \in |\mathsf{Th}^{\mathsf{op}}|$, the image of $\mu_T : \mathbf{models}(T) \rightarrow \mathscr{P} \circ \mathbf{Mod}(T)$ is the subcategory of $\mathbf{Mod}(T)$ corresponding to each canonical representation of a class of models in $|\mathbf{models}(T)|$. The map μ_T is called the *projection of the category of models* of the theory T.

The intuition behind the previous definition is the following. For any theory T, the functor $\mathbf{M}$ assigns a structure in the category Struct_{SC} representing the class of models for T. Notice that the target of functor $\mathbf{M}$, when applied to a theory T is not necessarily a model but a structure representing the category of models of T. The reader may have already noticed that the functor $\mathbf{M}$ is contravariant with respect to category Th, reflecting the existing opposite direction of morphisms between categories of models with respect to those between signatures found in institutions (see Def. 2.4). The functor $\mathbf{Mods}$ maps the structure representing the class of models of a theory $T = \langle \Sigma, \Gamma \rangle$ to a category whose objects are canonical representations of models of Γ. Finally, for any theory T, the functor μ_T relates each of these structures to the corresponding subcategory of $\mathbf{Mod}(T)$.

Example 2.8 [Tableau Method for First-Order Predicate Logic] Let us start by presenting the well-known tableaux method for first-order logic [57]. Let us denote by $\mathbb{I}_{FOL} = \langle \mathbf{Sign}, \mathbf{Sen}, \mathbf{Mod}, \{\models^{\Sigma}\}_{\Sigma \in |\mathsf{Sign}|} \rangle$ the institution of first-order predicate logic [38, Exs. 2 and 3]. Let $\Sigma \in |\mathsf{Sign}|$ and $S \subseteq \mathbf{Sen}(\Sigma)$; then a *tableau* for S is a tree such that:

(i) the nodes are labeled with sets of formulae (over Σ) and the root node is labeled with S,

(ii) if u and v are two connected nodes in the tree (u being an ancestor of v), then the label of v is obtained from the label of u by applying one of the following rules:

$$\frac{X \cup \{A \wedge B\}}{X \cup \{A \wedge B, A, B\}} \ [\wedge] \qquad \frac{X \cup \{A \vee B\}}{X \cup \{A \vee B, A\} \quad X \cup \{A \vee B, B\}} \ [\vee]$$

$$\frac{X \cup \{\neg\neg A\}}{X \cup \{\neg\neg A, A\}} \ [\neg_1] \qquad \frac{X \cup \{A\}}{X \cup \{A, \neg\neg A\}} \ [\neg_2] \qquad \frac{X \cup \{A, \neg A\}}{\mathbf{Sen}(\Sigma)} \ [false]$$

$$\frac{X \cup \{\neg(A \wedge B)\}}{X \cup \{\neg(A \wedge B), \neg A \vee \neg B\}} \ [DM_1] \qquad \frac{X \cup \{\neg(A \vee B)\}}{X \cup \{\neg(A \vee B), \neg A \wedge \neg B\}} \ [DM_2]$$

$$[t \text{ is a ground term.}] \ \frac{X \cup \{(\forall x)P(x)\}}{X \cup \{(\forall x)P(x), P(t)\}} \ [\forall]$$

$$[c \text{ is a new constant.}] \ \frac{X \cup \{(\exists x)P(x)\}}{X \cup \{(\exists x)P(x), P(c)\}} \ [\exists]$$

A sequence of nodes $s_0 \xrightarrow{\tau_0^{\alpha_0}} s_1 \xrightarrow{\tau_1^{\alpha_1}} s_2 \xrightarrow{\tau_2^{\alpha_2}} \ldots$ is a *branch* if: *a)* s_0 is the root node of the tree, and *b)* for all $i \leq \omega$, $s_i \rightarrow s_{i+1}$ occurs in the tree, $\tau_i^{\alpha_i}$ is an instance of one of the rules presented above, and α_i are the formulae of s_i to which the rule was applied. A branch $s_0 \xrightarrow{\tau_0^{\alpha_0}} s_1 \xrightarrow{\tau_1^{\alpha_1}} s_2 \xrightarrow{\tau_2^{\alpha_2}} \ldots$ in a tableau is *saturated* if there exists $i \leq \omega$ such that $s_i = s_{i+1}$. A branch $s_0 \xrightarrow{\tau_0^{\alpha_0}} s_1 \xrightarrow{\tau_1^{\alpha_1}} s_2 \xrightarrow{\tau_2^{\alpha_2}} \ldots$ in a tableau is *closed* if there exists $i \leq \omega$ and $\alpha \in \mathbf{Sen}(\Sigma)$ such that $\{\alpha, \neg\alpha\} \subseteq s_i$.

Let $s_0 \xrightarrow{\tau_0^{\alpha_0}} s_1 \xrightarrow{\tau_1^{\alpha_1}} s_2 \xrightarrow{\tau_2^{\alpha_2}} \ldots$ be a branch in a tableau. Examining the rules presented above, it is straightforward to see that every s_i, with $i < \omega$, is a set of formulae. In each step, we have either the application of a rule decomposing one formula of the set into its constituent parts with respect to its major connective, while preserving satisfiability, or the application of the rule [false] denoting the fact that the corresponding set of formulae is unsatisfiable. Thus, the limit set of the branch is a set of formulae containing subformulae (and "*instances*" in the case of quantifiers) of the original set of

33

formulae for which the tableau was built. As a result of this, every open branch represents, by means of the set of formulae occurring in the leaf, the class of models satisfying them.

In order to define the tableau method as a satisfiability calculus, we have to provide formal definitions for the categories supporting tableaux structures, for the functors **M** and **Mods** and for the natural transformation μ.

First, given $\Sigma \in |\mathbf{Sign}|$ and $\Gamma \subseteq \mathbf{Sen}(\Sigma)$, we define $Str^{\Sigma,\Gamma} = \langle \mathcal{O}, \mathcal{A} \rangle$ such that $\mathcal{O} = 2^{\mathbf{Sen}(\Sigma)}$ and $\mathcal{A} = \{ \alpha : \{A_i\}_{i \in \mathcal{I}} \to \{B_j\}_{j \in \mathcal{J}} \mid \alpha = \{\alpha_j\}_{j \in \mathcal{J}} \}$, where for all $j \in \mathcal{J}$, α_j is a branch in a tableau for $\Gamma \cup \{B_j\}$ with leaves $\Delta \subseteq \{A_i\}_{i \in \mathcal{I}}$ $Str^{\Sigma,\Gamma}$ can be proved to be a category. Then, we can prove that $\langle Str^{\Sigma,\Gamma}, \cup, \emptyset \rangle$, where $\cup : Str^{\Sigma,\Gamma} \times Str^{\Sigma,\Gamma} \to Str^{\Sigma,\Gamma}$ is the typical bi-functor on sets and functions, and $\emptyset$ is the neutral element for $\cup$, is a strict monoidal category.

Second, using the previous definition we can introduce the class of legal tableaux (denoted by Struct_{SC}), together with a class of arrows, and prove it is a category. Struct_{SC} is defined as $\langle \mathcal{O}, \mathcal{A} \rangle^{\mathsf{op}}$ where $\mathcal{O} = \{ \langle Str^{\Sigma,\Gamma}, \cup, \emptyset \rangle \mid \Sigma \in |\mathbf{Sign}| \wedge \Gamma \subseteq \mathbf{Sen}(\Sigma) \}$, and $\mathcal{A} = \{ \hat{\sigma} : \langle Str^{\Sigma,\Gamma}, \cup, \emptyset \rangle \to \langle Str^{\Sigma',\Gamma'}, \cup, \emptyset \rangle \mid \sigma : \langle \Sigma, \Gamma \rangle \to \langle \Sigma', \Gamma' \rangle \in ||\mathsf{Th}|| \}$, the homomorphic extensions of the morphisms in $||\mathsf{Th}||$ to sets of formulae preserving the application of rules (i.e., the structure of the tableaux).

Third, the functor **M** must be understood as the relation between a theory in $|\mathsf{Th}|$ and its corresponding category of structures representing legal tableaux. So, for every theory $\langle \Sigma, \Gamma \rangle$, **M** associates to it the strict monoidal category [69, Sec. 1, pp. 157] $\langle Str^{\Sigma,\Gamma}, \cup, \emptyset \rangle$, and for every theory morphism $\sigma : \langle \Sigma, \Gamma \rangle \to \langle \Sigma', \Gamma' \rangle \in ||\mathsf{Th}||$ observed in the opposite direction, **M** associates to it a morphism $\hat{\sigma} : Str^{\Sigma,\Gamma} \to Str^{\Sigma',\Gamma'}$ which is the homomorphic extension of σ to the structure of the tableaux, also observed in the opposite direction. Then, **M** : $\mathsf{Th}^{\mathsf{op}} \to \mathsf{Struct}_{SC}$ is defined as $\mathbf{M}(\langle \Sigma, \Gamma \rangle) = \langle Str^{\Sigma,\Gamma}, \cup, \emptyset \rangle$ and for any $\sigma : \langle \Sigma, \Gamma \rangle \to \langle \Sigma', \Gamma' \rangle \in ||\mathsf{Th}||$, $\mathbf{M}(\sigma^{\mathsf{op}}) = \hat{\sigma}^{\mathsf{op}}$, where $\hat{\sigma} : \langle Str^{\Sigma,\Gamma}, \cup, \emptyset \rangle \to \langle Str^{\Sigma',\Gamma'}, \cup, \emptyset \rangle$ is the homomorphic extension of σ to the structures in $\langle Str^{\Sigma,\Gamma}, \cup, \emptyset \rangle$.

Fourth, the functor **Mods** provides the means for obtaining theory presentations characterising classes of models from structures of the form $Str^{\Sigma,\Gamma}$ by identifying the sets of formulae in the leaves of the open branches of a tableau. To this effect, **Mods** : $\mathsf{Struct}_{SC} \to \mathsf{Cat}$ is defined on objects as $\mathbf{Mods}(\langle Str^{\Sigma,\Gamma}, \cup, \emptyset \rangle) = \langle \mathcal{O}, \mathcal{A} \rangle$ where:

- $\mathcal{O} = \bigcup_{\langle \Sigma, \Delta \rangle \in |\mathsf{Th}|} \left\{ \langle \Sigma, \tilde{\Delta} \rangle \in |\mathsf{Th}| \;\middle|\; \begin{array}{l} (\exists \alpha : \Delta \to \emptyset \in ||Str^{\Sigma,\Gamma}||) \\ (\forall \alpha' : \Delta' \to \Delta \in ||Str^{\Sigma,\Gamma}||) \\ (\Delta' = \Delta) \wedge (\tilde{\Delta} \to \emptyset \in \alpha) \wedge \\ \neg(\exists \varphi)(\{\neg\varphi, \varphi\} \subseteq \tilde{\Delta}) \} \end{array} \right\},$

(i.e., 1. the existentially quantified $\alpha : \Delta \to \emptyset \in ||Str^{\Sigma,\Gamma}||$ is a tableau,

34

2. stating that for any $\alpha' : \Delta' \to \Delta \in ||Str^{\Sigma,\Gamma}||$, the equation $\Delta' = \Delta$ holds, expresses that α is saturated, and 3. requesting that $\widetilde{\Delta}$, where $\widetilde{\Delta} \to \emptyset$ is a branch of α, is not inconsistent, expresses that it is the set of formulae at the leaf of an open branch), and

- $\mathcal{A} = \{id_T : T \to T \mid T \in \mathcal{O}\}$, (i.e., only the identities);

and on morphisms as for all $\sigma : \langle \Sigma, \Gamma \rangle \to \langle \Sigma', \Gamma' \rangle \in ||\mathsf{Th}||$, $\mathbf{Mods}(\widehat{\sigma}^{op})(\langle \Sigma, \delta \rangle) = \langle \Sigma', \mathbf{Sen}(\sigma)(\delta) \rangle$. This is proved to be a functor.

Finally, μ has to relate the structures representing saturated tableaux with the model satisfying the set of formulae denoted by the source of the morphism; then we can define $\mu_{\langle \Sigma, \Delta \rangle} : \mathbf{models}(\langle \Sigma, \Delta \rangle) \to \mathscr{P} \circ \mathbf{Mod}(\langle \Sigma, \Delta \rangle)$ as for all $\langle \Sigma, \delta \rangle \in |\mathbf{models}(\langle \Sigma, \Delta \rangle)|$, $\mu_{\langle \Sigma, \Delta \rangle}(\langle \Sigma, \delta \rangle) = \mathbf{Mod}(\langle \Sigma, \delta \rangle)$ and prove it to be a natural transformation.

Therefore, we conclude that $\langle \mathsf{Sign}, \mathbf{Sen}, \mathbf{Mod}, \{\models^{\Sigma}\}_{\Sigma \in |\mathsf{Sign}|}, \mathbf{M}, \mathbf{Mods}, \mu \rangle$ is a satisfiability calculus. The reader interested in the details of the proofs is pointed to [59, Ex. 3.2].

As we mentioned in the introduction, model theory and proof systems are closely related and, in general, logical properties such as soundness and completeness are established by relating the families of entailment and satisfaction relations as we showed in Def. 2.5. As a consequence of having refined the notions of entailment and satisfaction by introducing concrete representations (i.e. proof calculus and satisfiability calculus, respectively), soundness and completeness can be reformulated in terms of the structures used for representing proofs and models.

The following proposition gives an alternative definition of soundness and completeness.

Proposition 2.9 *Let the structure* $\langle \mathsf{Sign}, \mathbf{Sen}, \mathbf{Mod}, \{\vdash^{\Sigma}\}_{\Sigma \in |\mathsf{Sign}|}, \{\models^{\Sigma}\}_{\Sigma \in |\mathsf{Sign}|} \rangle$ *be a logic, the structure* $\langle \mathsf{Sign}, \mathbf{Sen}, \{\vdash^{\Sigma}\}_{\Sigma \in |\mathsf{Sign}|}, \mathbf{P}, \mathbf{Pr}, \pi \rangle$ *be a proof calculus and the structure* $\langle \mathsf{Sign}, \mathbf{Sen}, \mathbf{Mod}, \{\vdash^{\Sigma}\}_{\Sigma \in |\mathsf{Sign}|}, \{\models^{\Sigma}\}_{\Sigma \in |\mathsf{Sign}|}, \mathbf{M}, \mathbf{Mods}, \mu \rangle$ *be a satisfiability calculus. Therefore, if* $T = \langle \Sigma, \Gamma \rangle \in |\mathsf{Th}_0|$ *and* $\alpha \in \mathbf{Sen}(\Sigma)$:

[Soundness] *If there exists* $\tau \in |\mathbf{proof}(T)|$ *such that* $\pi_T(\tau) = \alpha$, *then for all* $M \in |\mathbf{models}(T)|$ *and* $\mathcal{M} \in |\mu_T(M)|$, $\mathcal{M} \models^{\Sigma} \alpha$.

[Completeness] *If for all* $M \in |\mathbf{models}(T)|$ *and* $\mathcal{M} \in |\mu_T(M)|$, $\mathcal{M} \models^{\Sigma} \alpha$, *then there exists* $\tau \in |\mathbf{proof}(T)|$ *such that* $\pi_T(\tau) = \alpha$.

Therefore, soundness can be reformulated in order to support the known fact stating that the evidence of the existence of a counterexamples is a sufficient fact to conclude that there cannot exists a proof.

Corollary 2.10 *Let the structure* $\langle \mathsf{Sign}, \mathbf{Sen}, \mathbf{Mod}, \{\vdash^{\Sigma}\}_{\Sigma \in |\mathsf{Sign}|}, \{\models^{\Sigma}\}_{\Sigma \in |\mathsf{Sign}|} \rangle$

be a logic, the structure $\langle \mathbf{Sign}, \mathbf{Sen}, \{\vdash^\Sigma\}_{\Sigma \in |\mathsf{Sign}|}, \mathbf{P}, \mathbf{Pr}, \pi \rangle$ be a proof calculus and the structure $\langle \mathbf{Sign}, \mathbf{Sen}, \mathbf{Mod}, \{\models^\Sigma\}_{\Sigma \in |\mathsf{Sign}|}, \mathbf{M}, \mathbf{Mods}, \mu \rangle$ be a satisfiability calculus. Therefore, for all $T = \langle \Sigma, \Gamma \rangle \in |\mathsf{Th}_0|$ and $\alpha \in \mathbf{Sen}(\Sigma)$, if there exists $M \in |\mathbf{models}(T)|$ and $\mathcal{M} \in |\mu_T(M)|$ such that $\mathcal{M} \models^\Sigma \alpha$ does not hold, then there is no $\tau \in |\mathbf{proof}(T)|$ such that $\pi_T(\tau) = \alpha$.

Now, on the one hand, Def. 2.7 provides the means for defining specific mechanisations of the satisfiability relation $\models_\Sigma$, with $\Sigma \in |\mathsf{Sign}|$, but, on the other hand, being able to use Coro. 2.12 requires asserting that a model $\mathcal{M}$ does not satisfies a formula α, written above as "$\mathcal{M} \models_\Sigma \alpha$ does not hold". Luckily, most of the logical languages have some form of negation in their syntax that, from a semantical point of view, translates into a complementation of the notion of satisfaction. This notion is usually referred to as for an institution to "have negation", understood as, for the language of that institution, to have a syntactic device whose behaviour, from a model-theoretic perspective, is that of a negation. The next definition formalises this notion.

Definition 2.11 Given a institution $\mathbb{I}$, we say that $\mathbb{I}$ *has negation* if for every signature $\Sigma \in |\mathsf{Sign}|$, $\alpha \in \mathbf{Sen}(\Sigma)$, there exists a formula in $\mathbf{Sen}(\Sigma)$, usually denoted as $\neg \alpha$, such that for all $\mathcal{M} \in \mathbf{Mod}(\Sigma)$,

$$\mathcal{M} \models^\Sigma \neg \alpha \text{ iff } \mathcal{M} \models^\Sigma \alpha \text{ does not hold.}$$

Therefore, Coro. 2.10 can be reformulated as follows.

Corollary 2.12 *Let the structure* $\langle \mathbf{Sign}, \mathbf{Sen}, \mathbf{Mod}, \{\vdash^\Sigma\}_{\Sigma \in |\mathsf{Sign}|}, \{\models^\Sigma\}_{\Sigma \in |\mathsf{Sign}|} \rangle$ *be a logic, the structure* $\langle \mathbf{Sign}, \mathbf{Sen}, \{\vdash^\Sigma\}_{\Sigma \in |\mathsf{Sign}|}, \mathbf{P}, \mathbf{Pr}, \pi \rangle$ *be a proof calculus and the structure* $\langle \mathbf{Sign}, \mathbf{Sen}, \mathbf{Mod}, \{\models^\Sigma\}_{\Sigma \in |\mathsf{Sign}|}, \mathbf{M}, \mathbf{Mods}, \mu \rangle$ *be a satisfiability calculus such that* $\langle \mathbf{Sign}, \mathbf{Sen}, \mathbf{Mod}, \{\models^\Sigma\}_{\Sigma \in |\mathsf{Sign}|} \rangle$ *has negation. Therefore, for all* $T = \langle \Sigma, \Gamma \rangle \in |\mathsf{Th}_0|$ *and* $\alpha \in \mathbf{Sen}(\Sigma)$, *if there exists* $M \in |\mathbf{models}(T)|$ *and* $\mathcal{M} \in |\mu_T(M)|$ *such that* $\mathcal{M} \models^\Sigma \neg \alpha$, *then there is no* $\tau \in |\mathbf{proof}(T)|$ *such that* $\pi_T(\tau) = \alpha$.

3 Satisfiability subcalculus, effectiveness and the foundations for combining deduction and model finding

In the introduction we mentioned the tool Dynamite [64] as the result from combining the capabilities of the bounded model checker Alloy [60] and a theorem prover for the language of first-order relational logic [68], implemented on top of the theorem prover PVS. In this section we present the formal elements underlying this way of combining (bounded) counterexample finding with theorem proving from a language independent setting.

As we mentioned in Sec. 1, in [50], Meseguer not only developed the idea of formalising the notion of proof calculus as an "implementation" of an entailment system, but also explored the possibility of restricting a proof calculus in such a way that the result is a subcalculus for a restriction of the language with specific properties. The next definition, introduced in [59] presentes a model-theoretic counterpart of Meseguer's definitions of proof subcalculus.

Definition 3.1 [Satisfiability subcalculus] A *satisfiability subcalculus* is a structure of the form $\langle \mathbf{Sign}, \mathbf{Sen}, \mathbf{Mod}, \mathbf{Sign}_0, \mathbf{ax}, \{\models^\Sigma\}_{\Sigma \in |\mathbf{Sign}|}, \mathbf{M}, \mathbf{Mods}, \mu \rangle$ satisfying the following conditions:

- $\langle \mathbf{Sign}, \mathbf{Sen}, \mathbf{Mod}, \{\models^\Sigma\}_{\Sigma \in |\mathbf{Sign}|} \rangle$ is an institution,

- $\mathbf{Sign}_0$ is a subcategory of $\mathbf{Sign}$ called the subcategory of admissible signatures; the restriction of the functor $\mathbf{Sen}$ to $\mathbf{Sign}_0$ will be denoted by $\mathbf{Sen}_0$,

- $\mathbf{ax} : \mathbf{Sign}_0 \to \mathbf{Set}$ is a subfunctor of the functor obtained by composing $\mathbf{Sen}_0$ with the powerset functor, i.e., there is a natural inclusion $\mathbf{ax}(\Sigma) \subseteq \mathscr{P}(\mathbf{Sen}_0(\Sigma))$ for each $\Sigma \in \mathbf{Sign}_0$. Each $\Gamma \in \mathbf{ax}(\Sigma)$ is called a set of admissible axioms. This defines a subcategory $\mathbf{Th}_{ax}$ of $\mathbf{Th}$ whose objects are theory presentations $T = \langle \Sigma, \Gamma \rangle$ with $\Sigma \in \mathbf{Sign}_0$ and $\Gamma \in \mathbf{ax}(\Sigma)$, and whose morphisms are axiom-preserving theory morphisms H such that H is in $\mathbf{Sign}_0$.

- $\mathbf{M} : \mathbf{Th}_{ax}{}^{\mathrm{op}} \to \mathbf{Struct}_{SC}$ is a functor. Let $T \in |\mathbf{Th}_{ax}{}^{\mathrm{op}}|$, then $\mathbf{M}(T) \in |\mathbf{Struct}_{SC}|$ is the model structure of T,

- $\mathbf{Mods} : \mathbf{Struct}_{SC} \to \mathbf{Cat}$ is a functor. Let $T \in |\mathbf{Th}_{ax}{}^{\mathrm{op}}|$, then $\mathbf{Mods}(\mathbf{M}(T))$ is the set of canonical models of T; the composite functor $\mathbf{Mods} \circ \mathbf{M} : \mathbf{Th}_{ax}{}^{\mathrm{op}} \to \mathbf{Cat}$ will be denoted by $\mathbf{models}$, and

- $\mu : \mathbf{models} \Rightarrow \mathscr{P} \circ \mathbf{Mod}$ is a natural transformation such that, for each $T = \langle \Sigma, \Gamma \rangle \in |\mathbf{Th}_{ax}{}^{\mathrm{op}}|$, the image of $\mu_T : \mathbf{models}(T) \to \mathscr{P} \circ \mathbf{Mod}(T)$ is the subcategory of $\mathbf{Mod}(T)$ corresponding to each canonical representation of a class of models in $|\mathbf{models}(T)|$. The map μ_T is called the *projection of the category of models* of the theory T.

There are no major differences with respect to [50, Def. 14], except for the lack of restriction on the possible conclusions that the sub-calculus can draw. Notice that in the case of proof theoretic approaches, the introduction of a functor restricting the conclusions, as a sub functor of $\mathbf{Sen}$, is a key element of the definition introduced for restricting the set of theorems of interest, in contrast with satisfiability calculi, where models only relate to a given theory presentation, there is not such need.

Example 3.2 [Tableau Method as a satisfiability subcalculus for the quantifier-free and ground fragment of first-order predicate logic] This example strongly relays on Ex. 2.8 as the language for which we present a satisfiability subcalculus is a restriction of the language of first-order predicate logic.

We first proceed to define the basic restriction of the language of first order predicate logic by determining Sign_0 and **ax**:

- $\mathsf{Sign}_0 = \mathsf{Sign}$,
- **ax** is the composition of a functor $Qf : \mathsf{Sign}_0 \to \mathsf{Set}$ yielding, for each $\Sigma \in |\mathsf{Sign}|$, the restriction of $\mathbf{Sen}(\Sigma)$ to the quantifier-free sentences, with $\mathscr{P}_{fin}$.

Once we established the restriction of the language, $\mathbf{M}$ is defined exactly as in Ex. 2.8 but considering only those tableaux that do not contain any application of rules $[\forall]$ and $[\exists]$. Notice that these rules are not required as they can only be applied to sets of formulae containing a quantified formula which, by the restriction stated before, do not exists.

Finally, $\mathbf{Mods}$ and μ are defined exactly as in Ex. 2.8.

The next definition introduces the notion of effectiveness of the procedure for constructing structures characterising models for sets of sentences over a logical (sub)language. To this end, we follow Meseguer's approach [50, Def. 16], which, in turn, adopts the axiomatic view of computability outlined by Shoenfield in [52]. The elementary notions are those of a *finite object*, a *space* of finite objects, and *recursive functions*. In Shoenfield's own words, a *finite object* is an "object which can be specified by a finite amount of information", a *space* is "an infinite class X of finite objects such that, given a finite object x, we can decide whether or not x belongs to X". Now, given spaces X and Y, a recursive function $f : X \to Y$ is then a total function that can be computed by an algorithm (i.e., by a terminating program, disregarding space and time limitations); spaces and recursive functions form a category Space. Effectiveness is then obtained by restricting sentences and axioms over selected signatures to be organised in a space.

Definition 3.3 [Effective satisfiability subcalculus] An *effective satisfiability subcalculus* is a structure $\mathbb{Q}$ of the form: $\langle \mathsf{Sign}, \mathbf{Sen}, \mathbf{Mod}, \mathsf{Sign}_0, \mathbf{Sen}_0, \mathbf{ax}, \{\models^{\Sigma}\}_{\Sigma \in |\mathsf{Sign}|}, \mathbf{M}, \mathbf{Mods}, \mu \rangle$ satisfying the following conditions:

- $\langle \mathsf{Sign}, \mathbf{Sen}, \mathbf{Mod}, \{\models^{\Sigma}\}_{\Sigma \in |\mathsf{Sign}|} \rangle$ is an institution.
- Sign_0 is a subcategory of Sign called the subcategory of admissible signatures; let $J : \mathsf{Sign}_0 \hookrightarrow \mathsf{Sign}$ be the inclusion functor.
- $\mathbf{Sen}_0 : \mathsf{Sign}_0 \to \mathsf{Space}$ is a functor such that $\mathcal{U} \circ \mathbf{Sen}_0 = \mathbf{Sen} \circ J$, where $\mathcal{U} : \mathsf{Space} \to \mathsf{Set}$ is the obvious forgetful functor.
- $\mathbf{ax} : \mathsf{Sign}_0 \to \mathsf{Space}$ is a subfunctor of the functor obtained by composing $\mathbf{Sen}_0$ with the functor $\mathscr{P}_{fin} : \mathsf{Space} \to \mathsf{Space}$, that sends each space to the space of its finite subsets. This defines a subcategory Th_{ax} of Th whose

objects are theories $T = \langle \Sigma, \Gamma \rangle$ with $\Sigma \in \mathsf{Sign}_0$ and $\Gamma \in \mathbf{ax}(\Sigma)$, and whose morphisms are axiom-preserving theory morphisms H such that H is in Sign_0.

- $\mathbf{M} : \mathsf{Th}_{ax}{}^{\mathsf{op}} \to \mathsf{Struct}_{SC}$ is a functor. Let $T \in |\mathsf{Th}_{ax}{}^{\mathsf{op}}|$, then $\mathbf{M}(T) \in |\mathsf{Struct}_{SC}|$ is the model structure of T.

- $\mathbf{Mods} : \mathsf{Struct}_{SC} \to \mathsf{Space}$ is a functor. Let $T \in |\mathsf{Th}_{ax}{}^{\mathsf{op}}|$, then $\mathbf{Mods}(\mathbf{M}(T))$ is the set of canonical models of T; the composite functor $\mathbf{Mods} \circ \mathbf{M} : \mathsf{Th}_{ax}{}^{\mathsf{op}} \to \mathsf{Space}$ will be denoted by $\mathbf{models}$.

- $\mu : \mathbf{models} \Rightarrow \mathscr{P} \circ \mathbf{Mod}$ is a natural transformation such that, for each $T = \langle \Sigma, \Gamma \rangle \in |\mathsf{Th}_{ax}{}^{\mathsf{op}}|$, the image of $\mu_T : \mathbf{models}(T) \to \mathscr{P} \circ \mathbf{Mod}(T)$ is the subcategory of $\mathbf{Mod}(T)$ corresponding to each canonical representation of a class of models in $|\mathbf{models}(T)|$. The map μ_T is called the *projection of the category of models* of the theory T.

- $\mathcal{U}(\mathbb{Q}) = \langle \mathsf{Sign}, \mathsf{Sen}, \mathbf{Mod}, \mathsf{Sign}_0, \mathcal{U} \circ \mathbf{ax}, \{\models^{\Sigma}\}_{\Sigma \in |\mathsf{Sign}|}, \mathbf{M}, \mathcal{U} \circ \mathbf{Mods}, \mu \circ \mathcal{U} \rangle$ is a satisfiability subcalculus, where $\mu \circ \mathcal{U}$ denotes the natural transformation formed by $\{\mu_T \circ \mathcal{U} : \mathcal{U} \circ \mathbf{models}(T) \to \mathscr{P} \circ \mathbf{Mod}\}_{T \in |\mathsf{Th}_{ax}{}^{\mathsf{op}}|}$.

Notice that the only differences between Def. 3.1 and Def. 3.3 are that: a) the restriction Sen_0 of the functor Sen must satisfy $\mathcal{U} \circ \mathsf{Sen}_0 = \mathsf{Sen} \circ J$, and b) all occurrences of the category Set involved in the definition are replaced by Space. Condition a establishes that the restriction $\mathsf{Sen}_0 : \mathsf{Sign}_0 \to \mathsf{Space}$ of the functor $\mathsf{Sen} : \mathsf{Sign} \to \mathsf{Set}$ is coherent with the inclusion functor J and the forgetful functor $\mathcal{U}$, and Cond. b ensures decidability.

Example 3.4 [Truth tables as an effective satisfiability subcalculus for the quantifier-free and ground fragment of first-order predicate logic] Let $\mathcal{X}$ be a set of first-order variables and $\mathbb{I}_{\mathrm{FOL}}$ be the institution for first-order predicate logic. Let Σ be a set of propositional variables then, the set of propositional sentences over those variables (denoted as $\mathcal{L}_{\Sigma}$) is defined as follows:

$$\mathcal{L}_{\Sigma} := p \mid \neg\alpha \mid \alpha \vee \beta \text{ where } p \in \Sigma \text{ and } \alpha, \beta \in \mathcal{L}_{\Sigma}$$

an *assignment* for Σ is a function $val_{\Sigma} : \Sigma \to \{\bot, \top\}$. Given $\alpha \in \mathcal{L}_{\Sigma}$, we say that an *assignment val* satisfies α (denoted as $val \models \alpha$) if and only if:

$$val \models p \text{ iff } val(p) = \top$$
$$val \models \neg\alpha \text{ iff } val \models \alpha \text{ does not hold}$$
$$val \models \alpha \vee \beta \text{ iff } val \models \alpha \text{ or } val \models \beta$$

Given a set of formulae $\Gamma \in 2^{\mathcal{L}_{\Sigma}}$ we say that a formula α *can be obtained from* Γ if and only if at least one of the following conditions hold:

- $\alpha \in \Gamma$
- α is of the form $\neg\beta_1$
- α is of the form $\beta_1 \vee \beta_2$

where β_1 and β_2 can be obtained from Γ.

The reader should note that, if we define Γ as a set of propositional variables then a formula α *can be obtained from* Γ if and only if $\alpha \in \mathcal{L}_\Gamma$; furthermore, we can tell if a *truth assignment* val_Γ satisfies the formula α (noted $val_\Gamma \models \alpha$).

Given $\Gamma_1, \Gamma_2 \in \mathcal{L}_\Sigma$, if all formula $\alpha \in \Gamma_2$ can be obtained from Γ_1, then we can define a *Truth table* from Γ_1 to Γ_2 as a function $t : assigns_{\Gamma_1} \rightarrow assigns_{\Gamma_2}$. Each set $assigns_\Gamma$ is the set of all functions with type $\Gamma \rightarrow \{\top, \bot\}$; in particular, the set $assigns_\Sigma$ is the set of all possible *truth assignments* for Σ. In order for t to be a *Truth table* the following condition must also hold:

$$t(val_{\Gamma_1})(\alpha) = \top \text{ if and only if } val_{\Gamma_1} \models \alpha, \text{ for all } val_{\Gamma_1} \in assigns_{\Gamma_1}, \text{ for } \alpha \in \Gamma_2.$$

Note that given two *Truth tables* $t : assigns_{\Gamma_1} \rightarrow assigns_{\Gamma_2}$ and $t' : assigns_{\Gamma_2} \rightarrow assigns_{\Gamma_3}$, the composition $t' \circ t : assigns_{\Gamma_1} \rightarrow assigns_{\Gamma_3}$ is also a *Truth table*. Next, we have to provide formal definitions for the categories supporting *Truth table* structures. Given a set of propositional variables Σ and a set of formulae $\Gamma \in 2^{\mathcal{L}_\Sigma}$, we define $Str^{\Sigma,\Gamma} = \langle \mathcal{O}, \mathcal{A} \rangle$ such that $\mathcal{O} = 2^{\Gamma'}$ where Γ' is the set of all subformulae of the formulae in Γ, and $\mathcal{A} = \{t : \Gamma_1 \rightarrow \Gamma_2 \mid \Gamma_1, \Gamma_2 \subseteq 2^{\Gamma'}\}$, where all formula $\alpha \in \Gamma_2$ can be obtained from Γ_1 and t is the *Truth table* from Γ_1 to Γ_2. Note that a structure $Str^{\Sigma,\Gamma}$ has identities and composition, and it can be proved to be a category.

Now we can define the effective satisfiability subcalculus for $\mathbb{I}_{FOL}$ as follows:

(i) In this case any signature is an admissible signature, therefore $\mathsf{Sign}_0 = \mathsf{Sign}$. Then, $\mathbf{Sen}_0$ is the restriction of the functor $\mathbf{Sen}$ to the category Sign_0. Note that $\mathbf{Sen}_0(\Sigma)$ is a recursive infinite set of finite objects, and therefore, it can be proved that the image of $\mathbf{Sen}_0$ is a space. Since $\mathbf{Sen}_0$ is a subfunctor of $\mathbf{Sen}$ it is easy to observe that $\mathcal{U} \circ \mathbf{Sen}_0 = \mathbf{Sen} \circ J$.

(ii) $\mathbf{ax}$ is the composition of a functor $Qf : \mathsf{Sign}_0 \rightarrow \mathsf{Set}$ yielding, for each $\Sigma \in |\mathsf{Sign}|$, the restriction of $\mathbf{Sen}_0(\Sigma)$ to the quantifier-free sentences, with $\mathscr{P}_{fin}$.

(iii) In order to define $\mathbf{M}$ we first need to map each first order formula to a boolean combination of propositional variables and then introduce the class of legal Truth tables for those formulas. We will call $\mathrm{prop}(\Sigma) = \{v_p \mid p$ is a formula in Γ, with $\Gamma \in \mathbf{ax}(\Sigma)\}$ for $\Sigma \in \mathsf{Sign}_0$. Then, we define the function $Tr : Qf(\Sigma) \rightarrow \mathcal{L}_{\mathrm{prop}(\Sigma)}$ as follows:

$$\begin{aligned}
Tr(P(t_1, \ldots, t_k)) &= v_{``P(t_1, \ldots, t_k)"} \\
Tr(t = t') &= v_{``t = t'"}, \\
Tr(\neg\alpha) &= \neg Tr(\alpha), \\
Tr(\alpha \vee \beta) &= Tr(\alpha) \vee Tr(\beta).
\end{aligned}$$

where P is a predicate symbol and $t, t', t_1 \ldots t_k$ are terms.

We will also note Tr as its extension to sets of formulae (i.e., $Tr(\Gamma)$ with $\Gamma \in \mathbf{ax}(\Sigma)$). Now we can define Struct_{SC} as $\langle \mathcal{O}, \mathcal{A} \rangle$ where

- $\mathcal{O} = \{\left\langle Str^{\mathsf{prop}(\Sigma),\, Tr(\Gamma)}, \cup, \emptyset \right\rangle \mid \Sigma \in |\mathbf{Sign}_0| \wedge \Gamma \in \mathbf{ax}(\Sigma)\}$, and

- $\mathcal{A} = \{\hat{\sigma} : \left\langle Str^{\mathsf{prop}(\Sigma),\, Tr(\Gamma)}, \cup, \emptyset \right\rangle \to \left\langle Str^{\mathsf{prop}(\Sigma'),\, Tr(\Gamma')}, \cup, \emptyset \right\rangle \mid \sigma : \langle \Sigma, \Gamma \rangle \to \langle \Sigma', \Gamma' \rangle \in \|\mathbf{Th}\|\}$.

Finally, we can define $\mathbf{M}$ in the following way:

- $\mathbf{M}(\langle \Sigma, \Gamma \rangle) = \left\langle Str^{\mathsf{prop}(\Sigma),\, Tr(\Gamma)}, \cup, \emptyset \right\rangle$, for each $\langle \Sigma, \Gamma \rangle \in |\mathbf{Th}_{ax}|$.

- $\mathbf{M}(\sigma^{\mathsf{op}}) = \widehat{\sigma^{\mathsf{op}}}$, for each theory morphism $\sigma : \langle \Sigma, \Gamma \rangle \to \langle \Sigma', \Gamma' \rangle \in \|\mathbf{Th}_{ax}\|$, where $\hat{\sigma} : \left\langle Str^{\mathsf{prop}(\Sigma),\, Tr(\Gamma)}, \cup, \emptyset \right\rangle \to \left\langle Str^{\mathsf{prop}(\Sigma'),\, Tr(\Gamma')}, \cup, \emptyset \right\rangle$ is the homomorphic extension of σ.

(iv) **Mods** provides the means for obtaining the set of canonical models from structures of the form $Str^{\mathsf{prop}(\Sigma),\, Tr(\Gamma)}$ by identifying the "rows" of the truth table that satisfy each formula in Γ (i.e. , the *truth assignments* of the propositional variables for which the *truth assignments* for each formula is $\top$). **Mods** : $\mathbf{Struct}_{SC} \to \mathbf{Space}$ is defined on objects as $\mathbf{Mods}(\left\langle Str^{\mathsf{prop}(\Sigma),\, Tr(\Gamma)}, \cup, \emptyset \right\rangle) = \langle \mathcal{O}, \mathcal{A} \rangle$ where:

- $\mathcal{O} = \left\{ val_{\mathsf{prop}(\Sigma)}\big|_{Tr(\Gamma)} \;\middle|\; \begin{array}{l} val_{\mathsf{prop}(\Sigma)} \in assigns_{\mathsf{prop}(\Sigma)}, \\ t : \emptyset \to Tr(\Gamma) \in \|Str^{\mathsf{prop}(\Sigma),\, Tr(\Gamma)}\|, \\ (\forall \alpha \in Tr(\Gamma))\; t(val_{\mathsf{prop}(\Sigma)})(\alpha) = \top \end{array} \right\}$

where $val_{\mathsf{prop}(\Sigma)}\big|_{Tr(\Gamma)}$ is the restriction of the function $val_{\mathsf{prop}(\Sigma)}$ to the set of propositional variables that appear in $Tr(\Gamma)$.

- $\mathcal{A} = \{id_v : v \to v \mid v \in \mathcal{O}\}$.

and on morphisms as for all $\sigma : \langle \Sigma, \Gamma \rangle \to \langle \Sigma', \Gamma' \rangle \in \|\mathbf{Th}_{ax}\|$, $\mathbf{Mods}(\widehat{\sigma^{\mathsf{op}}})(val_{\mathsf{prop}(\Sigma')}\big|_{Tr(\Gamma')}) = val_{\mathsf{prop}(\Sigma)}\big|_{Tr(\Gamma)}$, such that $val_{\mathsf{prop}(\Sigma)}(v_p) = val_{\mathsf{prop}(\Sigma')}(\sigma(v_p))$ for all the variables v_p that appear in $Tr(\Gamma)$. Each object $\langle \mathcal{O}, \mathcal{A} \rangle$ is a set of functions with a finite fixed domain, therefore there is at most a finite amount of functions, thus we can prove that $\langle \mathcal{O}, \mathcal{A} \rangle$ is a space.

(v) μ has to relate the structures representing truth assignments with the first order models satisfying the set of formulae denoted by those truth assignments; then we can define $\mu_{\langle \Sigma, \Delta \rangle} : \mathbf{models}(\langle \Sigma, \Delta \rangle) \to \mathscr{P} \circ \mathbf{Mod}(\langle \Sigma, \Delta \rangle)$ as for each $val_{\mathsf{prop}(\Sigma)} \in |\mathbf{models}(\langle \Sigma, \Delta \rangle)|$, $\mu_{\langle \Sigma, \Delta \rangle}(val_{\mathsf{prop}(\Sigma)}) = \mathbf{Mod}(\langle \Sigma, \widehat{\Delta} \rangle)$, where $\widehat{\Delta} = \{P(t_1, \ldots, t_k) \mid val_{\mathsf{prop}(\Sigma)}(v_{\text{``}}P(t_1, \ldots, t_k)\text{''}) = \top\} \cup \{\neg P(t_1, \ldots, t_k) \mid val_{\mathsf{prop}(\Sigma)}(v_{\text{``}}P(t_1, \ldots, t_k)\text{''}) = \bot\} \cup \{t = t' \mid val_{\mathsf{prop}(\Sigma)}(v_{\text{``}t = t'\text{''}}) = \top\} \cup \{\neg t = t' \mid val_{\mathsf{prop}(\Sigma)}(v_{\text{``}t = t'\text{''}}) = \bot\}$. In order to prove that μ is a natural family of functors we have to show that $\mu_{\langle \Sigma, \Delta \rangle} \circ \mathbf{models}(\sigma^{\mathsf{op}})(val_{\mathsf{prop}(\Sigma')}) = (\mathscr{P} \circ \mathbf{Mod}(\sigma^{\mathsf{op}})) \circ \mu_{\langle \Sigma', \Delta' \rangle}(val_{\mathsf{prop}(\Sigma')})$, for $\sigma : \langle \Sigma, \Delta \rangle \to \langle \Sigma', \Delta' \rangle$. It is easy to observe that:

- $\mu_{\langle \Sigma, \Delta \rangle} \circ \mathbf{models}(\sigma^{\mathsf{op}})(val_{\mathsf{prop}(\Sigma')}) = \mathbf{Mod}(\langle \Sigma, \widehat{\Delta} \rangle)$.

- $(\mathscr{P} \circ \mathbf{Mod}(\sigma^{\mathsf{op}})) \circ \mu_{\langle \Sigma', \Delta' \rangle}(val_{\mathsf{prop}(\Sigma')}) = \mathbf{Mod}(\langle \Sigma, \widehat{\Delta} \rangle)$.

where $\widehat{\Delta}$, as defined above, is the set of first order predicates that correspond to the *truth assignment* $val_{\mathsf{prop}(\Sigma)}$, and $val_{\mathsf{prop}(\Sigma)}$ is the map of $val_{\mathsf{prop}(\Sigma')}$ to the signature Σ.

The notion of effective satisfiability subcalculus provides the theoretical foundations for those analysis commands relying on model finding, much in the same way that proof calculus provide theoretical support for the proof commands; the combination results from applying Coro. 2.12. Applying such a corollary requires the language to have negation, in the sense of Def. 2.11 which, even when it might be satisfied by the institution underlying the effective satisfiability subcalculus, there is no guarantee that it is satisfied by the restriction of the language for which the subcalculus is effective.

Proposition 3.5
Let the structure $\langle \mathsf{Sign}, \mathbf{Sen}, \mathbf{Mod}, \mathsf{Sign}_0, \mathbf{Sen}_0, \mathsf{ax}, \{\models^{\Sigma}\}_{\Sigma \in |\mathsf{Sign}|}, \mathbf{M}, \mathbf{Mods}, \mu \rangle$
be an effective satisfiability subcalculus, then
$\left\langle \mathsf{Sign}_0, \mathbf{Sen}_0, \mathbf{Mod}_0, \{\models_0^{\Sigma}\}_{\Sigma \in |\mathsf{Sign}_0|} \right\rangle$ *is an institution, where* $\mathbf{Mod}_0$ *stands for the functor* $\mathbf{Mod}$ *restricted to the subcategory* $\mathsf{Sign}_0{}^{\mathsf{op}}$ *(usually denoted as* $\mathbf{Mod}|_{\mathsf{Sign}_0{}^{\mathsf{op}}}$*) and* $\models_0^{\Sigma}$ *for the restriction of* $\models^{\Sigma}$ *to the models in* $\mathbf{Mod}_0(\Sigma)$ *and the formulae in* $\mathbf{Sen}_0(\Sigma)$ *(usually denoted as* $\models_0^{\Sigma} = \models^{\Sigma}|_{\mathbf{Mod}_0 \times \mathbf{Sen}_0}$*).*

We already shown how Coro. 2.12 can be used to conclude the unprovability of a given formula α from a theory presentation T, by using a satisfiability calculus in order to construct a structure $M \in |\mathbf{models}(T)|$ and then, having to find a model $\mathcal{M}$ such that $\mathcal{M} \models T$ and $\mathcal{M} \models \alpha$ does not hold which, under the presence of negation in the syntax of the logical language (see Def. 2.11), is equivalent to construct a model $\mathcal{M}$ such that $\mathcal{M} \models T$ and $\mathcal{M} \models \neg \alpha$. Effectiveness, as it was introduced by Def. 3.3, states that M is the result of a constructive push-button process but, for that to hold, the language of the effective satisfiability subcalculus must have negation (i.e. the institution $\left\langle \mathsf{Sign}_0, \mathbf{Sen}_0, \mathbf{Mod}_0, \{\models_0^{\Sigma}\}_{\Sigma \in |\mathsf{Sign}_0|} \right\rangle$ has to have negation).

Corollary 3.6 *Let the structure* $\langle \mathsf{Sign}, \mathbf{Sen}, \mathbf{Mod}, \{\vdash^{\Sigma}\}_{\Sigma \in |\mathsf{Sign}|}, \{\models^{\Sigma}\}_{\Sigma \in |\mathsf{Sign}|} \rangle$ *be a logic, the structure* $\langle \mathsf{Sign}, \mathbf{Sen}, \{\vdash^{\Sigma}\}_{\Sigma \in |\mathsf{Sign}|}, \mathbf{P}, \mathbf{Pr}, \pi \rangle$ *be a proof calculus and the structure* $\langle \mathsf{Sign}, \mathbf{Sen}, \mathbf{Mod}, \mathsf{Sign}_0, \mathbf{Sen}_0, \mathsf{ax}, \{\models^{\Sigma}\}_{\Sigma \in |\mathsf{Sign}|}, \mathbf{M}, \mathbf{Mods}, \mu \rangle$ *be an effective satisfiability subcalculus such that* $\left\langle \mathsf{Sign}_0, \mathbf{Sen}_0, \mathbf{Mod}_0, \{\models_0^{\Sigma}\}_{\Sigma \in |\mathsf{Sign}|} \right\rangle$ *has negation. Therefore, for all* $T = \langle \Sigma, \Gamma \rangle \in |\mathsf{Th}_0|$ *and* $\alpha \in |\mathbf{Sen}_0(\Sigma)|$*, if there exists* $M \in |\mathbf{models}(T)|$ *and* $\mathcal{M} \in |\mu_T(M)|$ *such that* $\mathcal{M} \models^{\Sigma} \neg \alpha$*, then there is no* $\tau \in |\mathbf{proof}(T)|$ *such that* $\pi_T(\tau) = \alpha$*.*

As we mentioned at the beginning of this section, our focus is in combining automatic model finding capabilities as part of the process of analysis of software descriptions. While Def. 3.3 provides the formal framework for describing such effective procedures and, as we said before, Coro. 3.6 expose the link between the result of such procedures and the unprovability of a formula, there is still a missing piece in the puzzle in order to guarantee automatic counterexample finding.

Corollary 3.6 properly connects the existence of a model satisfying the negation of a formula with the impossibility of proving the formula itself, but it provides no guide on how to use the effective procedure for building a model structure $M \in |\mathbf{models}(T)|$ for finding a model $\mathcal{M} \in |\mu_T(M)|$ such that $\mathcal{M} \models^\Sigma \neg \alpha$. To solve that, $\neg \alpha$ has to be involved in the process of building M in a way that every model $\mathcal{M} \in |\mu_T(M)|$ satisfies $\neg \alpha$. In general, the mechanism used to internalise $\neg \alpha$ in the process for building models for T strongly depend on the specific procedure for building model structures and, under certain conditions, it can be done by simply adding $\neg \alpha$ to the axioms in T. Such a condition is know, analogous to what we did for requiring an institution to have negation, as to "have conjunction", formally defined below.

Definition 3.7 Given a institution $\mathbb{I}$, we say that $\mathbb{I}$ *has conjunction* if for every signature $\Sigma \in |\mathsf{Sign}|$, $\{\alpha_i\}_{i \in \mathcal{I}} \subseteq \mathbf{Sen}(\Sigma)$, there exists a formula in $\mathbf{Sen}(\Sigma)$, usually denoted as $\bigwedge_{i \in \mathcal{I}} \alpha_i$, such that for all $\mathcal{M} \in \mathbf{Mod}(\Sigma)$,

$$\mathcal{M} \models^\Sigma \bigwedge_{i \in \mathcal{I}} \alpha_i \text{ iff } \mathcal{M} \models^\Sigma \alpha_i, \text{ for all } i \in \mathcal{I}$$

Remark 3.8 Notice that given a institution $\mathbb{I}$, $\Sigma \in |\mathsf{Sign}|$ and $\Gamma \subseteq \mathbf{Sen}(\Sigma)$, for all $\mathcal{M} \in \mathbf{Mod}(\Sigma)$,

$$\mathcal{M} \models^\Sigma \Gamma \text{ iff } \mathcal{M} \models^\Sigma \bigwedge_{\alpha \in \Gamma} \alpha$$

Therefore, Coro. 3.6 can be stated as follows.

Corollary 3.9 *Let the structure* $\langle \mathsf{Sign}, \mathbf{Sen}, \mathbf{Mod}, \{\vdash^\Sigma\}_{\Sigma \in |\mathsf{Sign}|}, \{\models^\Sigma\}_{\Sigma \in |\mathsf{Sign}|} \rangle$ *be a logic, the structure* $\langle \mathsf{Sign}, \mathbf{Sen}, \{\vdash^\Sigma\}_{\Sigma \in |\mathsf{Sign}|}, \mathbf{P}, \mathbf{Pr}, \pi \rangle$ *be a proof calculus and the structure* $\langle \mathsf{Sign}, \mathbf{Sen}, \mathbf{Mod}, \mathsf{Sign}_0, \mathbf{Sen}_0, \mathbf{ax}, \{\models^\Sigma\}_{\Sigma \in |\mathsf{Sign}|}, \mathbf{M}, \mathbf{Mods}, \mu \rangle$ *be an effective satisfiability subcalculus such that* $\langle \mathsf{Sign}_0, \mathbf{Sen}_0, \mathbf{Mod}_0, \{\models_0{}^\Sigma\}_{\Sigma \in |\mathsf{Sign}_0|} \rangle$ *has negation and conjunction. Therefore, for all* $T = \langle \Sigma, \Gamma \rangle \in |\mathbf{Th}_0|$ *and* $\alpha \in |\mathbf{Sen}_0(\Sigma)|$, *if there exists* $M \in |\mathbf{models}(\langle \Sigma, \Gamma \cup \{\neg \alpha\} \rangle)|$, *then there is no* $\tau \in |\mathbf{proof}(T)|$ *such that* $\pi_T(\tau) = \alpha$.

So far, we managed to provide the means for understanding how an effective procedure for building models can be used for short-cutting a proving attempt by deducing that no such proof exists but such usage is confined to theories and propositions consisting exclusively of formulae from the sublanguage formalised as the institution $\langle \mathsf{Sign}_0, \mathbf{Sen}_0, \mathbf{Mod}_0, \{\models_0{}^\Sigma\}_{\Sigma \in |\mathsf{Sign}_0|} \rangle$ for which such an effective procedure exists. We would like to get as much value as possible from the, usually big, effort invested in developing tools supporting specific effective satisfiability calculi.

The typical way of doing so is as follows: given an institution of interest $\mathbb{I} = \langle \mathbf{Sign}, \mathbf{Sen}, \mathbf{Mod}, \{\models^\Sigma\}_{\Sigma \in |\mathbf{Sign}|} \rangle$ and an effective satisfiability subcalculus $\mathbb{Q} = \langle \mathbf{Sign'}, \mathbf{Sen'}, \mathbf{Mod'}, \mathbf{Sign'_0}, \mathbf{Sen'_0}, \mathbf{ax'}, \{\models'^\Sigma\}_{\Sigma \in |\mathbf{Sign'}|}, \mathbf{M'}, \mathbf{Mods'}, \mu' \rangle$, we consider a semantics preserving translation from $\mathbb{I}$ to $\langle \mathbf{Sign'_0}, \mathbf{Sen'_0}, \mathbf{Mod'_0}, \{\models_0'^\Sigma\}_{\Sigma \in |\mathbf{Sign'_0}|} \rangle$, the institution underlying the decidable fragment of $\mathbb{Q}$.

The usual notion of morphism between institutions consists of three arrows between the components of the source and target institutions: 1) an arrow relating the categories of signatures, 2) an arrow relating the grammar functors, and 3) an arrow relating the models functors. Several notions of morphisms between institutions, and their properties, were investigated in [78,50,44]. More recently, in [79], all these notions of morphism were scrutinised in more detail by observing how the direction of the arrows modify its interpretation. Institution comorphisms can be used as a vehicle for borrowing proofs along logic translation [44]; for defining heterogeneous development environments for software specification and design [80,81], which provides the foundations of tools like HETS [82] and CafeOBJ [83]; for providing structured specifications in general [40], for providing semantics to specific features of formal languages [84]; for defining proof systems for structured specifications [85,86,87]; and for formalising data and specification refinements in [39,88,89], just to give a few examples.

Let us start by recalling some notions about mapping entailment systems. In general, given two entailment systems $\mathbb{E} = \langle \mathbf{Sign}, \mathbf{Sen}, \{\vdash^\Sigma\}_{\Sigma \in |\mathbf{Sign}|} \rangle$ and $\mathbb{E'} = \langle \mathbf{Sign'}, \mathbf{Sen'}, \{\vdash'^\Sigma\}_{\Sigma \in |\mathbf{Sign}|} \rangle$, if we aim at mapping sentences in $\mathbb{E}$ to sentences in $\mathbb{E'}$ by using a natural transformation $\alpha : \mathbf{Sen} \Rightarrow \mathbf{Sen'} \circ \Phi$ in a way that provability is preserved (i.e. $\Gamma \vdash^\Sigma \phi$ if and only if $\alpha_\Sigma(\Gamma) \vdash'^{\Phi(\Sigma)} \alpha_\Sigma(\phi)$), a functor $\Phi : \mathbf{Sign} \rightarrow \mathbf{Sign'}$ will not be enough. The reason is that for preserving provability, the proof theoretic structure of $\mathbb{E'}$ might require certain basic axioms for characterising the behaviour of its own logical symbols. Solving this issue requires resorting to a functor $\Phi : \mathbf{Sign} \rightarrow \mathbf{Th'_0}$ that, in turn, can be easily extended to a functor $\overline{\Phi} : \mathbf{Th_0} \rightarrow \mathbf{Th'_0}$, the α-extension to theories of Φ, as $\overline{\Phi}(\langle \Sigma, \Gamma \rangle) = \langle \Sigma', \overline{\Gamma'} \rangle$ such that $\Phi(\Sigma) = \langle \Sigma', \Gamma' \rangle$ and $\overline{\Gamma'} = \Gamma' \cup \alpha_\Sigma(\Gamma)$. Notice also that the natural transformation $\alpha : \mathbf{Sen} \Rightarrow \mathbf{Sen'} \circ \Phi$ can be extended to $\overline{\alpha} : \mathbf{Sen} \Rightarrow \mathbf{Sen'} \circ \overline{\Phi}$ between the functors $\mathbf{Sen} : \mathbf{Th_0} \rightarrow \mathbf{Set}$ and $\mathbf{Sen'} \circ \overline{\Phi} : \mathbf{Th'_0} \rightarrow \mathbf{Set}$ as $\alpha_{\langle \Sigma, \Gamma \rangle} = \alpha_\Sigma$.

Definition 3.10 [Sensibility and simplicity [50]] Let $\langle \mathbf{Sign}, \mathbf{Sen}, \{\vdash^\Sigma\}_{\Sigma \in |\mathbf{Sign}|} \rangle$ and $\langle \mathbf{Sign'}, \mathbf{Sen'}, \{\vdash'^\Sigma\}_{\Sigma \in |\mathbf{Sign'}|} \rangle$ be entailment systems, $\Phi : \mathbf{Th_0} \rightarrow \mathbf{Th'_0}$ be a functor and $\alpha : \mathbf{Sen} \Rightarrow \mathbf{Sen'} \circ \Phi$ a natural transformation. Φ is said to be

α-*sensible* if the following conditions are satisfied:

(i) there is a functor $\Phi^\diamond : \mathsf{Sign} \to \mathsf{Sign}'$ such that $\mathbf{sign}' \circ \Phi = \Phi^\diamond \circ \mathbf{sign}$, where $\mathbf{sign} : \mathsf{Th} \to \mathsf{Sign}$ and $\mathbf{sign}' : \mathsf{Th}' \to \mathsf{Sign}'$ are the forgetful functors from theory presentations to signatures, and

(ii) if $\langle \Sigma, \Gamma \rangle \in |\mathsf{Th}|$ and $\langle \Sigma', \Gamma' \rangle \in |\mathsf{Th}'|$ such that $\Phi(\langle \Sigma, \Gamma \rangle) = \langle \Sigma', \Gamma' \rangle$, then $(\Gamma')^\bullet = (\emptyset' \cup \alpha_\Sigma(\Gamma))^\bullet$, where $\emptyset' = \alpha_\Sigma(\emptyset)$ [5].

Φ is said to be α-*simple* if, instead of satisfying $(\Gamma')^\bullet = (\emptyset' \cup \alpha_\Sigma(\Gamma))^\bullet$ in Condition ii, the stronger condition $\Gamma' = \emptyset' \cup \alpha_\Sigma(\Gamma)$ is satisfied.

It is straightforward to see, based on the monotonicity of $^\bullet$, that α-simplicity implies α-sensibility. An α-sensible functor has the property that the associated natural transformation α depends only on signatures. This is a consequence of the following lemma.

Lemma 3.11 (Lemma 22, [50])
Let $\left\langle \mathsf{Sign}, \mathbf{Sen}, \{\vdash^\Sigma\}_{\Sigma \in |\mathsf{Sign}|} \right\rangle$ *and* $\left\langle \mathsf{Sign}', \mathbf{Sen}', \{\vdash'^\Sigma\}_{\Sigma \in |\mathsf{Sign}'|} \right\rangle$ *be entailment systems and* $\Phi : \mathsf{Th}_0 \to \mathsf{Th}'_0$ *a functor satisfying Cond. i of Def. 3.10. Then any natural transformation* $\alpha : \mathbf{Sen} \Rightarrow \mathbf{Sen}' \circ \Phi$ *can be obtained from a natural transformation* $\alpha^\diamond : \mathbf{Sen}(\Sigma) \Rightarrow \mathbf{Sen}' \circ \Phi^\diamond$ *by horizontally composing with the functor* $\mathbf{sign} : \mathsf{Th} \to \mathsf{Sign}$.

The next definition introduces institution comorphism.

Definition 3.12 [Institution comorphism [44]]
Let $\mathbb{I}$ and $\mathbb{I}'$ be institutions. Then, $\langle \rho^{Sign}, \rho^{Sen}, \rho^{Mod} \rangle : \mathbb{I} \longrightarrow \mathbb{I}'$ is an *institution comorphism* if and only if:

- $\rho^{Sign} : \mathsf{Sign} \to \mathsf{Sign}'$ is a functor,
- $\rho^{Sen} : \mathbf{Sen} \Rightarrow \mathbf{Sen}' \circ \rho^{Sign}$ is a natural transformation, (i.e., a natural family of functions $\rho^{Sen}_\Sigma : \mathbf{Sen}(\Sigma) \to \mathbf{Sen}'(\rho^{Sign}(\Sigma)))$, such that for each $\Sigma_1, \Sigma_2 \in |\mathsf{Sign}|$ and $\sigma : \Sigma_1 \to \Sigma_2$ morphism in Sign, the following diagram commutes

$$
\begin{array}{ccc}
\mathbf{Sen}(\Sigma_2) & \xrightarrow{\ \rho^{Sen}_{\Sigma_2}\ } & \mathbf{Sen}'(\rho^{Sign}(\Sigma_2)) \qquad \Sigma_2 \\
\Big\uparrow{\scriptstyle \mathbf{Sen}(\sigma)} & & \Big\uparrow{\scriptstyle \mathbf{Sen}'(\rho^{Sign}(\sigma))} \qquad \Big\uparrow{\scriptstyle \sigma} \\
\mathbf{Sen}(\Sigma_1) & \xrightarrow[\ \rho^{Sen}_{\Sigma_1}\ ]{} & \mathbf{Sen}'(\rho^{Sign}(\Sigma_1)) \qquad \Sigma_1
\end{array}
$$

- $\rho^{Mod} : \mathbf{Mod}' \circ \rho^{Sign^{op}} \Rightarrow \mathbf{Mod}$ [6] is a natural transformation, (i.e., the

---

[5] $\emptyset'$ is not necessarily the empty set of axioms. This fact will be clarified later on.

[6] The functor $\rho^{Sign^{op}} : \mathsf{Sign}'^{op} \to \mathsf{Sign}^{op}$ is the same as $\rho^{Sign} : \mathsf{Sign}' \to \mathsf{Sign}$ but considered

family of functors $\rho_\Sigma^{Mod} : \mathbf{Mod}'(\rho^{Sign^{op}}(\Sigma)) \to \mathbf{Mod}(\Sigma)$ is natural), such that for each $\Sigma_1, \Sigma_2 \in |\mathsf{Sign}|$ and $\sigma : \Sigma_1 \to \Sigma_2$ a morphism in Sign, the following diagram commutes

$$
\begin{array}{ccccc}
\mathbf{Mod}'(\rho^{Sign^{op}}(\Sigma_2)) & \xrightarrow{\ \rho_{\Sigma_2}^{Mod}\ } & \mathbf{Mod}(\Sigma_2) & & \Sigma_2 \\
\Big\downarrow{\scriptstyle \mathbf{Mod}'(\rho^{Sign^{op}}(\sigma^{op}))} & & \Big\downarrow{\scriptstyle \mathbf{Mod}(\sigma^{op})} & & \Big\downarrow{\scriptstyle \sigma} \\
\mathbf{Mod}'(\rho^{Sign^{op}}(\Sigma_1)) & \xrightarrow{\ \rho_{\Sigma_1}^{Mod}\ } & \mathbf{Mod}(\Sigma_1) & & \Sigma_1
\end{array}
$$

such that for any $\Sigma \in |\mathsf{Sign}|$, the function $\rho_\Sigma^{Sen} : \mathbf{Sen}(\Sigma) \to \mathbf{Sen}'(\rho^{Sign}(\Sigma))$ and the functor $\rho_\Sigma^{Mod} : \mathbf{Mod}'(\rho^{Sign^{op}}(\Sigma)) \to \mathbf{Mod}(\Sigma)$ preserves the following satisfaction condition: for any $\alpha \in \mathbf{Sen}(\Sigma)$ and $\mathcal{M}' \in |\mathbf{Mod}'(\rho^{Sign^{op}}(\Sigma))|$,

$$\mathcal{M}' \models'^{\rho^{Sign}(\Sigma)} \rho_\Sigma^{Sen}(\alpha) \ \text{ iff } \ \rho_\Sigma^{Mod}(\mathcal{M}') \models^\Sigma \alpha \ .$$

Intuitively, an institution comorphism $\rho : \mathbb{I} \longrightarrow \mathbb{I}'$ expresses how the satisfiability in a (potentially) less expressive institution $\mathbb{I}$ ca be encoded into a (potentially) more expressive institution $\mathbb{I}'$. In [44, Sec. 5.2], Tarlecki shows that institution comorphisms compose in a rather obvious component wise way, and that it can be proved that institutions together with institution comorphisms form a category, denoted as coIns.

The following results, presented in [44], characterise the relation between the satisfaction relation of $\mathbb{I}$ and $\mathbb{I}'$, in the presence of an institution comorphism.

Proposition 3.13 (Preservation of consequence [44]) *Let* $\mathbb{I}$ *and* $\mathbb{I}'$ *be the institutions* $\langle \mathsf{Sign}, \mathbf{Sen}, \mathbf{Mod}, \{\models^\Sigma\}_{\Sigma \in |\mathsf{Sign}|} \rangle$ *and* $\langle \mathsf{Sign}', \mathbf{Sen}', \mathbf{Mod}', \{\models'^\Sigma\}_{\Sigma \in |\mathsf{Sign}'|} \rangle$, *respectively. Let* $\rho : \mathbb{I} \to \mathbb{I}'$ *be an institution comorphism. Then, for all* $\Sigma \in |\mathsf{Sign}|$, $\Gamma \subseteq \mathbf{Sen}(\Sigma)$ *and* $\varphi \in \mathbf{Sen}(\Sigma)$, *if* $\Gamma \models^\Sigma \varphi$, *then* $\rho_\Sigma^{Sen}(\Gamma) \models'^{\rho^{Sign}(\Sigma)} \rho_\Sigma^{Sen}(\varphi)$.

In some cases institution comorphisms can be extended to what Meseguer introduced under the name *map of institutions* [50, Def. 27], and were more recently renamed by Goguen and Roşu as *theoroidal comorphism* [79, Def. 5.3], by reformulating the functor mapping signatures to act on theory presentations (i.e. $\rho^{Th} : \mathsf{Th} \to \mathsf{Th}'$).

This extension can be done in many ways being one of them when ρ^{Th} is ρ^{Sen}-sensible (see Def. 3.10) with respect to the *entailment system* induced by the consequence relations of the institutions $\mathbb{I}$ and $\mathbb{I}'$. In this way, the natural transformation ρ^{Sign} relating the categories of signatures of both logical

---

between the opposite categories.

languages, can be extended to ρ^{Th} : Sign → Th' enabling the restriction of the target class of models over which the consequence is preserved, and then, to a functor ρ^{Th} : Th → Th' defined in the following way: let $\Sigma \in |\text{Sign}|$, $\Gamma \in |\textbf{Sen}(\Sigma)|$, $\rho^{Th}(\langle \Sigma, \Gamma \rangle) = \langle \rho^{Sign}(\Sigma), \emptyset' \cup \rho_{\Sigma}^{Sen}(\Gamma) \rangle$. Additionally, given an institution comorphism $\langle \rho^{Sign}, \rho^{Sen}, \rho^{Mod} \rangle : \mathbb{I} \longrightarrow \mathbb{I}'$ we say it is *plain* if and only if ρ^{Th} is ρ^{Sen}-plain, and similarly we say it is *simple* if and only if ρ^{Th} is ρ^{Sen}-simple.

The interested reader is pointed to [50, Sec. 4], [44, Sec. 5] and [79, Sec. 5] for a thorough discussion on the matter.

Therefore, the combination of Prop. 3.13 and Coro. 3.9 results in the final statement of how soundness enables the use of an effective satisfiability subcalculus for a logical language, as a counterexample finder for a (potentially) different one.

Corollary 3.14 *Let the structure* $\langle \text{Sign}, \text{Sen}, \text{Mod}, \{\vdash^{\Sigma}\}_{\Sigma \in |\text{Sign}|}, \{\models^{\Sigma}\}_{\Sigma \in |\text{Sign}|} \rangle$ *be a logic, the structure* $\langle \text{Sign}, \text{Sen}, \{\vdash^{\Sigma}\}_{\Sigma \in |\text{Sign}|}, \mathbf{P}, \mathbf{Pr}, \pi \rangle$ *be a proof calculus, the structure* $\langle \text{Sign}', \text{Sen}', \text{Mod}', \text{Sign}'_0, \text{Sen}'_0, \text{ax}', \{\models'^{\Sigma}\}_{\Sigma \in |\text{Sign}'|}, \mathbf{M}', \text{Mods}', \mu' \rangle$ *be an effective satisfiability subcalculus such that* $\langle \text{Sign}'_0, \text{Sen}'_0, \text{Mod}'_0, \{\models'_0{}^{\Sigma}\}_{\Sigma \in |\text{Sign}'_0|} \rangle$ *has negation and conjunction and* $\rho = \langle \rho^{Sign}, \rho^{Sen}, \rho^{Mod} \rangle : \langle \text{Sign}, \text{Sen}, \text{Mod}, \{\models^{\Sigma}\}_{\Sigma \in |\text{Sign}|} \rangle \longrightarrow \langle \text{Sign}'_0, \text{Sen}'_0, \text{Mod}'_0, \{\models'_0{}^{\Sigma}\}_{\Sigma \in |\text{Sign}'_0|} \rangle$ *a comorphism between institutions, being* ρ^{Th} : $\text{Th}_0 \to \text{Th}'_0$ *the theoroidal extension of* ρ^{Sign} : Sign → Sign'_0. *Therefore, for all* $T = \langle \Sigma, \Gamma \rangle \in |\text{Th}_0|$ *and* $\alpha \in |\textbf{Sen}_0(\Sigma)|$, *if there exists* $M \in |\textbf{models}'(\rho^{Th}(\langle \Sigma, \Gamma \cup \{\neg\alpha\} \rangle))|$, *then there is no* $\tau \in |\textbf{proof}(T)|$ *such that* $\pi_T(\tau) = \alpha$.

Corollary 3.14 provides the formal support for using a model finder to look for counterexamples of judgements of the shape $\Gamma \vdash^{\Sigma} \alpha$ at any point of a proof, enabling the capability to check whether the application of a given proof command has modified the provability of α from Γ.

The reader should note that Coro. 3.14 only guaranties that, given a theory presentation $T = \langle \Sigma, \Gamma \rangle$ and a formula α, whenever a model structure M is built for $\rho^{Th}(\langle \Sigma, \Gamma \cup \{\neg\alpha\} \rangle)$ using an effective satisfiability subcalculus, we can conclude the impossibility of constructing a proof structure for α from Γ; but not being able to do so does not provide any solid information about its existence, because there could still be a model in the source institution satisfying the axioms in T and not satisfying α. That, of course, does not invalidate the confidence gained in the validity of the judgement $\gamma \models^{\Sigma} \alpha$, by not founding a counterexample.

Depending on how precise the natural transformation ρ^{Mod} is, regarding

47

the representation of the target category of models over the source one, we can derive stronger conclusion.

Definition 3.15 [Model expansion over model translation] Let $\mathbb{I}$ and $\mathbb{I}'$ be the institutions $\langle \mathsf{Sign}, \mathbf{Sen}, \mathbf{Mod}, \{\models_\Sigma\}_{\Sigma \in |\mathsf{Sign}|} \rangle$ and $\langle \mathsf{Sign}', \mathbf{Sen}', \mathbf{Mod}', \{\models'^\Sigma\}_{\Sigma \in |\mathsf{Sign}'|} \rangle$, respectively. Let $\rho : \mathbb{I} \to \mathbb{I}'$ be an institution comorphism. Then, $\mathbb{I}$ has the ρ-*expansion property* if for all $\langle \Sigma, \Gamma \rangle \in |\mathsf{Th}_0^{\mathbb{I}}|$, $\mathcal{M} \in |\mathbf{Mod}^{\mathbb{I}}(\langle \Sigma, \Gamma \rangle)|$, there exists $\mathcal{M}' \in |\mathbf{Mod}^{\mathbb{I}'}(\rho^{Th}(\langle \Sigma, \Gamma \rangle))|$ such that $\mathcal{M} = \rho^{Mod}(\mathcal{M}')$.

The intuition behind the previous definition is that, given a theoroidal institution comorphism $\rho : \mathbb{I} \to \mathbb{I}'$, $\mathbb{I}$ has the ρ-expansion property whenever every $\mathbb{I}$-model is the target of some $\mathbb{I}'$-models, in a way that the satisfaction of $\mathbb{I}$-formulae is reflected in $\mathbb{I}'$.

Theorem 3.16 (Reflection of consequence [44]) *Let* $\mathbb{I}$ *and* $\mathbb{I}'$ *be the institutions* $\langle \mathsf{Sign}, \mathbf{Sen}, \mathbf{Mod}, \{\models_\Sigma\}_{\Sigma \in |\mathsf{Sign}|} \rangle$ *and* $\langle \mathsf{Sign}', \mathbf{Sen}', \mathbf{Mod}', \{\models'^\Sigma\}_{\Sigma \in |\mathsf{Sign}'|} \rangle$, *respectively. Let* $\rho : \mathbb{I} \to \mathbb{I}'$ *be an institution comorphism. Then, for all* $\Sigma \in |\mathsf{Sign}|$, $\Gamma \subseteq \mathbf{Sen}(\Sigma)$ *and* $\varphi \in \mathbf{Sen}(\Sigma)$, *if every* $\mathcal{M} \in \mathbf{Mod}(\langle \Sigma, \Gamma \rangle)$ *has the* ρ-*expansion property, then* $\Gamma \models_\Sigma \varphi$ *if and only if* $\rho_\Sigma^{Sen}(\Gamma) \models_{\rho^{Sign}(\Sigma)} \rho_\Sigma^{Sen}(\varphi)$.

Finally, Thm. 3.16 states that, given a theoroidal institution comorphism $\rho : \mathbb{I} \to \mathbb{I}'$, such that $\mathbb{I}$ has the ρ-expansion property, then an effective satisfiability subcalculus for $\mathbb{I}'$ (i.e. $\mathbb{I}'$ is the fragment of the language of the effective satisfiability subcalculus for which the procedure is indeed effective) constitutes a semantics-based decision procedure for $\mathbb{I}$.

4 Case-study: first-order predicate logic

First-order predicate logic provides a well-known, and simple, example for showing the value of using theoroidal comorphisms as a tool for reusing tools designed for one language in the analysis of software specifications written in "another". Let us consider the effective satisfiability subcalculus, presented in Ex. 3.4, for the quantifier-free and ground fragment of *FOL*. Intuitively, the theories for which we are capable of constructing models for, are those that do not resort to any quantification and, of course, have no free variables (i.e. all terms appearing in the formulae are ground), but Coro. 3.14 provides the mathematical machinery needed for using off-the-shelve constraint-solving tools in order to enable counterexample searching capabilities.

The reader might note that such a semantics preserving translation contradicts the intuition mentioned after Def. 3.12 where we slide the misleading, but widely spread, idea that the source logical system of an institution comorphism is less expressive than the target one. A more precise interpretation is to consider institution comorphisms as encodings that, in general, satisfy the intuition mentioned before but, under some specific conditions, might loose expressivity / representation capability, while, as we will show in the forthcoming section, still preserve the satisfaction condition. A more thorough study of the conditions under which this type of institution comorphisms can be defined will be left for further investigation.

Let $\mathcal{X}$ be a set of first order variable, $\mathbb{L}_{\text{FOL}} = \langle \mathbf{Sign}, \mathbf{Sen}, \mathbf{Mod}, \{\vdash^{\Sigma}\}_{\Sigma \in |\mathbf{Sign}|}, \{\models^{\Sigma}\}_{\Sigma \in |\mathbf{Sign}|} \rangle$ be the structure formalising first-order predicate logic over $\mathcal{X}$ and $\mathbb{P}_{\text{FOL}} = \langle \mathbf{Sign}, \mathbf{Sen}, \{\vdash^{\Sigma}\}_{\Sigma \in |\mathbf{Sign}|}, \mathbf{P}, \mathbf{Pr}, \pi \rangle$ be a proof calculus for $\mathbb{L}$.

Let $\mathbb{Q}_{\text{Prop}}$ be the effective satisfiability subcalculus $\langle \mathbf{Sign}', \mathbf{Sen}', \mathbf{Mod}', \mathbf{Sign}'_0, \mathbf{Sen}'_0, \mathbf{ax}', \{\models'^{\Sigma}\}_{\Sigma \in |\mathbf{Sign}'|}, \mathbf{M}', \mathbf{Mods}', \mu' \rangle$, where $\langle \mathbf{Sign}', \mathbf{Sen}', \mathbf{Mod}', \{\models'^{\Sigma}\}_{\Sigma \in |\mathbf{Sign}'|} \rangle$ is the institution of propositional logic [7]. Then, we can define a theoroidal comorphism from the underlying institution of $\mathbb{L}_{\text{FOL}}$ to the underlying institution of $\mathbb{Q}_{\text{Prop}}$ by parameterising the translation of first-order formulae with a natural number used to enforce finite bounds to the domains of interpretation of first-order formulae.

Definition 4.1 $\gamma^{Sign} : \mathbf{Sign} \to \mathbf{Sign}'$ is defined as the functor such that:

- for all $\Sigma \in |\mathbf{Sign}|$, $\gamma^{Sign}(\Sigma) = \{v_p | p \text{ is a ground atomic formula in } \mathbf{Sen}(\Sigma)\}$, and
- for all $\sigma : \Sigma \to \Sigma' \in ||\mathbf{Sign}||$, $\gamma^{Sign}(\sigma) = \tau$, where $\tau(v_p) = v_{\mathbf{Sen}(\sigma)(p)}$.

Proposition 4.2 γ^{Sign} *is a functor.*

Proof Note that $\gamma^{Sign}(\sigma)$ is defined in terms of $\mathbf{Sen}(\sigma)$. Since $\mathbf{Sen}$ is a functor it can be proved that γ^{Sign} preserves identities and composition. ∎

Definition 4.3 Let $n \in \mathbb{N}$, $\Sigma = \langle \{f_i\}_{i \in \mathcal{I}}, \{P_j\}_{j \in \mathcal{J}} \rangle$ and $\Sigma' = \langle \{f_i\}_{i \in \mathcal{I}} \cup \{c_k\}_{1 \leq k \leq n}, \{P_j\}_{j \in \mathcal{J}} \rangle$ such that $\Sigma, \Sigma' \in |\mathbf{Sign}|$.

(i) First, we define $Tr_v^n : \mathbf{Sen}(\Sigma) \to \mathbf{Sen}(\Sigma')$ for mapping first-order logic sentences into quantifier-free and ground first-order logic sentences. This will be done by turning existencial quantifiers into finite disjunctions over Σ' in a way that the fresh new constant symbols $\{c_k\}_{1 \leq k \leq n}$ play the role of the only elements in the domain of interpretation.

Let $v : \mathcal{X} \to \{c_k\}_{1 \leq k \leq n}$ be a function mapping the first-order variable

---

[7] Note that in this particular case $\langle \mathbf{Sign}', \mathbf{Sen}', \mathbf{Mod}', \{\models^{\Sigma}\}_{\Sigma \in |\mathbf{Sign}'|} \rangle$ and $\langle \mathbf{Sign}'_0, \mathbf{Sen}'_0, \mathbf{Mod}'_0, \{\models'^{\Sigma}_0\}_{\Sigma \in |\mathbf{Sign}'_0|} \rangle$ can be assumed to be the same institution due to the fact that propositional logic is decidable.

symbols in $\mathcal{X}$ to constant symbols in $\{c_k\}_{1\leq k\leq n}$, then Tr_v^n is defined as follows [8]:

$$Tr_v^n(P(t_1,\ldots,t_k)) = P(Tr_v^n(t_1),\ldots,Tr_v^n(t_k)) \text{ , for all } P \in \{P_j\}_{j\in\mathcal{J}}$$
$$Tr_v^n(\alpha \vee \beta) = Tr_v^n(\alpha) \vee Tr_v^n(\beta)$$
$$Tr_v^n(\neg\alpha) = \neg Tr_v^n(\alpha)$$
$$Tr_v^n((\exists x)\alpha) = \bigvee_{i=1}^n Tr_{v\{x\mapsto c_i\}}^n(\alpha)$$

$$Tr_v^n(x) = v(x) \text{ , for all } x \in \mathcal{X}$$
$$Tr_v^n(f(t_1,\ldots,t_k)) = f(Tr_v^n(t_1),\ldots,Tr_v^n(t_k)) \text{ , for all } f \in \{f_i\}_{i\in\mathcal{I}}$$

(ii) Second, we define a partial function $Tr_{Int} : \mathbf{Sen}(\Sigma') \to \mathbf{Sen}(\Sigma')$ mapping quantifier-free and ground first-order sentences by interpreting the terms as the fresh new constant symbols $\{c_k\}_{1\leq k\leq n}$.

Let $\alpha \in \mathbf{Sen}(\Sigma')$ and $Term(\alpha)$ be the set of terms mentioned in α, excluding those in $\{c_k\}_{1\leq k\leq n}$, then Tr_{Int} is defined as follows:

$$Tr_{Int}(\alpha) = \bigvee_{f\in[Term(\alpha)\to\{c_k\}_{1\leq k\leq n}]} \left[Tr_{Int\,f}(\alpha) \wedge \bigwedge_{t\in Term(\alpha)} t = f(t) \right]$$

$$Tr_{Int\,f}(P(t_1,\ldots,t_k)) = P(f(t_1),\ldots,f(t_k)), \text{ for all } P \in \{P_j\}_{j\in\mathcal{J}},$$
$$Tr_{Int\,f}(t = t') = f(t) = f(t'),$$
$$Tr_{Int\,f}(\neg\alpha) = \neg Tr_{Int\,f}(\alpha),$$
$$Tr_{Int\,f}(\alpha \vee \beta) = Tr_{Int\,f}(\alpha) \vee Tr_{Int\,f}(\beta).$$

(iii) Third, we define a partial function $Tr_{Prop} : \mathbf{Sen}(\Sigma') \to \mathbf{Sen}'(\gamma^{Sign}(\Sigma'))$ for mapping quantifier-free and ground first-order sentences, whose only terms are in $\{c_k\}_{1\leq k\leq n}$, to propositional sentences, as follows:

$$Tr_{Prop}(P(c_1,\ldots,c_k)) = v_{``P(c_1,\ldots,c_k)"}, \text{ for all } P \in \{P_j\}_{j\in\mathcal{J}},$$
$$Tr_{Prop}(c = c') = v_{``c = c'"},$$
$$Tr_{Prop}(\neg\alpha) = \neg Tr_{Prop}(\alpha),$$
$$Tr_{Prop}(\alpha \vee \beta) = Tr_{Prop}(\alpha) \vee Tr_{Prop}(\beta).$$

Then $\gamma_\Sigma^{Sen} : \mathbf{Sen}(\Sigma) \to \mathbf{Sen}'(\gamma^{Sign}(\Sigma'))$ is defined as follows:

$$\gamma_\Sigma^{Sen}(\alpha) = Tr_{Prop}\left(Tr_{Int}\left(Tr_\emptyset^n(\alpha)\right)\right)$$

In the previous definition γ_Σ^{Sen} eliminates quantifiers replacing them with finite disjunctions and produces all the possible interpretations of the terms over the domain $\{c_1,\ldots,c_n\}$. Then, the last stage in the translation, replaces all atomic formulae (in which there are no term other than those in $\{c_1,\ldots,c_n\}$) by propositional variables labeled with the atomic formula they represent.

---

[8] Let $v : \mathcal{X} \to \{c_k\}_{1\leq k\leq n}$ be a function mapping the first-order variable symbols in $\mathcal{X}$ to constant symbols in $\{c_k\}_{1\leq k\leq n}$, then $v\{x \mapsto c_i\}(y) = \begin{cases} v(y) & \text{; if } x \neq y. \\ c_i & \text{; if } x = y. \end{cases}$

Proposition 4.4 γ^{Sen} *is a natural family of functions.*

Proof The proof follows by first observing that given $\Sigma \in |\mathsf{Sign}|$, γ_Σ^{Sen} (see Def. 4.3) is a function. Therefore, we need to prove that the following diagram commutes:

$$
\begin{array}{ccccc}
\mathbf{Sen}(\Sigma_2) & \xrightarrow{\;\;\gamma_{\Sigma_2}^{Sen}\;\;} & \mathbf{Sen}'(\gamma^{Sign}(\Sigma_2)) & & \Sigma_2 \\[2mm]
\mathbf{Sen}(\sigma) \uparrow & & \mathbf{Sen}'(\gamma^{Sign}(\sigma)) \uparrow & & \uparrow \sigma \\[2mm]
\mathbf{Sen}(\Sigma_1) & \xrightarrow{\;\;\gamma_{\Sigma_1}^{Sen}\;\;} & \mathbf{Sen}'(\gamma^{Sign}(\Sigma_1)) & & \Sigma_1
\end{array}
$$

where $\sigma : \Sigma_1 \to \Sigma_2 \in ||\mathsf{Sign}||$ is an homomorphism between two first-order signatures. Note that:

- each γ_Σ^{Sen} is the function mapping first-order Σ-formulae into propositional formulae,

- given $\sigma : \Sigma \to \Sigma' \in ||\mathsf{Sign}||$, $\mathbf{Sen}(\sigma)$ is a function mapping first-order Σ-formulae to first-order Σ'-formulae, and

- given $\sigma : \Sigma \to \Sigma' \in ||\mathsf{Sign}||$, $\mathbf{Sen}'(\gamma^{Sign}(\sigma))$ is a function mapping propositional $\gamma^{Sign}(\Sigma)$-formulae to propositional $\gamma^{Sign}(\Sigma')$-formulae.

Then, the proof follows by observing that translating a first-order formulae across signatures and then mapping them to propositional formulae yields the same result as first mapping the first-order formula to a propositional one, and then translating the propositional formula. ∎

Definition 4.5 Let $n \in \mathbb{N}$, $\gamma^{Sign} : \mathsf{Sign} \to \mathsf{Sign}'$ be the functor of Def. 4.1 and $\gamma^{Sen} : \mathbf{Sen} \to \mathbf{Sen}' \circ \gamma^{Sign}$ be the natural family of functions of Def. 4.3. Then, we define $\gamma^{Th_0} : \mathsf{Th}_0 \to \mathsf{Th}'_0$ as:

$$\gamma^{Th_0}(\langle \Sigma, \Gamma \rangle) = \langle \gamma^{Sign}(\Sigma), \{\gamma_\Sigma^{Sen}(\alpha) | \alpha \in \Gamma \} \rangle \ .$$

Proposition 4.6 *The functor* $\gamma^{Th_0} : \mathsf{Th}_0 \to \mathsf{Th}'_0$ *is* γ^{Sen}*-sensible.*

Proof It follows directly from the definition of γ^{Th_0} by observing it is explicitly constructed in terms of γ^{Sign} and γ^{Sen}. ∎

The next definition provides the usual definition of model for propositional logic. A model is a function assigning a truth value from $\{\top, \bot\}$ to each extralogical (also referred to as rigid) symbol, appearing in the signature. It is easy to note that for such a model, not depending on any domain of discourse for interpreting objects, there is no possible notion of homomorphism that can be regarded as an arrow between two models thus, forcing us to consider them as organised as a discrete category.

51

Definition 4.7 Let $n \in \mathbb{N}$ and $\Sigma = \langle \{f_i\}_{i \in \mathcal{I}}, \{P_j\}_{j \in \mathcal{J}} \rangle \in |\mathbf{Sign}|$. Then we define $\gamma_\Sigma^{Mod} : \mathbf{Mod}'(\gamma^{Sign}(\Sigma)) \to \mathbf{Mod}(\Sigma)$ as follows: for all $val : \gamma^{Sign}(\Sigma) \to \{\bot, \top\} \in |\mathbf{Mod}'(\gamma^{Sign}(\Sigma))|$, $\gamma_\Sigma^{Mod}(val) = \langle \mathcal{S}, \mathcal{F}, \mathcal{P} \rangle$ such that:

- $\mathcal{S} = \{c_1, \dots, c_n\}$,
- $\mathcal{F} = \{\overline{f} | f \in \{f_k\}_{k \in \mathcal{K}}\}$, where
$$\overline{f} = \{\langle c_1, \dots, c_k \rangle \mapsto c | c_1, \dots, c_k, c \in \mathcal{S}, val\left(v_{c=f(c_1,\dots,c_k)}\right) = \top\}.$$
- $\mathcal{P} = \{\overline{P} | P \in \{P_j\}_{j \in \mathcal{J}}\}$, where
$$\overline{P} = \{\langle c_1, \dots, c_k \rangle | c_1, \dots, c_k \in \mathcal{S}, val\left(v_{P(c_1,\dots,c_k)}\right) = \top\}, \text{ and}$$

and for all $Id_{val} : val \to val \in ||\mathbf{Mod}'(\gamma^{Sign}(\Sigma))||$, $\gamma_\Sigma^{Mod}(Id_{val}) = Id_{\gamma_\Sigma^{Mod}(val)}$

Proposition 4.8 γ_Σ^{Mod} *is a functor.*

Proof γ_Σ^{Mod} preserves identities and, since the source category is discrete, the compositions are trivially preserved. ∎

Proposition 4.9 γ^{Mod} *is a natural transformation and the functors γ_Σ^{Mod} preserve the satisfaction condition.*

Proof We need to prove that $\mathbf{Mod}(\sigma^{op}) \circ \gamma_{\Sigma_2}^{Mod} = \gamma_{\Sigma_1}^{Mod} \circ \mathbf{Mod}'(\gamma^{Sign^{op}}(\sigma^{op}))$, with $\sigma : \Sigma_1 \to \Sigma_2 \in ||\mathbf{Sign}||$. It follows from observing that:

- $\mathbf{Mod}(\sigma^{op})(\mathcal{M})$ yields a first-order model obtained by capturing elements of $\mathcal{M}$ according to the signature morphism σ.
- $\mathbf{Mod}'(\gamma^{Sign^{op}}(\sigma^{op}))(\mathcal{M}')$ yields a propositional valuation obtained by capturing the values in $\mathcal{M}'$ according to the signature morphism $\gamma^{Sign}(\sigma)$.
- $\gamma^{Sign}(\sigma)$, as it was defined in Def. 4.1, is the signature morphism in the category of signatures of propositional logic obtained from σ.

With these observations it can also be proved that the functor γ_Σ^{Mod} preserves the satisfaction condition. ∎

Proposition 4.10 *For all $n \in \mathbb{N}$, $\langle \gamma^{Tho}, \gamma^{Sen}, \gamma^{Mod} \rangle : \mathbb{I}_{FOL}(\mathcal{X}) \to Prop$ is a theoroidal comorphism between institutions.*

Proof The proof follows directly from Props. 4.2, 4.4, 4.6, 4.8 and 4.9. ∎

Finally, the institution comorphism $\langle \gamma^{Sign}, \gamma^{Sen}, \gamma^{Mod} \rangle$, together with γ^{Tho}, the theoroidal extension of γ^{Sign}, presented above, satisfy the hypothesis of Coro. 3.14, thus providing an effective procedure, formalised in $\mathbb{Q}_{Prop}$, for bounded counterexample finding that can be applied in the critical parts of a proof being developed within the proof calculus formalised in $\mathbb{P}_{FOL}$.

5 Conclusions

In this work we showed how effective satisfiability sub-calculi, a special type of satisfiability calculi, all of which were presented in [59], can be combined with proof calculi, as they were presented in the context of *General logics* by Meseguer in [50], in order to provide the foundations for methodological approaches to software analysis. This was done by relating, in an abstract categorical setting, the construction of counterexamples, using model finders, with the absence of proofs.

This methodology is based on the fact that searching of counterexamples is usually entangled with theorem proving in software analysis. As we mentioned in the preceding sections, there are many uses for counterexample finding capabilities, among which we find: 1) gaining confidence on the correctness of the specification and the satisfaction of the property, 2) understanding the relevance of each hypothesis in the a proof, and 3) the analysis of the appropriateness of the addition of new hypothesis that might not be provable from the current set of hipothesis. This was exemplified by formalising a bounded counterexample finder as an effective satisfiability subcalculus for propositional logic, and then combining it with a proof calculus for first order logic with equality by means of a semantics preserving translation.

In [90] we presented the tool HETEROGenius as an implementation of a framework based on the (initially intuitive) notion of *heterogeneous hybrid analysis*. The idea behind HETEROGenius is to consider software analysis as a task developed by combining different techniques, following certain methodology. This can be done by considering an *analysis structure* where nodes are judgements of the form $\Gamma \vdash_\Sigma \alpha$ and arrows relate judgements by applying a specific technique thus, providing some insight on its validity. The reader should note that the formalisation of both, proof calculi and satisfiability calculi, are not suitable for the implementation of analysis structures as the latter requires different tools to operate over the same structure, thus internalising their combination.

References

[1] Pnueli, A.: The temporal logic of programs. In: Proceedings of 18th. Annual IEEE Symposium on Foundations of Computer Science, Los Alamitos, CA, USA, IEEE Computer Society, IEEE Computer Society (1977) 46–57

[2] Pnueli, A.: The temporal semantics of concurrent programs. Theoretical Computer Science **13**(1) (1981) 45–60

[3] Manna, Z., Pnueli, A.: Temporal Verification of Reactive Systems. Springer-Verlag, New York, NY, USA (1995)

[4] Ben-Ari, M., Manna, Z., Pnueli, A.: The temporal logic of branching time. In: Proceedings of the 8th. ACM SIGPLAN-SIGACT Symposium on Principles of Programming Languages, Williamsburg, Virginia, Association for the Computer Machinery, ACM Press (1981) 164–176

[5] Emerson, E.A., Halpern, J.Y.: "sometimes" and "not never" revisited: on branching versus linear time temporal logic. Journal of the ACM **33**(1) (1986) 151–178

[6] Fischer, M.J., Ladner, R.E.: Propositional modal logic of programs. In Hopcroft, J.E., Friedman, E.P., Harrison, M.A., eds.: Proceedings of the 9th. annual ACM symposium on theory of computing, Boulder, Colorado, United States, ACM Press (1977) 286–294

[7] Harel, D., Kozen, D., Tiuryn, J.: Dynamic logic. Foundations of Computing. The MIT Press, Cambridge, MA, USA (2000)

[8] Henriksen, J.G., Thiagarajan, P.: Dynamic linear time temporal logic. Annals of Pure and Applied Logic **96**(1–3) (1999) 187–207

[9] van Benthem, J., Doets, K.: Higher-order logic. In Gabbay, D., Guenthner, F., eds.: Handbook of Philosophical Logic. Volume 1. second edn. Kluwer Academic Publishers (2001) 275–329

[10] Henkin, L.A.: The logic of equality. The American Mathematical Monthly **84**(8) (1977) 597–612

[11] Goguen, J.A., Thatcher, J.W., Wagner, E.G., Wright, J.B.: Abstract data types as initial algebras and the correctness of data representations. In: Computer Graphics, Pattern Recognition and Data Structure with the IEEE Computer Society and in cooperation with the ACM Special Interest Group on Computer Graphics, IEEE Computer Society (May 1975) 89–93

[12] Turing, A.M.: On computable numbers, with an application to the entscheidungsproblem. Proceedings of the London Mathematical Society **s2-42**(1) (1937) 230–265

[13] Hoare, C.A.R.: An axiomatic basis for computer programming. Communications of the ACM **26**(1) (1969) 53–56

[14] Burstall, R.M.: Proving properties of programs by structural induction. The Computer Journal **12**(1) (1969) 41–48

[15] Floyd, R.W.: Assigning meaning to programs. In Schwartz, J.T., ed.: Proceedings of Symposia Applied Mathematics of the American Mathematical Society – Mathematical Aspects of Computer Science. Volume 19., American Mathematical Society (April 1966) 19–32 Reprinted in [91].

[16] Parnas, D.L.: A technique for software module specification with examples. Communications of the ACM **15**(5) (1972) 330–336

[17] Dijkstra, E.W.: Guarded commands, nondeterminacy and formal derivation of programs. Communications of the ACM **18**(8) (1975) 453–457

[18] Liskov, B.H.: A design methodology for reliable software systems. In: Proceedings of American Federation of Information Processing Societies '72 Fall Joint Computer Conference - Part I. Volume 41 of AFIPS Conference Proceedings., AFIPS / ACM / Thomson Book Company, Washington D.C. (December 1972) 191–199

[19] Hoare, C.A.R. In: Chapter II: Notes on data structuring. Volume 8 of A.P.I.C. Studies in data processing. Academic Press (1972) 94–185

[20] Hoare, C.A.R.: Proof of correctness of data representations. Acta Informatica **1**(4) (1972) 271–281

[21] Hoare, C.A.R.: Recursive data structures. International Journal of Computer and Information Science **4**(2) (1975) 105–132

[22] Liskov, B.H., Zilles, S.N.: Programming with abstract data types. ACM SIGPLAN Notices **9**(4) (1974) 50–59 Also in [92].

[23] Liskov, B.H., Zilles, S.N.: Specification techniques for data abstractions. ACM SIGPLAN Notices **10**(6) (1975) 72–87 Also in [93].

[24] Liskov, B.H. In: Chapter 1: An introduction to formal specifications of data abstractions. Volume 1 of Current trends in programming methodology. Prentice Hall (1977) 1–32

[25] Guttag, J.V.: Abstract data types and the development of data structures. Communications of the ACM **20**(6) (1977) 396–404

[26] Guttag, J.V., Horowitz, E., Musser, D.R.: Abstract data types and software validation. Communications of the ACM **21**(12) (1978) 1048–1064

[27] Goguen, J.A., Thatcher, J.W., Wagner, E.G. In: Chapter 5: An initial algebra approach to the specification, correctness, and implementation of abstract data types. Volume 4 of Current trends in programming methodology. Prentice Hall (1977) 80–149

[28] de Carvalho, R.L., Maibaum, T.S.E., Pequeno, T.H.C., Pereda, A.A., Veloso, P.A.S.: A model theoretic approach to the theory of abstract data types and data structures. Research Report CS-80-22, Department of Computer Science, University of Waterloo (April 1980)

[29] de Carvalho, R.L., Maibaum, T.S.E., Pequeno, T.H.C., Pereda, A.A., Veloso, P.A.S.: A model theoretic approach to the theory of abstract data types and data structures. In Yau, S.S., ed.: Proceedings of International Computer Symposium – (ICS'82), IEEE Computer Society (December 1982)

[30] Maibaum, T.S.E.: Conservative extensions, interpretations between theories and all that! In Bidoit, M., Dauchet, M., eds.: Proceedings of CAAP/FASE – 7th International Joint Conference Theory and Practice of Software Development (TAPSOFT'97). Volume 1214 of Lecture Notes in Computer Science., Springer-Verlag (1997) 40–66

[31] Ehrich, H.D.: On the theory of specification, implementation, and parametrization of abstract data types. Journal of the ACM **29**(1) (1982) 206–227

[32] Maibaum, T.S.E., Veloso, P.A.S.: A logical approach to abstract data types. Technical report, Department of Computing, Imperial College, and Departamento de Informatica, PUC/RJ (1981)

[33] Maibaum, T.S.E., Sadler, M.R., Veloso, P.A.S.: Logical specification and implementation. Technical report, Department of Computing, Imperial College (1983)

[34] Maibaum, T.S.E., Sadler, M.R., Veloso, P.A.S.: A straightforward approach to parameterised specifications. Technical report, Department of Computing, Imperial College (1983)

[35] Maibaum, T.S.E., Sadler, M.R., Veloso, P.A.S.: Logical specification and implementation. In Joseph, M., Shyamasundar, R., eds.: Proceedings of the Fourth Conference on Foundations of Software Technology and Theoretical Computer Science. Volume 181 of Lecture Notes in Computer Science., Springer-Verlag (December 1984) 13–30

[36] Maibaum, T.S.E., Veloso, P.A.S., Sadler, M.R.: A theory of abstract data types for program development: Bridging the gap? In Ehrig, H., Floyd, C., Nivat, M., Thatcher, J.W., eds.: Proceedings of Mathematical Foundations of Software Development – International Joint Conference on Theory and Practice of Software Development (TAPSOFT'85), Volume 2: Colloquium on Software Engineering (CSE). Volume 186 of Lecture Notes in Computer Science., Springer-Verlag (March 1985) 214–230

[37] Karp, C.C.: Languages with expressions of infinite length. North Holland, Amsterdam (1964)

[38] Goguen, J.A., Burstall, R.M.: Introducing institutions. In Clarke, E.M., Kozen, D., eds.: Proceedings of the Carnegie Mellon Workshop on Logic of Programs. Volume 184 of Lecture Notes in Computer Science., Springer-Verlag (1984) 221–256

[39] Tarlecki, A.: Bits and pieces of the theory of institutions. In Pitt, D.H., Abramsky, S., Poigné, A., Rydeheard, D.E., eds.: Proceedings of the Category Theory and Computer Programming, tutorial and workshop. Volume 240 of Lecture Notes in Computer Science., Springer-Verlag (1986) 334–363

[40] Sannella, D., Tarlecki, A.: Specifications in an arbitrary institution. Information and computation **76**(2–3) (1988) 165–210

[41] Durán, F., Meseguer, J.: Structured theories and institutions. Theoretical Computer Science **1–3**(309) (2003) 357–380

[42] Sannella, D., Tarlecki, A.: Toward formal development of programs from algebraic specifications: Implementations revisited. Acta Informatica **25**(3) (1988) 233–281 See also [94].

[43] Sannella, D., Tarlecki, A.: Toward formal development of programs from algebraic specifications: model-theoretic foundations. In Kuich, W., ed.: Proceedings of the 19th. Colloquium on Automata, Languages and Programming. Volume 623 of Lecture Notes in Computer Science., Vienna, Austria, Springer-Verlag (July 1992) 656–671 See also [95].

[44] Tarlecki, A.: Moving between logical systems. [96] 478–502

[45] Arrais, M., Fiadeiro, J.L.: Unifying theories in different institutions. [96] 81–101

[46] Mossakowski, T.: Different types of arrow between logical frameworks. In Meyer, F., Monien, B., eds.: Proceedings of 23rd International Colloquium on Automata, Languages and Programming (ICALP '96). Volume 1099 of Lecture Notes in Computer Science., Springer-Verlag (1996) 158–169

[47] Tarlecki, A.: Towards heterogeneous specifications. In Gabbay, D., de Rijke, M., eds.: Frontiers of Combining Systems. Volume 2 of Studies in Logic and Computation. Research Studies Press (2000) 337–360

[48] Bernot, G., Coudert, S., Gall, P.L.: Towards heterogeneous formal specification. In Wirsing, M., Nivat, M., eds.: Proceedings of the 5th. International Conference Algebraic on Methodology and Software Technology – AMAST 1996. Volume 1101 of Lecture Notes in Computer Science., Munich, Germany, Springer-Verlag (July 1996) 458–472

[49] Mossakowski, T.: Foundations of heterogeneous specification. In Wirsing, M., Pattinson, D., Hennicker, R., eds.: Proceedings of the 16th. International Workshop on Recent Trends in Algebraic Development Techniques WADT 2002. Volume 2755 of Lecture Notes in Computer Science., Frauenchiemsee, Germany, Springer-Verlag (September 2002) 359–375

[50] Meseguer, J.: General logics. In Ebbinghaus, H.D., Fernandez-Prida, J., Garrido, M., Lascar, D., Artalejo, M.R., eds.: Proceedings of the Logic Colloquium '87. Volume 129., Granada, Spain, North Holland (1989) 275–329

[51] Fiadeiro, J.L., Maibaum, T.S.E.: Generalising interpretations between theories in the context of π-institutions. In Burn, G., Gay, D., Ryan, M., eds.: Proceedings of the First Imperial College Department of Computing Workshop on Theory and Formal Methods, London, UK, Springer-Verlag (1993) 126–147

[52] Schoenfield, J.R.: Degrees of unsolvability. Number 2 in Mathematical studies. North Holland (1971)

[53] Beth, E.W.: The Foundations of Mathematics. North Holland (1959)

[54] Beth, E.W.: Semantic entailment and formal derivability. In Hintikka, J., ed.: The Philosophy of Mathematics. Oxford University Press (1969) 9–41 Reprinted from [97].

[55] Herbrand, J.: Investigation in proof theory. In Goldfarb, W.D., ed.: Logical Writings. Harvard University Press (1969) 44–202 Translated to english from [98].

[56] Gentzen, G.: The collected papers of gerhard gentzen. In Szabo, M.E., ed.: Investigation into logical deduction. North Holland (1969) 68–131 Translated to english from [99].

[57] Smullyan, R.M.: First-order Logic. Dover Publishing (1995)

[58] Robinson, J.A.: A machine-oriented logic based on the resolution principle. Journal of the ACM **12**(1) (1965) 23–41

[59] Lopez Pombo, C.G., Castro, P., Aguirre, N.M., Maibaum, T.S.E.: Satisfiability calculus: An abstract formulation of semantic proof systems. Fundamenta Informaticae **166**(4) (2019) 297–347

[60] Jackson, D.: Alloy: a lightweight object modelling notation. ACM Transactions on Software Engineering and Methodology **11**(2) (2002) 256–290

[61] Owre, S., Rajan, S., Rushby, J.M., Shankar, N., Srivas, M.: PVS: Combining specification, proof checking, and model checking. In Alur, R., Henzinger, T.A., eds.: Proceedings of the 9th. Computer Aided Verification (CAV). Volume 1102 of Lecture Notes in Computer Science., New Brunswick, NJ, Springer-Verlag (July/August 1996) 411–414

[62] Dowek, G., Felty, A., Herbelin, H., Huet, G., Murthy, C., Parent, C., Paulin-Mohring, C., Werner, B.: The coq proof assistant user's guide (version 5.8). Technical Report 154, INRIA, Rocquencourt, France (1993)

[63] Nipkow, T., Paulson, L.C., Wenzel, M.: Isabelle/HOL – A proof assistant for higher-order logic. Volume 2283 of Lecture Notes in Computer Science. Springer-Verlag, Berlin, Germany (2002)

[64] Frias, M.F., Lopez Pombo, C.G., Moscato, M.M.: Alloy Analyzer+PVS in the analysis and verification of Alloy specifications. [100] 587–601

[65] Blanchette, J.C., Nipkow, T.: Nitpick: A counterexample generator for higher-order logic based on a relational model finder. In Kaufmann, M., Paulson, L.C., eds.: Proceedings of First International Conference on Interactive Theorem Proving (ITP 2010). Volume 6172 of Lecture Notes in Computer Science., Berlin, Heidelberg, Springer-Verlag (July 2010) 131–146

[66] Torlak, E., Jackson, D.: Kodkod: A relational model finder. [100] 632–647

[67] Blanchette, J.C.: Picking Nits: A User's Guide to Nitpick for Isabelle/HOL. Institut f ur Informatik, Technische Universit at M unchen. (April 2020) Available https://isabelle.in.tum.de/doc/nitpick.pdf.

[68] Jackson, D.: Automating first-order relational logic. In: Proceedings of the 8th ACM SIGSOFT international symposium on Foundations of software engineering, San Diego, California, United States, Association for the Computer Machinery, ACM Press (2000) 130–139

[69] McLane, S.: Categories for working mathematician. Graduate Texts in Mathematics. Springer-Verlag, Berlin, Germany (1971)

[70] Fiadeiro, J.L.: Categories for software engineering. Springer-Verlag (2005)

[71] Cassano, V., Lopez Pombo, C.G., Maibaum, T.S.E.: Entailment systems for default reasoning. In Martí-Oliet, N., Palomino Tarjuelo, M., eds.: Proceedings of 21st International Workshop on Algebraic Development Techniques (WADT 2012), Salamanca, Spain (June 2012) 28–30

[72] Reiter, R.: A logic for default reasoning. Artificial Intelligence **13**(1-2) (1980) 81–132

[73] Lopez Pombo, C.G.: Fork algebras as a tool for reasoning across heterogeneous specifications. PhD thesis, Departamento de Computación, Facultad de Ciencias Exactas y Naturales, Universidad de Buenos Aires (2007) Promotor: Marcelo F. Frias.

[74] Frias, M.F., Baum, G.A., Maibaum, T.S.E.: Interpretability of first-order dynamic logic in a relational calculus. In de Swart, H., ed.: Proceedings of the 6th. Conference on Relational Methods in Computer Science (RelMiCS) - TARSKI. Volume 2561 of Lecture Notes in Computer Science., Oisterwijk, The Netherlands, Springer-Verlag (October 2002) 66–80

[75] Haeberer, A.M., Veloso, P.A.S.: Partial relations for program derivation: adequacy, inevitability and expressiveness. In: Proceedings of IFIP TC2 working conference on constructing programs from specifications, IFIP TC2: Software: Theory and Practice, North Holland (1991) 310–352

[76] Frias, M.F.: Fork algebras in algebra, logic and computer science. Volume 2 of Advances in logic. World Scientific Publishing Co., Singapore (2002)

[77] Lopez Pombo, C.G., Castro, P., Aguirre, N.M., Maibaum, T.S.E.: Satisfiability calculi: the semantic counterpart of proof calculi in general logics. In Martí-Oliet, N., Palomino Tarjuelo, M., eds.: Proceedings of 21st International Workshop on Algebraic Development Techniques (WADT 2012) and IFIP International Federation for Information Processing (2013). Volume 7841 of Lecture Notes in Computer Science., Salamanca, Spain, Springer-Verlag (June 2013) 195–211

[78] Goguen, J.A., Burstall, R.M.: Institutions: abstract model theory for specification and programming. Journal of the ACM **39**(1) (1992) 95–146

[79] Goguen, J.A., Roşu, G.: Institution morphisms. Formal Aspects of Computing **13**(3-5) (2002) 274–307

[80] Mossakowski, T., Tarlecki, A.: Heterogeneous logical environments for distributed specifications. In Corradini, A., Montanari, U., eds.: Proceedings of 19th International Workshop in Algebraic Development Techniques. Volume 5486 of Lecture Notes in Computer Science., Pisa, Italy, Springer-Verlag (June 2009) 266–289

[81] Lopez Pombo, C.G., Castro, P., Aguirre, N.M., Maibaum, T.S.E.: A heterogeneous characterisation of component-based system design in a categorical setting. In Ciobanu, G., Ipate, F., eds.: Proceedings of 11th International Colloquium Theoretical Aspects of Computing - ICTAC 2014. Volume 8687 of Lecture Notes in Computer Science., Springer-Verlag (September 2014) 314–332

[82] Mossakowski, T., Maeder, C., Luttich, K.: The heterogeneous tool set, Hets. [100] 519–522

[83] Diaconescu, R., Futatsugi, K.: Logical foundations of CafeOBJ. Theoretical Computer Science **285**(2) (2002) 289–318

[84] Castro, P., Aguirre, N.M., Lopez Pombo, C.G., Maibaum, T.S.E.: Categorical foundations for structured specifications in Z. Formal Aspects of Computing **27**(5-6) (2015) 831–865

[85] Borzyszkowski, T.: Logical systems for structured specifications. Theoretical Computer Science **286** (2002) 197–245

[86] Mossakowski, T., Tarlecki, A.: A relatively complete calculus for structured heterogeneous specifications. In Muscholl, A., ed.: Proceedings of 17th International Conference on Foundations of Software Science and Computation Structures (FOSSACS 2014), held as Part of the European Joint Conferences on Theory and Practice of Software. Volume 8412 of Lecture Notes in Computer Science., Springer-Verlag (2014) 441–456

[87] Lopez Pombo, C.G., Frias, M.F.: 16. In: (Heterogeneous) Structured Specifications in Logics Without Interpolation. Volume 17 of Outstanding Contributions to Logic. Springer International publishing (2018)

[88] Castro, P., Aguirre, N.M., Lopez Pombo, C.G., Maibaum, T.S.E.: Towards managing dynamic reconfiguration of software systems in a categorical setting. In Cavalcanti, A., D'eharbe, D., Gaudel, M.C., Woodcock, J., eds.: Proceedings of Theoretical Aspects of Computing - ICTAC 2010, 7th International Colloquium. Volume 6255 of Lecture Notes in Computer Science., Natal, Rio Grande do Norte, Brazil, Springer-Verlag (September 2010) 306–321

[89] Castro, P., Aguirre, N.M., Lopez Pombo, C.G., Maibaum, T.S.E.: A categorical approach to structuring and promoting Z specifications. In Pasareanu, C.S., Salaün, G., eds.: Proceedings of 9th International Symposium Formal Aspects of Component Software – FACS 2012. Volume 7684 of Lecture Notes in Computer Science., Springer-Verlag (2013) 73–91

[90] Gimenez, M., Moscato, M.M., Lopez Pombo, C.G., Frias, M.F.: HETEROGenius: a framework for hybrid analysis of heterogeneous software specifications. In Aguirre, N.M., Ribeiro, L., eds.: Proceedings of Latin American Workshop on Formal Methods 2013. (August 2013) 1045–1058 Workshop affiliated to [101].

[91] Floyd, R.W. In: Assigning meaning to programs. Volume 14 of Studies in Cognitive Systems. Springer-Verlag (1993) 65–81 Reprint of [15].

[92] Liskov, B.H., Zilles, S.N.: Programming with abstract data types. In: Proceedings of ACM SIGPLAN Symposium on Very High Level Languages, Association for the Computer Machinery, ACM Press (1974) 50–59 Also in [22].

[93] Liskov, B.H., Zilles, S.N.: Specification techniques for data abstractions. In Shooman, M.L., Yeh, R.T.Y., eds.: Proceedings of the International Conference on Reliable Software, Los Angeles, California, ACM Press (1975) 72–87 Also in [23].

[94] Sannella, D., Tarlecki, A.: Toward formal development of programs from algebraic specifications: implementations revisited. Technical Report 17, Laboratory for foundations of computer science, The University of Edinburgh (1986) Preliminar version of [42].

[95] Sannella, D., Tarlecki, A.: Toward formal development of programs from algebraic specifications: model-theoretic foundations. Technical Report 204, Laboratory for foundations of computer science, The University of Edinburgh (1992)

[96] Haveraaen, M., Owe, O., Dahl, O.J., eds. In Haveraaen, M., Owe, O., Dahl, O.J., eds.: Proceedings of Selected papers from the 11th Workshop on Specification of Abstract Data Types Joint with the 8th COMPASS Workshop on Recent Trends in Data Type Specification. Volume 1130 of Lecture Notes in Computer Science., Springer-Verlag (1996)

[97] Beth, E.W.: Semantic entailment and formal derivability. Mededlingen van de Koninklijke Nederlandse Akademie van Wetenschappen, Afdeling Letterkunde **18**(13) (1955) 309–342 Reprinted in [54].

[98] Herbrand, J.: Recherches sur la theorie de la demonstration. PhD thesis, Université de Paris (1930) English translation in [55].

[99] Gentzen, G.: Untersuchungen tiber das logische schliessen. Mathematische Zeitschrijt **39** (1935) 176–210 and 405–431 English translation in [56].

[100] Grumberg, O., Huth, M., eds. In Grumberg, O., Huth, M., eds.: Proceedings of the 13th. International Conference on Tools and Algorithms for the Construction and Analysis of Systems (TACAS 2007). Volume 4424 of Lecture Notes in Computer Science., Braga, Portugal, Springer-Verlag (April 2007)

[101] D'Argenio, P.R., Melgratti, H., eds. In D'Argenio, P.R., Melgratti, H., eds.: Proceedings of 24th International Conference on Concurrency Theory – CONCUR 2013. Volume 8052 of Lecture Notes in Computer Science., Springer-Verlag (2013)

A Dedicated to Tomás Esteban Eduardo Maibaum in his 70th. Birthday

This dedication is being written by me (Carlos G. Lopez Pombo), on behalf of the authors of this paper. The joke of calling Tom by the Spanish translation of his names (the amount of which would certainly fit the latin tradition) was never funny, and after some time I realised that it was not meant to be as he is one of us. Tom was born in Hungary and left with his family being a kid, in the aftermath of WWII; he was raised in Canada, where he grew, and got a degree in pure mathematics from the University of Toronto; he moved to England where he got a PhD in computer science from Queen Mary and Royal Holloway, Colleges of the University of London. Held academic positions in King's College and Imperial College and in both places was appointed head of the department of computer science. Returned to Canada where he still hold the position of Tier I Canada Research Chair in the Foundations of Software Engineering and is Emeritus Professor in the Department of Computing and Software at McMaster University. None of the preceding data really matters because he is one of us; not even his passionate love for soccer, entangled with his ragging hate towards Maradona and Argentina's futbol team counts; he is one of us.

Anyone can tell that he is not really Hungarian, Canadian or English; he gives hugs and kisses, opens his home, shares his table and most notably, jokes about the type of things that polite people would never dare mention, to then, laugh about it in your face; he is the kind of generous and loving Argentinian friend anyone would pray to have.

In 2010 I already had a couple of papers with Tom but never had really worked with him. I met him in person for the first time in Natal, Brasil, for ICTAC 2010 (there might be some dispute whether he is one of us or one of them, a part of Tom's heart is certainly Carioca, not necessarily Brazilian). There, we had long discussions about formal specification of software systems over countless *chope*; it would take a couple of years for me to understand how much he hated our joint paper accepted in that conference. As I mentioned in the introduction, Tom and Institutions are not a match. Nonetheless, he invited me to visit him in Canada and, six month later, I was heading to Canada to work with him for the first time. There was never a discussion, I was staying at

59

his place, as his kind and generous heart always dictate. There, I met Jan, his wife, and part of my admiration for Tom's amazing work in computer science shifted to Jan's cooking. I visited Tom and Jan many times over the years, at the beginning in Canada, and nowadays in England, where they currently live. Mum and dad are the lawful nicknames they won for their warm kindness and caring. Luckily for me, Tom like me a lot more than how much he hates the papers I forced him to coauthor with me.

A Rely-Guarantee Specification of Mixed-Criticality Scheduling

Cliff B Jones

School of Computing
Newcastle University, UK
`cliff.jones@newcastle.ac.uk`

Alan Burns

Department of Computer Science
University of York, UK
`alan.burns@york.ac.uk`

Abstract

The application considered is mixed-criticality scheduling. The core formal approaches used are Rely-Guarantee conditions and the Timeband framework; these are applied to give a layered description of job scheduling which includes resilience to jobs overrunning their expected execution time. A novel formal modelling idea is proposed to handle the relationship between actual time and its approximation in hardware clocks.

Dedication

One of the authors could have provided many anecdotes about his long association with Tom Maibaum. We thought however that a technical contribution would be more appropriate for someone who has made so many contributions to the subject. It is a pleasure to dedicate this paper to Tom — in the full expectation that he will not agree with all of the content! (We must also explain that the poetic extract is there for scientific reasons and has nothing to do with advancing ages.)

> The Moving Finger writes; and, having writ,
> Moves on: nor all thy Piety nor Wit
> Shall lure it back to cancel half a Line,
> Nor all thy Tears wash out a Word of it.
>
> *Rubaiyat of Omar Khayyam*
> (Translated by Edward FitzGerald)

61

1   Introduction

The objective of the research described in this paper is to develop a framework based on time bands and rely-guarantee conditions for formally specifying and reasoning about properties of mixed-criticality scheduling (MCS); the key correctness issues revolve around timing. The background ideas are summarised in Section 3 after the application area is outlined in Section 2.

The following paragraphs relate this objective to the wider topic of Cyber Physical Systems (CPS).

Correctness in safety-critical CPS can be considered from two perspectives: (i) (pre-run-time) verification, and (ii) survivability. Pre-run-time *verification* of a safety-critical system is the process of ensuring, prior to deployment, that the run-time behaviour of the system will be consistent with expectations. Verification assumptions are made regarding the kinds of circumstances that will be encountered by the system during run-time and guarantees are used to specify the required runtime behaviour of the system (provided that the assumptions hold).

In contrast, **survivability** addresses expectations of system behaviour in the event that the assumptions fail to hold in full (in which case a fault or error is said to have occurred during run-time). Survivability may further be considered to comprise two notions: robustness and resilience [BDBB18]. Informally, the robustness of a system is a measure of the severity and number of faults it can tolerate without compromising the quality of service it offers while resilience refers to the degree of fault for which it can provide degraded yet acceptable quality of service.

Section 2 outlines the application area while Section 3 briefly sketches published ideas on the timeband framework and rely-guarantee thinking together with the application of both of these formalisms to the specification of cyber physical systems. Section 4 tackles the thorny issue of the passage of time (see the quotation at the head of this paper): coming up with a satisfactory way to relate real physical time to values manipulated by programs held up writing this paper for some ... time! These ideas are brought together in Section 5 to write layered descriptions of MCS covering both optimistic and resilient modes. The customary summary and statement of future work are given in Section 6.

2   Mixed-criticality scheduling

The implementation of any real-time system requires a run-time scheduler that will follow the rules that define the required behaviour of the scheduling approach that has been chosen to deliver the temporal properties of the application. A human scheduling specialist will choose the basic approach, for example a fixed priority scheme with priorities assigned via the deadline monotonic algorithm, or the Earliest Deadline First protocol. Appropriate scheduling analysis will then be applied to a specification of the application to determine whether all deadlines can be met at run-time by the chosen scheduling approach.

Typical characteristics of an application are the number of jobs or tasks involved, the worst-case execution times of these entries, their deadlines and possible constraints on their arrival patterns. The dynamic run-time scheduler will rely on the validity of these parameters and will guarantee to manage the order of execution in accordance with the rules of the chosen scheduling protocol.

An increasingly important trend in the design of real-time systems is the integration of components with different levels of criticality on a common hardware platform. Criticality is a designation of the level of assurance against failure needed for a system component. A mixed-criticality system is one that has two or more distinct levels (for example safety critical, mission critical and low-critical). Perhaps up to five levels may be identified (see, for example, the IEC 61508, DO-178B and DO-178C, DO-254 and ISO 26262 standards). Typical names for the levels are ASILs (Automotive Safety and Integrity Levels), DALs (Design Assurance Levels or Development Assurance Levels) and SILs (Safety Integrity Levels).

A key aspect of MCS is that system parameters, such as the worst-case execution time (WCET) of a job, become dependent on the criticality level of the job. So the same code will have a higher WCET if it is defined to be safety-critical (as a higher level of assurance is required) than it would if it is just considered to be mission critical or indeed non-critical. Criticality also has a role when the system becomes overloaded; the jobs of the lower level of criticality may have to be abandoned to protect the integrity of the safety-critical (high integrity) jobs.

A mixed criticality (MC-) scheduler is one that manages a set of mixed criticality jobs (or tasks, but jobs only in this paper) so that all deadlines are met if all jobs execute for no more than a lower bound on their execution time. In addition, the MC-scheduler must ensure that all high criticality jobs meet their deadlines if any job executes for more than its lower bound (but less than a conservative upper bound defined for each job).

It must be emphasised that the internal details of MC-scheduler, and the theory used to define the associated schedulability analysis (for example the EDF-VD or AMC protocols) are not the emphasis in this paper — there is plenty of prior research on that [BD17]. Nor is there an explanation of how previously-proposed MC-scheduling algorithms can be shown to satisfy particular sets of rely-guarantee (R/G) specifications — that is (important) future work. This paper only seeks to provide a clear and intuitive specification of the formalism. The history of formal methods (such as Hoare Logic) prompts the belief that there is a good likelihood that methods can be developed for showing that specific MC-scheduling algorithms satisfy (or fail to so do) particular R/G specifications.

3   Background approaches

This section describes previously published ideas on which the developments in this paper are based.

$$\underbrace{\sigma_0}_{pre} \quad \cdots \quad \underbrace{\sigma_i \; \sigma_{i+1}}_{rely} \quad \cdots \quad \underbrace{\sigma_j \; \sigma_{j+1}}_{guar} \quad \cdots \quad \sigma_f$$

$$\underbrace{\phantom{\sigma_0 \quad \cdots \quad \sigma_i \; \sigma_{i+1} \quad \cdots \quad \sigma_j \; \sigma_{j+1} \quad \cdots \quad \sigma_f}}_{post}$$

pre/*rely* are assumptions the developer can make
guar/*post* are commitments that the code must achieve

Fig. 1. Picturing the parts of a Rely-Guarantee specification

3.1 Rely-guarantee reasoning for concurrency

Pre and post conditions are used to document the intended behaviour of sequential programs. Such specifications can be said to document the "Why" rather than the "How" of a component. Furthermore, developments of Tony Hoare's "axiomatic approach" [Hoa69,Hoa71] provide ways of evolving verified implementations in a top-down style. (Even if the development is not actually undertaken in this way, such a structure provides understandable documentation.) Key to layering such a description is a property that is often referred to as "compositionality": the specification of a component describes all that need be achieved by its implementation; such specifications insulate a component from considerations about its environment and facilitate the verification of one design step before proceeding to further stages of development.

Finding compositional development methods for concurrent software proved challenging with many initial methods (e.g. [AM71,Ash75,Owi75,OG76]) needing to reason jointly about the combination of one thread with its sibling threads and/or environment. This negates the ability to achieve top-down design. The Rely-Guarantee approach [Jon81,Jon83a,Jon83b] offers compositional specifications for a class of shared-variable concurrent programs. Just as pre conditions record assumptions about the context in which a component can be deployed, a rely condition indicates what interference a component must tolerate. Thus pre and rely conditions are information to the developer and warnings to anyone who wishes to deploy the specified component. A similar comparison can be made between the two conditions that record properties that the developed code must satisfy: post conditions describe the relation required of starting and finishing states [1] whereas guarantee conditions indicate an upper bound on the impact that steps of the component can have on its environment. A picture of these components of a specification is given in Figure 1.

In [Hoa69], Hoare offered proof rules that justify development to the main sequential programming constructs. It is not surprising that the proof rules which justify steps of development employing parallelism are more complicated: they essentially need to show the compatibility of the rely and guarantee con-

---

[1] Pre and post conditions are as in [Hoa69] except that in VDM [Jon80] post conditions are relations over initial and final states.

ditions. [2] The current paper does not go into these details because description rather than proof is the objective here.

One observation that does carry over from development methods for sequential programs to many applications of the Rely-Guarantee approach is the importance of data abstraction and reification [Jon07]. Although predicates over states provide an element of procedural abstraction, specifications of significant systems can only be made brief and perspicuous by using abstract data types that match the problem. Subsequent development steps must show that representations of the abstractions preserve the properties of the specification. Development and justification of more concrete representations is variously referred to as "refinement" or "reification".

3.2 Time bands

The motivation for the timeband framework comes from a number of observations about complex time-sensitive systems. Of relevance to this paper are the following:

- systems can be best understood by distinguishing different granularities (of time), i.e. there are different abstract views of the dynamics of the system

- it is useful to view certain actions (events) as atomic and "instantaneous" in one time band, while allowing them to have internal state and behaviour that takes time at a more detailed level of description

- the durations of certain actions are important, but the measuring of time must not be made artificially precise and must allow for tolerance (non-determinacy) in the temporal domain.

Key references include [BHJ20,BH10,WWB12,WOBW10,BBT07,BB06].

The central notion in the framework is that of a time band that is defined by its *granularity*, G, (e.g. 1 millisecond) and its *precision*, ρ, (e.g. 5 microseconds). Granularity defines the unit of time of the band; precision bounds the maximum duration of an event that is deemed to be instantaneous in its band.

Whilst it is the case that system descriptions can be given on a single time axis, inevitably, this has to be a fine granularity and it becomes difficult to "see the wood for the trees." It is much clearer if the behaviour of a system is given in terms of a finite set of ordered *bands*. System activities are described in some band B if they engage in significant events at the time scale represented by B, i.e. they have dynamics that give rise to changes that are observable or meaningful in the granularity of band B.

A complete system specification must address all dynamic behaviours. At the lowest level, circuits (e.g. gates) have propagation delays measured in nanoseconds or even picoseconds; at intermediate levels, tasks/threads have rates and deadlines that are usually expressed in tens of milliseconds; at yet-

---

[2] A significant reworking [HJC14,JHC15,HJ18] presents the original rely-guarantee ideas in a more algebraic style.

higher levels, missions can change every hour; and maintenance may need to be undertaken every month.

Understanding the behaviour of circuits allows the worst-case execution time of tasks to be predicted. At a higher band this allows deadlines to be checked and the schedulability of whole missions to be verified.

In this paper, behaviour of the application jobs and the scheduler is placed in a band that reflects the deadlines of the jobs; this might be a band with a granularity of one millisecond, or a finer granularity if that is required. The precision in this band will be sufficiently short so that the duration of certain actions, for example a context switch, can be ignored.

Precision is employed, in Section 4.1, to constrain the difference between external 'real' time and any interval interpretation of time as delivered by a hardware clock.

3.3 Specifying resilient CPS

As indicated in Section 3.1, the Rely-Guarantee approach was originally conceived for developments where a specified system was to be decomposed into concurrent processes. The general idea has however been shown to be applicable to contexts where a component is being specified which will execute in an environment that evolves in parallel with the specified component. Examples include [HJJ03,JHJ07] but these suffered from the fact that time was treated on a single (i.e. the finest) band.

In [BHJ20], the timeband approach was used to make the rely and guarantee conditions more intelligible. This indicated that combining the timeband and rely-guarantee approaches can be used to specify CPS. A particular issue with CPS is that they need to be resilient in the sense that they are likely to have layers of required behaviour:

- optimistic (or optimal) behaviour is required when everything is performing in accord with the strongest rely conditions — the control system is required to meet its strongest guarantee condition;

- when some rely conditions are not satisfied, something in the environment is not behaving in an optimal way (this can be caused by a timing problem) — a weaker rely condition can describe a less desirable environment assumption under which the control system can only achieve a weaker guarantee condition;

- such layering of rely and guarantee conditions can be repeated over as many levels as required.

Such nested conditions (combined with time bands) are illustrated in [BHJ20, §4]. Another idea that appears to be useful in specifying CPS is the setting of "may/must" levels (again often linked to time): [BHJ20, §4.3] contains an example where a short period of aberrant behaviour can be flagged but the control system is required to report a longer period of misbehaviour. This pattern of specification appears to be useful quite frequently.

66

4 Handling time

Specifying the sort of scheduling problem described in Section 2 presents additional challenges not faced in, for example, [BHJ20]:

- internal machine clocks must be linked to the passage of actual time
- state variables are needed that record the amount of time used by a job.

What follows is a novel approach to these two problems linking the passage of time with the values recorded in computer clocks. The simple scheduling task considered in the body of the paper concerns a finite number of "one shot" jobs; extensions to address tasks are mentioned in Section 6.2.

4.1 *ClockValue* vs. *Time*

The first step is to distinguish an abstract notion of *Time* from what clocks record in a computer (a clock will contain a *ClockValue*). Consider a collection of *States* indexed by the abstract notion of *Time*:

$$\Sigma = Time \rightarrow State$$

This is a function; *Time* should be "dense" like the real numbers (so Σ cannot be modelled as a list) — but fortunately it transpires that little need be said about *Time* because specifications of operations (e.g. the scheduler and the jobs that it controls) are written with respect to the t component of *State*:

$$State :: t \quad : \quad ClockValue$$
$$\cdots$$

For a given $\sigma : \Sigma$ at time α (because the identifier t is used for a component of *State* above, $\alpha \in Time$ is used here), its *ClockValue* $(\sigma(\alpha).t)$ can differ from α; that is an issue for a fine time band and time bands need to be chosen such that the allowable difference is within the precision of the coarser band so that it can essentially be assumed that the *ClockValue* in the machine is always sufficiently close to *Time*.[3]

Assume that the precision of the band is ρ, equality $=_\rho$ is with respect to that precision. Then the relationship between t and α is defined by the following predicate:

$$P_t(\sigma) \stackrel{def}{=} \forall \alpha \in Time \cdot \sigma(\alpha).t =_\rho \alpha$$

4.2 Recording execution time

A *State* contains an indexed collection of *Jobs* in its *curr* field (and *exec* which is a subset [4] of the domain of that mapping indicating the jobs that are scheduled for execution).

---

[3] At the finer time band, issues such as clock drift could also be formalised. In a distributed system, there would be a local *State* for each processor and their clocks could also differ within the appropriate precision.

[4] The *exec* field is a set to cover multi-processors.

$$State :: t \quad : \; ClockValue$$
$$curr : I \xrightarrow{m} Job$$
$$exec : I\text{-}\mathbf{set}$$

Among other fields (see below) a *Job* has a record of how long it has been executing:

$$Job :: e \quad : \; Duration$$
$$\ldots$$

Neither the scheduler nor any job can change t or e which are instead linked to the autonomous (i.e. not under the control of software) progress of time: the key properties are that, if $i \in exec$ over a period of time from α_1 to α_2, then the e field for the indexed *State* must advance as much as the difference in the *Time* [5] i.e. $e_2 - e_1$ must be equal, within the precision of the time band, to $\alpha_2 - \alpha_1$; furthermore, when $i \notin exec$ the e field of that *Job* remains unchanged.

Thus the link between *Time* and e is defined by a predicate over Σ:

$$P_e(\sigma) \stackrel{def}{=}$$
$$\forall \alpha_1, \alpha_2 \in Time, i \in Index \cdot$$
$$((\forall \alpha \mid \alpha_1 \leq \alpha \leq \alpha_2 \cdot i \in \sigma(\alpha).exec) \Rightarrow$$
$$\sigma(\alpha_2).curr(i).e - \sigma(\alpha_1).curr(i).e =_\rho \alpha_2 - \alpha_1) \wedge$$
$$((\forall \alpha \mid \alpha_1 \leq \alpha \leq \alpha_2 \cdot i \notin \sigma(\alpha).exec) \Rightarrow$$
$$\sigma(\alpha_2).curr(i).e = \sigma(\alpha_1).curr(i).e)$$

Although *Time* is dense and progresses outside the influence of the software (*Scheduler* or *Job*s), it is precisely that software that brings about discrete changes to *State*. Essentially, real time is about the Σ function whereas programs actually bring about discrete changes in *State*s (except, of course, neither *Scheduler* nor *Job*s can write to t or e whose values are constrained by P_t/P_e above).

Although the focus in Section 5 is on specifications for the scheduler and the jobs to which it is allocating time, the progress of *Time* is really a third concurrent process. What could be thought of as a guarantee condition of this enigmatic process (the conjunction of P_e and P_t) can be used as an assumption in any reasoning about the more tangible components (*Scheduler* and *Job*s).

5 Job-Based Scheduling

As outlined in Section 2, scheduling work can be divided into two parts. A human scheduler considers the likely arrival pattern –and estimates of the *worst case execution time*– of jobs and chooses a scheduling algorithm for the run-time scheduling software (which comprises the second part). The aim of the software component is to ensure that jobs complete execution by their respective deadlines. The rely conditions of the combined scheduling activities would detail the inputs to the static part of scheduling. In this section, the focus is

---

[5] The difference between two values of type *Time* is a *Duration* as is the difference between two values of type *Duration*.

on specifying the run-time scheduling software using rely and guarantee conditions.

In safety-critical situations, resilience is crucial and minor deviation from the estimated run times must not be allowed to cause highly-critical (hi-crit) jobs to miss their deadlines. The categorisation of jobs as hi/lo-crit is part of the human, off-line, process. [6] Here, nested rely and guarantee conditions are used to specify an optimistic mode in which all jobs can meet their deadlines and a fault-tolerant mode in which only hi-crit jobs are guaranteed to meet their deadlines.

In real scheduling there is likely to be a *task level* above jobs but this is not addressed in the current paper.

5.1 Starting and ending *Job*s

The run-time Scheduler manages the execution of *Job*s (indexed by $i \in I$ — the set I is an arbitrary index set). As indicated in Section 4.2, *curr* contains information about those jobs that have started and not yet finished.

The information stored for each job is as follows:

$$Job :: \quad e \quad : \quad Duration$$
$$d \quad : \quad Time$$
$$C \quad : \quad Duration$$
$$X \quad : \quad Duration$$

As mentioned in Section 4.1, the time (e) that a job has been executing cannot be changed directly by the scheduler and is updated in accordance with P_e. The deadline by which a job should complete (d) is set when a job starts (see *START* below) — it is shown to be of type *Time* because deadlines relate to the external world but P_t ensures that software can use t: *ClockValue* as an acceptable surrogate. The C field contains the expected maximum execution time of the job but the X field distinguishes between lo-crit (where $X = 0$) and hi-crit jobs where the latter have a non-zero *Duration* that can be allocated if necessary.

The arrival of jobs is not controlled by the scheduler; the *START* operation is specified as follows:

$$START \ (D\!: Duration, C\!: Duration, X\!: Duration) \ i\!: I$$

ext rd t $\quad : \quad ClockValue$

$\quad$ **wr** $curr \ : \ I \xrightarrow{m} Job$

post $i \notin \textbf{dom} \ curr \wedge$
$\quad curr' = curr \cup \{i \mapsto mk\text{-}Job(0, D + t, C, X)\}$

The execution time (e) at the start of a job is set to zero; the D argument is the relative deadline — adding the clock time gives the absolute deadline (d); and C is an estimate of WCET.

---

[6] In reality, there could be many levels of criticality but the approach can be illustrated with just two.

Notice that starting a Job does not make it execute — that is the role of the *Scheduler*. Thus, jobs start and are added to *curr*; the scheduler moves their index to *exec*.

Ending a job just removes it from *curr*.

END $(i\!:\!I)$

ext wr *curr* : $I \xrightarrow{m} Job$

post $curr' = \{i\} \lhd curr$

5.2 Dynamic scheduler

The *exec* field of a *State* records the indexes of *Jobs* that are actively executing (thus *exec* contains a subset of the domain of *curr*); the scheduler moves job indexes into and out of *exec*. In fact, that is all it can do [7] and that makes its way of achieving its specification rather indirect.

These specifications are anyway expressed at two levels: an optimistic mode in which all jobs can be scheduled successfully and a resilient mode in which lo-crit jobs can be abandoned if necessary to meet the deadlines of hi-crit jobs.

5.2.1 Optimistic mode

The overall scheduling objective is to make sure that jobs can finish by their respective deadlines; if all jobs were of equal criticality, this could be expressed by requiring that the following optimistic invariant is maintained:

$inv\text{-}State_O : State \to \mathbb{B}$

$inv\text{-}State_O(mk\text{-}State(t, curr,)) \quad \triangleq$
$\qquad \forall mk\text{-}Job(e, d, C,) \in \mathbf{rng}\ curr \cdot C - e \le d - t$

This states that all jobs currently in the system must have room to finish by their deadline time (d). A corollary of this is that each job would terminate no later than its deadline. (It is shown below that a more conservative invariant must be preserved to achieve resilience.)

Preserving $inv\text{-}State_O$ can be viewed as the key obligation of the scheduler but the only way in which the *SCHEDULER* can achieve this is by allocating time to *Jobs* in *curr* which entails moving their index into *exec* (P_e then governs the increase in their e field).

Anyone familiar with the literature on the Rely-Guarantee approach might wonder if such invariants should be couched as guarantee conditions of the form:

$inv\text{-}State(st) \ \Rightarrow \ inv\text{-}State(st')$

The reason for preferring the invariant is that *Time* is advancing even if the scheduler is inactive. A guarantee condition puts constraints on what happens over steps of the relevant process; maintaining the invariant imposes a stronger requirement that the scheduler does something often enough.

---

[7] In some resilient modes, the scheduler can re-allocate "budgets" and/or terminate jobs.

To realise the maintenance of this invariant, the rely condition of the scheduler must cover:

- reliance on all *Jobs* respecting their C
- for each job, the values of its C and d are unchanging (see second conjunct of the rely condition and remember that jobs can arrive in –and leave from– *curr*)
- furthermore the value of e for each job is increasing (in line with t/α).

$SCHEDULER_O$

ext rd t $\quad$: $ClockValue$
$\quad$ **rd** $curr$: $I \xrightarrow{m} Job$
$\quad$ **wr** $exec$: I-**set**
rely $(\forall mk\text{-}Job(e',\,,C,) \in \textbf{rng } curr' \cdot e' \leq C) \,\wedge$
$\quad\quad \forall i \in (\textbf{dom } curr \cap \textbf{dom } curr') \cdot$
$\quad\quad\quad curr'(i).d = curr(i).d \,\wedge$
$\quad\quad\quad curr'(i).C = curr(i).C \,\wedge$
$\quad\quad\quad curr'(i).e \geq curr(i).e$

Correspondingly, the specification of each job is defined as follows:

$JOB(i)$

ext rd t $\quad$: $ClockValue$
$\quad$ **rd** e $\quad$: $Duration$
$\quad$ **rd** d $\quad$: $ClockValue$
$\quad$ **rd** C $\quad$: $Duration$
rely $t' \geq t \,\wedge$
$\quad\quad C' = C \wedge d' = d \wedge e' \geq e \,\wedge$
$\quad\quad C - e' \leq d - t'$
guar $e' \leq C$

Although the guarantee conditions of jobs imply the rely condition of the scheduler, it cannot be implemented unless the developer can also assume that P_e is satisfied. Notice that the value C has two roles: each job relies on its environment behaving according to whatever model or measuring process was used to derive C, but the job also has a contract with the scheduler not to execute for more than C. The scheduler is assumed to have used some form of analysis to verify (offline usually) that if all jobs respect their guarantee conditions then it will indeed provide the necessary capacity to each job. Hence the job can rely upon receiving C before its deadline.

It should again be noted that this specification of the Scheduler's behaviour does not include the actual details of the scheduling algorithm or dispatching policy — it is just a specification of what the Scheduler must achieve (its obligations). For a specific set of jobs it may not be possible to derive a valid scheduler that can meet this specification.

71

5.2.2 Resilient mode

In resilient mode, the scheduler only guarantees that hi-crit jobs get serviced and lo-crit jobs $(X = 0)$ might be terminated or fail to complete by their deadlines. [8] The specification does not require such terminations, it simply specifies a lower bound on the scheduler.

To see that $inv\text{-}State_O$ is not strong enough as an invariant to handle mixed criticality, consider the following example which shows that there is an issue when resilience to overrunning hi-crit jobs is included. Suppose there was a hi-crit job (a) with: $e_a = 10$, $d_a = 56$, $C_a = 15$ and $X_a = 3$. There might also be some other lo-crit jobs so $curr$ would contain:

$$\left\{ \begin{array}{l} a \mapsto mk\text{-}Job(10, 56, 15, 3), \\ b \mapsto \cdots \end{array} \right\}$$

If this situation existed at $t = 52$, there would be insufficient time to complete the hi-crit job (a) by its deadline. (Presumably some other job with an earlier deadline would have been using the resource.) A scheduler could abandon execution of any lo-crit jobs such as b and employ the eXtra allowance stored for a — in the example there is an extra allowance of 3 units of time to be allocated to a but it is too late to meet the deadline (56) so this does not help. Therefore the situation must not be allowed to arise at $t = 52$ — it is clear that the scheduler has not kept enough "fat" to be able to complete a by its deadline. The conservative invariant below requires that all of the extra allocations can be accommodated.

As indicated at the beginning of Section 5.2, the optimistic invariant preserves enough resource to be able to complete all jobs whether hi or lo-crit. In contrast, $inv\text{-}State_R$ enshrines a cautious approach of making sure that hi-crit jobs can meet their deadlines even if they all use their extra time allocation:

$inv\text{-}State_R : State \rightarrow \mathbb{B}$

$inv\text{-}State_R(mk\text{-}State(t, curr,)) \quad \triangle$
$\quad \forall mk\text{-}Job(e, d, C, X) \in \mathbf{rng}\ curr \cdot X > 0 \ \Rightarrow \ C + X - e \leq d - t$

In resilient mode $(SCHEDULER_R)$, the weaker rely condition concerns only hi-crit jobs and accepts that their execution might need the extra (X) execution time. So the invariant only requires that the scheduler concerns itself with hi-crit jobs. [9]

Notice that this represents what the scheduler must do — it is at liberty to attempt to schedule more jobs than required including some that are marked $(X = 0)$ as lo-crit.

The specifications are:

---

[8] A third possibility is that some lo-crit jobs do complete by their deadlines. It is just that the scheduler is not required to achieve this.

[9] Many schedulers live more dangerously and hold only a global reserve ("fat") or work with $3/4$ of X — this would require a different specification.

$SCHEDULER_R$

ext rd t : $ClockValue$
    rd $curr$: $I \xrightarrow{m} Job$
    wr $exec$: I-**set**
rely $(\forall mk\text{-}Job(e',, C, X) \in \mathbf{rng}\ curr' \cdot X > 0 \Rightarrow e' \leq C + X) \wedge$
      $\forall i \in (\mathbf{dom}\ curr \cap \mathbf{dom}\ curr') \cdot$
          $curr'(i).d = curr(i).d \wedge$
          $curr'(i).C = curr(i).C \wedge$
          $curr'(i).e \geq curr(i).e$

In resilient mode each hi-crit job promises to stay within its extended execution time; lo-crit jobs make no promises.

$JOB(i)$

ext rd t : $ClockValue$
    rd e : $Duration$
    rd d : $ClockValue$
    rd C : $Duration$
    rd X : $Duration$
rely $t' \geq t \wedge$
    $C' = C \wedge d' = d \wedge e' \geq e \wedge X' = X \wedge$
    $C + X - e' \leq d - t'$
guar $X > 0 \Rightarrow e' \leq C + X$

It is important to realise that the design of the scheduler must create code that satisfies both $SCHEDULER_O$ and $SCHEDULER_R$: all jobs will meet their deadlines providing none are greedy and hi-crit jobs will get the extra resources to meet their deadlines — if necessary at the expense of lo-crit jobs being abandoned.

6 Conclusions

The formal methods basis for this paper is the timebands framework and the rely-guarantee approach. These ideas have previously been shown to be applicable to the specification of Cyber Physical Systems (CPS). Time bands have been used to avoid the confusion that arises when coarse-grained concepts are discussed at a fine granularity. Rely-guarantee conditions both help separate documentation of components and –when nested– help distinguish resilient modes of operation from the ideal behaviour of a system.

The targeted application of this paper is Mixed Criticality Scheduling; tackling MCS has required an important extension to the previously used notations.

6.1 Summary

The objective in writing this paper was to take existing ideas on the timeband framework and rely-guarantee approaches and to extend them so that they can be useful in specifying MCS. To achieve this, a novel approach to viewing time as a separate index has been proposed: assumptions about the relationship between actual *Time* and what happens inside a computer are recorded essentially as guarantee conditions on the unstoppable progress of "the moving finger".

With MCS, the trigger that indicates that ideal behaviour cannot be achieved is related to time: if hi-crit jobs need more resource than their optimistic estimates, a scheduler has to take action such as abandoning lo-crit jobs. Layered rely-guarantee conditions cope well with describing such nested modes.

The important task of relating the passage of *Time* in the real world with what is going on inside the computer has been handled by having a model in which there is a function from *Time* to machine states; this function cannot be affected by programs but programs do bring about discrete changes in the machine states. Crucially, the relationship between the *Time* index and values in the machine states is defined by a predicate that can be thought of as a guarantee condition. Appropriate definition of the precision of the time band concerns issues such as clock accuracy and drift.

6.2 Further work

Of course, much work remains to be done. This introductory paper is restricted to scheduling jobs. Sketches for describing the "task level" using the same formal ideas exist and show that they appear to suffice. This material will be the subject of a companion paper that will also say more on the transition between modes.

There is extensive published work on MC scheduling and implementation, but little on their formal specification. The Rely-Guarantee (R/G) approach has proved to be a useful formalism for specifying non-real-time safety-critical systems and the main contribution here is to extend R/G to (i) time and (ii) multiple criticalities. Such a formalism will prove to be essential since the notion of mixed criticality has subtle semantics: concepts such as correctness, resilience and robustness are rarely straightforward or intuitive for such systems.

It is important to remember that the material in the body of this paper concerns only specifications. These specifications set a necessary condition on implementations but they are at liberty to achieve more. A typical scheduler will ensure that jobs with the earliest deadline are executed first (EDF); more useful schedulers might abandon lo-crit jobs in stages if so doing provides enough resource for the hi-crit jobs. The usefulness of the specifications in the body of this paper has to be judged by seeing how easy it is to show that such implementations satisfy the specifications proposed here.

An ambitious extension that has not yet been worked on would be to specify probability distributions on assumptions about timing and on the commitment to timely job completion.

Acknowledgements

This paper relates to one aspect of research that is on going with Sanjoy Baruah and Iain Bate. The authors also acknowledge useful suggestions made by Ian Hayes on an earlier draft of this paper.

This research has been supported in part by EPSRC (UK) grants, STRATA and MCCps and Leverhulme grant RPG-2019-020.

References

[AM71] E. A. Ashcroft and Z. Manna. Formalization of properties of parallel programs. In B. Meltzer and D. Michie, editors, *Machine Intelligence, 6*, pages 17–41. Edinburgh University Press, 1971.

[Ash75] Edward A Ashcroft. Proving assertions about parallel programs. *Journal of Computer and System Sciences*, 10(1):110–135, 1975.

[BB06] A. Burns and G.D. Baxter. Time bands in systems structure. In *Structure for Dependability*, pages 74–90. Springer, 2006.

[BBT07] G. Baxter, A. Burns, and K. Tan. Evaluating timebands as a tool for structuring the design of socio-technical systems. In P. Bust, editor, *Contemporary Ergonomics 2007*, pages 55–60. Taylor & Francis, 2007.

[BD17] A. Burns and R.I. Davis. A survey of research into mixed criticality systems. *ACM Computer Surveys*, 50(6):1–37, 2017.

[BDBB18] A. Burns, R. Davis, S. K. Baruah, and I. Bate. Robust mixed-criticality systems. *IEEE Transactions on Computers*, 67(10):1478–1491, 2018.

[BH10] Alan Burns and Ian J. Hayes. A timeband framework for modelling real-time systems. *Real-Time Systems*, 45(1–2):106–142, 6 2010.

[BHJ20] Alan Burns, Ian J. Hayes, and Cliff B. Jones. Deriving specifications of control programs for cyber physical systems. *The Computer Journal*, 63(5):774–790, 2020.

[HJ18] I. J. Hayes and C. B. Jones. A guide to rely/guarantee thinking. In Jonathan Bowen, Zhiming Liu, and Zili Zhan, editors, *Engineering Trustworthy Software Systems – Third International School, SETSS 2017*, volume 11174 of *Lecture Notes in Computer Science*, pages 1–38. Springer-Verlag, 2018.

[HJC14] Ian J. Hayes, Cliff B. Jones, and Robert J. Colvin. Laws and semantics for rely-guarantee refinement. Technical Report CS-TR-1425, Newcastle University, 7 2014.

[HJJ03] Ian Hayes, Michael Jackson, and Cliff Jones. Determining the specification of a control system from that of its environment. In Keijiro Araki, Stefani Gnesi, and Dino Mandrioli, editors, *FME 2003: Formal Methods*, volume 2805 of *Lecture Notes in Computer Science*, pages 154–169. Springer Verlag, 2003.

[Hoa69] C. A. R. Hoare. An axiomatic basis for computer programming. *Communications of the ACM*, 12(10):576–580, 1969.

[Hoa71] C. A. R. Hoare. Proof of a program: FIND. *Communications of the ACM*, 14(1):39–45, January 1971.

[JHC15] Cliff B. Jones, Ian J. Hayes, and Robert J. Colvin. Balancing expressiveness in formal approaches to concurrency. *Formal Aspects of Computing*, 27(3):465–497, 2015.

[JHJ07] Cliff B. Jones, Ian J. Hayes, and Michael A. Jackson. Deriving specifications for systems that are connected to the physical world. In Cliff B. Jones, Zhiming Liu, and Jim Woodcock, editors, *Formal Methods and Hybrid Real-Time Systems: Essays in Honour of Dines Bjørner and Zhou Chaochen on the Occasion of Their 70th Birthdays*, volume 4700 of *Lecture Notes in Computer Science*, pages 364–390. Springer Verlag, 2007.

[Jon80] C. B. Jones. *Software Development: A Rigorous Approach.* Prentice Hall International, Englewood Cliffs, N.J., USA, 1980.

[Jon81] C. B. Jones. *Development Methods for Computer Programs including a Notion of Interference.* PhD thesis, Oxford University, 6 1981. Printed as: Programming Research Group, Technical Monograph 25.

[Jon83a] C. B. Jones. Specification and design of (parallel) programs. In *Proceedings of IFIP'83*, pages 321–332. North-Holland, 1983.

[Jon83b] C. B. Jones. Tentative steps toward a development method for interfering programs. *Transactions on Programming Languages and System*, 5(4):596–619, 1983.

[Jon07] C. B. Jones. Splitting atoms safely. *Theoretical Computer Science*, 375(1–3):109–119, 2007.

[OG76] S. S. Owicki and D. Gries. An axiomatic proof technique for parallel programs I. *Acta Informatica*, 6:319–340, 1976.

[Owi75] S. S. Owicki. *Axiomatic Proof Techniques for Parallel Programs.* PhD thesis, Department of Computer Science, Cornell University, 1975. Published as technical report 75-251.

[WOBW10] J. Woodcock, M. Oliveira, A. Burns, and K. Wei. Modelling and implementing complex systems with timebands. In *Proc. IEEE Conference on Secure System Integration and Reliability Improvement (SSIRI)*, pages 1–13, 2010.

[WWB12] K. Wei, J. Woodcock, and A. Burns. Modelling temporal behaviour in complex systems with timebands. In M. Hinchey and L. Coyle, editors, *Conquering Complexity*, pages 277–307. Spinger, 2012.

On Refining Choreographies*

Ugo de'Liguoro

Università di Torino, Italy
deligu@di.unito.it

Hernán Melgratti

ICC, Universidad de Buenos Aires, and Conicet, Argentina
hernan.melgratti@gmail.com

Emilio Tuosto

Gran Sasso Science Institute, L'Aquila, Italy
emilio.tuosto@gssi.it

Abstract

We put our recent results on choreographic refinement into the context of action refinement of concurrency theory. More precisely, we cast our approach in some categories discussed in the literature.

This exercise is our contribution to the laudatio of Tom Maibaum; it allowed us to identify interesting new directions, one of which is inspired by a paper of Tom.

1 Introduction

We frame a recently proposed approach for the refinement of choreographic models in the traditional research stream on refinement of concurrent systems.

A choreography specifies how components (often called *participants* or *roles*) coordinate with each other through message exchange. In [36], W3C envisages a choreography as a contract consisting of a *global view* that yields a blueprint of the overall communications, the so-called *application-level* protocol. This blueprint can be *projected* on *local views*, namely specifications of participants involved in the protocol, which realise the expected communications. This shapes the ground for the following engineering approach:

$$\text{Global view} \xrightarrow{\quad\text{projection}\quad} \text{Local view} \xleftarrow{\quad\text{compliance}\quad} \text{Local systems} \qquad (1)$$

* Research supported by the EU H2020 RISE programme under the Marie Skłodowska-Curie grant agreement No 778233

where the 'projection' operation produces local views from the global ones and the 'compliance' checking verifies that the behaviour of each participant adheres to the one of the corresponding local view.

Choreographic approaches are appealing because, unlike in orchestration, coordination is not centralised (see [7] for a deeper discussion). Moreover, global views allow developers to work independently on different components.

Choreographic approaches however suffer a main drawback: the lack of support for modular development. This shortcoming is present in standards such as BPMN or in workflow patterns and languages [8] and it has also been reported for choreographic programming [13].

Refinement is a well-established approach for the designing and implementation of software, with roots in stepwise-refinement methodology introduced in [46]:

"program is gradually developed in a sequence of refinement steps. In each step, one or several instructions of the given program are decomposed into more detailed instructions."

Step-wise refinement is complex when programs are concurrent or distributed. A key source of troubles is the fact that refinement usually breaks atomicity, dependencies, and conflict. We discuss this in more details in Section 4.

In [20,21] we propose a refinement approach for a choreographic framework of message-passing systems. To the best of our knowledge, this is the first attempt in this direction. The basic idea is inspired by the *action refinement* developed in concurrency theory (described below). We introduce specific syntax for underspecified parts of the global view that can be replaced with complex protocols. This is a rather straightforward mechanism; however it could spoil desired properties of global views and hence compromise their realisability. We tackle this problem by extending a typing discipline for non-refinable global views to refinable ones so that type-preserving refinements ensure realisability.

2   Refining Tom's Refinement

Refinement is among the many topics Tom has contributed to. An original aspect of his approach to refinement is the use of techniques based on algebraic specifications [25] and recently on model transformation [26].

Tom's work on on protocol refinement [37] is the most close to our approach. In some sense, our approach can be envisaged as *refinement* of some ideas presented in [37]. This work advocates a top-down step-wise refinement development of communication protocols. The authors identify a main source of problems; in their own words (bold text is ours):

"the difficulties in constructing and verifying protocol specifications, with the conventional methods, are mainly due to the complexity of the issues faced by each protocol entity, and the fact that the relations between a **protocol-service specification** and its **protocol-entity specifications** are not always straightforward."

This sentence could be rewritten in the terminology of choreographies by replacing "protocol-service" with "global" and "protocol-entity" with "local"! The way of making the relations between these specification straightforward is by means of projections. Our typing discipline establishes a connection between the semantics of global types and their projections when refining interactions.

An unorthodox approach to action refinement in terms of refinement of temporal logic specifications is in [27]. This work advocates the use of temporal logic as a specification language of reactive systems consisting of interacting objects. More precisely, an object is an "isolated" components with a private (local) state and an public interface of *actions*. The only means that objects have to access each others private states is by "invoking" (that is synchronising on) actions. The intended behaviour of an action is specified, at a given level, in terms of formulae of a temporal logic. Actions, meant to be atomic at a level of abstraction, may be refined by more complex objects at lower levels when their behaviour relies on operations that are not primitive. In logical terms this amounts to *refine* the "next" operator of the logic used to specify the behaviour of at a given level of abstraction with the "eventually" modality at the lower level.

Section 6 discusses interesting future directions inspired by the ideas in [27].

3 Refinement of Choreographies

Our approach to the refinement of choreographies has been introduced in [20] and further developed in [21]. We recap the salient aspects of our framework.

Fix a set $\mathcal{P}$ of *participants* (ranged over by A, B, etc.) and a disjoint set $\mathcal{M}$ of *messages* (ranged over by m, x, etc.). The elements of $\mathcal{L} = \mathcal{L}^! \cup \mathcal{L}^?$ (ranged over by l) will be used to label the events of our event structures. We write $A\,B!m \in \mathcal{L}^!$ and $A\,B?m \in \mathcal{L}^?$ instead of $((A, B), !, m) \in \mathcal{L}^!$ and $((A, B), ?, m) \in \mathcal{L}^?$. The *subject* of a label l, written $\mathsf{sbj}(l)$, is defined as $\mathsf{sbj}(A\,B!m) = \mathsf{sbj}(B\,A?m) = \{A\}$.

3.1 Global choreographies

Global views of message-passing systems are formalised in terms of global choreographies. The syntax of *refinable choreographies* is adapted from [20,21].

Definition 3.1 [Refinabable Choreographies] The set $\mathcal{G}$ of *refinable choreographies* consists of the terms G derived by the grammar

$$
\begin{array}{llll}
\mathsf{G} ::= \mathbf{0} & & \text{empty} & (2) \\
\quad \mid \; \mathsf{A} \overset{m}{\longrightarrow} \mathsf{B} \quad \text{where} \quad \mathsf{A} \neq \mathsf{B} & & \text{interaction} & (3) \\
\quad \mid \; \mathsf{G}; \mathsf{G}' & & \text{sequential} & (4) \\
\quad \mid \; \mathsf{G} + \mathsf{G}' & & \text{choice} & (5) \\
\quad \mid \; \mathsf{A} \overset{\overline{m}}{\dashrightarrow} \overline{\mathsf{B}} & & \text{refinable action} & (6)
\end{array}
$$

Let $\mathcal{P}(\mathsf{G})$ be the set of participants occurring in G.

Let us first focus on *ground* choreographies (g-choreographies for short), that is a terms of $\mathcal{G}$ derived without using the last production (6); as we will see,

79

refinable actions are our technical devise for the refinement of choreographies.

G-choreographies, borrowed from [42], specify (a possibly empty $\mathbf{0}$) set of interactions built our of sequential $\_;\_$, and non-deterministic $\_ + \_$ composition. (The syntax in [42] encompasses iteration and parallel composition which we drop for simplicity.) An interaction $A \xrightarrow{m} B$ represents the exchange of message m between participants A and B; intuitively, A sends m to B which on turn is expected to receive it.

Example 3.2 The g-choreography $G_{(3.2)} = A \xrightarrow{m} C; C \xrightarrow{m} B + A \xrightarrow{n} C; C \xrightarrow{n} B$ specifies a protocol where A non-deterministically decides whether to send m or n to C. In either case, C forwards the message received from A to B. ◇

We use *event structures* to give semantics to g-choreographies. An *event structure labelled over a fixed a set of labels* $\mathcal{L}$ [38] is a tuple $\mathcal{E} = (E, \leq, \#, \lambda)$ where

- E is a set of (atomic) *events*,
- $\leq \, \subseteq \, E \times E$ is a partial order (the *causality* relation),
- $\# \subseteq E \times E$ is a symmetric and irreflexive relation (the *conflict* relation),
- and $\lambda : E \to \mathcal{L}$ is a *labelling* map

satisfying the following conditions: (i) each event has only finitely many predecessors, namely if $e \in E$ then $\{e' \in E \mid e' \leq e\}$ is finite, and (ii) conflicts are hereditary, namely if $e, e', e'' \in E$ then $e \# e'$ & $e' \leq e'' \implies e \# e''$.

As we will see, our semantics is partial. In fact, not every g-choreography $G \in \mathcal{G}$ is "meaningful" because G can specify protocols where the behaviour of some participant depends on choices made by others that are not properly propagated. We show this in the following example.

Example 3.3 A faithful implementation of

$$G_{(3.3)} = A \xrightarrow{m} C; B \xrightarrow{m} C + A \xrightarrow{n} C; B \xrightarrow{n} C$$

could lead to problems. In fact, unlike C, B is oblivious of the decision of A; hence, e.g., B could send message m while A decided to send message n. ◇

A typical way to tackle the problem above is to find *well-formedness* conditions ruling out problematic g-choreographies as the one in Example 3.3. We consider here *well-branchedness*. The events labelled by actions of a same subject form an event structure. More precisely, the *projection* of an event structure $\mathcal{E} = (E, \leq, \#, \lambda)$ on a participant $A \in \mathcal{P}$ is the structure

$$\mathcal{E} \restriction A = (E \restriction A, \leq \restriction A, \# \restriction A, \lambda \restriction A) \qquad \text{where}$$

$E \restriction A = \{e \in E \mid \mathsf{sbj}(\lambda(e)) = A\}$

$\leq \restriction A \, = \, \leq \, \cap (E \restriction A \times E \restriction A)$ and $\# \restriction A = \# \cap (E \restriction A \times E \restriction A)$

$\lambda \restriction A = \lambda|_{E \restriction A}$, namely the restriction of λ to $E \restriction A$

Some auxiliary notations and definitions are useful. If $\mathcal{E} = (E, \leq, \#, \lambda)$ is an event structure then $\min(\mathcal{E}), \max(\mathcal{E}) \subseteq E$ are the minimal and the maximal elements in the poset $(E, \leq)$. Given a family $\{\mathcal{E}_i\}_{i \in I}$ of event structures, we define the sum $\sum_{i \in I} \mathcal{E}_i$ as the operation that takes the disjoint union of $\mathcal{E}_i$ while preserving their orders and labellings and introducing conflicts among events of different members of the family. Formally, if $\mathcal{E}_i = (E_i, \leq_i, \#_i, \lambda_i)$ for $i \in I$ $\sum_{i \in I} \mathcal{E}_i = (\biguplus_{i \in I} E_i, \leq, \#, \lambda)$ where, writing $\iota_i : E_i \to \biguplus_{i \in I} E_i$ for the injections, the following hold:

$$\iota_i(e) \leq \iota_j(e') \iff i = j \ \& \ e \leq_i e'$$
$$\iota_i(e) \# \iota_j(e') \iff i \neq j \ \lor \ (i = j \ \& \ e \#_i e')$$
$$\lambda(\iota_i(e)) = \lambda_i(e)$$

We write $\mathcal{E}_0 + \mathcal{E}_1$ for $\sum_{i \in \{0,1\}} \mathcal{E}_i$ and $\sum_{i \in I} \mathcal{E}$ for $\sum_{i \in I} \mathcal{E}_i$ where $\mathcal{E}_i = \mathcal{E}$ for all $i \in I$.

Definition 3.4 [Well-branchedness [20,21]] Event structures $\mathcal{E}_0$ and $\mathcal{E}_1$ are *well-branched* (in symbols $wb(\mathcal{E}_0, \mathcal{E}_1)$) if, for $\mathcal{E} = \mathcal{E}_0 + \mathcal{E}_1 = (E, \leq, \#, \lambda)$, the following two conditions hold:

determinacy: $\forall B \in \mathcal{P} : (\mathcal{E}_0 \upharpoonright B = \epsilon \iff \mathcal{E}_1 \upharpoonright B = \epsilon) \ \&$
$\qquad\qquad \forall e, e' \in \min(E \upharpoonright B) : e \# e' \implies \lambda(e) \neq \lambda(e')$

awareness: $\exists A \in \mathcal{P} : \emptyset \neq \lambda(\min(E \upharpoonright A)) \subseteq \{l \in \mathcal{L}^! \mid \mathrm{sbj}(l) = A\} \ \&$
$\qquad\qquad \forall B \neq A \in \mathcal{P} : \lambda(\min(E \upharpoonright B)) \subseteq \{l \in \mathcal{L}^? \mid \mathrm{sbj}(l) = B\}$

We dub *active* the unique participant A satisfying the second condition and *passive* the others.

A set of events $x \subseteq E$ is a *configuration* of $\mathcal{E}$ if

(i) $e \leq e' \ \& \ e' \in x \implies e \in x$ (x is downward closed)

(ii) $\forall e, e' \in x. \ \neg(e \# e')$ (x is consistent)

The *domain of configurations* of $\mathcal{E}$ is the poset $\mathcal{D}(\mathcal{E})$ of the configurations of $\mathcal{E}$ ordered by subset inclusion. We say that a configuration x is *maximal* if it is such in $\mathcal{D}(\mathcal{E})$; $\mathcal{C}_{\max}(\mathcal{E})$ is the set of maximal configurations. Being conflict-free and maximal, configurations in $\mathcal{C}_{\max}(\mathcal{E})$ correspond to branches of events of $\mathcal{E}$.

Definition 3.5 [Sequential composition [20,21]] Let $\mathcal{E}, \mathcal{E}'$ be event structures and

$$(E'', \leq'', \#'', \lambda'') = \mathcal{E} \otimes \sum_{x \in \mathcal{C}_{\max}(\mathcal{E})} \mathcal{E}'_x$$

where the structures $\mathcal{E}'_x = (E_x, \leq_x, \#_x, \lambda_x)$ are disjoint copies of $\mathcal{E}'$, then

$$\mathrm{seq}(\mathcal{E}, \mathcal{E}') = (E'', \leq, \#'', \lambda'').$$

where $\leq \ = \ \leq'' \cup \bigcup_{x \in \mathcal{C}_{\max}(\mathcal{E})} \{(e, e') \in x \times E_x \mid \mathrm{sbj}(\lambda''(e)) = \mathrm{sbj}(\lambda''(e'))\}$.

81

The intuition of the definition of $\text{seq}(\mathcal{E}, \mathcal{E}')$ is that any branch $x \in C_{\max}(\mathcal{E})$ of $\mathcal{E}$ is concatenated to a (pairwise incompatible) copy of $\mathcal{E}'_x$, where events in $\mathcal{E}$ cause those of $\mathcal{E}'$ with labels having the same subject.

We can now give a denotational semantics of g-choreographies which is defined only on well-branched g-choreographies; also, we require

- each component to uniquely correspond to a participant of the g-choreography

- and communication among components to uniquely correspond to some communication events of the (semantics of the) g-choreography.

These requirements impose that the communication behaviour of a realisation of a g-choreography faithfully reflects the communication events of the g-choreography.

Definition 3.6 [Semantics, adapted from [20]] Let G be a g-choreography and $\epsilon = (\emptyset, \emptyset, \emptyset, \emptyset)$ be the empty event structure, where $\lambda_\emptyset = \emptyset$ is the empty map. The *semantics* $[\![G]\!]$ of G is the partial mapping assigning an event structure to G according to the following inductive clauses:

$$[\![0]\!] = \epsilon$$

$$[\![A \xrightarrow{m} B]\!] = (\{c_1, c_2\}, \{c_1 < c_2\}, \emptyset, \{c_1 \mapsto A\,B!m, \ c_2 \mapsto B\,A?m\})$$

$$[\![G; G']\!] = \text{seq}([\![G]\!], [\![G']\!])$$

$$[\![G + G']\!] = \begin{cases} [\![G]\!] + [\![G']\!] & \text{if } wb([\![G]\!], [\![G']\!]) \\ \perp & \text{otherwise} \end{cases}$$

where if either $[\![G]\!]$ or $[\![G']\!]$ is $\perp$, then $\text{seq}([\![G]\!], [\![G']\!]) = \perp$ and $[\![G]\!] + [\![G']\!] = \perp$.

Example 3.7 The semantics of $G_{(3.3)}$ in Example 3.3 is undefined. By Def. 3.6, $[\![G_{(3.3)}]\!]$ is defined if $wb(A \xrightarrow{m} C; B \xrightarrow{m} C, A \xrightarrow{n} C; B \xrightarrow{n} C)$ holds. We now verify that this is not the case. By definition, we have:

$$[\![A \xrightarrow{m} C; B \xrightarrow{m} C]\!] = \begin{array}{c} A\,C!m \\ \downarrow \\ A\,C?m \end{array} \quad \begin{array}{c} B\,C!m \\ \downarrow \\ B\,C?m \end{array} \qquad \text{and} \qquad [\![A \xrightarrow{n} C; B \xrightarrow{n} C]\!] = \begin{array}{c} A\,C!n \\ \downarrow \\ B\,C!n \\ \downarrow \nearrow \\ B\,C?n \end{array} \quad \begin{array}{c} A\,C?n \end{array}$$

The sum operation on event structures introduces conflicts between the events in $[\![A \xrightarrow{m} C; B \xrightarrow{m} C]\!]$ and those in $[\![A \xrightarrow{n} C; B \xrightarrow{n} C]\!]$, hence:

$$\mathcal{E} = [\![A \xrightarrow{m} C; B \xrightarrow{m} C]\!] + [\![A \xrightarrow{n} C; B \xrightarrow{n} C]\!] = $$

(recall that conflicts are hereditary, hence it is enough to put only minimal events in conflict). It is easy to verify that the awareness condition of Def. 3.4

is violated since both A and B have output minimal events on the two branches.

$\diamond$

Checking if a g-choreography is not well-branched (or, more generally, well-formed) directly on the event structure computed as in Def. 3.6 can be expensive. Therefore, we introduced a typing system [20] that statically verifies well-branchedness. This typing system establishes judgments of the form

$$\Pi \vdash G : \langle \phi, \Lambda \rangle \tag{7}$$

whose intended meaning is that, under the assumption that G is a g-choreography involving the participants in $\Pi \subseteq \mathcal{P}$, then G has a defined semantics and it is typed by the pair of maps $\langle \phi, \Lambda \rangle$ assigning to participants in Π respectively the labels of minimal and maximal events they execute in G. We refer the interested reader to [20,21] for the details of our typing discipline.

3.2 Refinement: semantics & typing

Let us turn our attention to refinable actions $A \xrightarrow{\overline{m}} \overline{B}$ (cf. production (6) of Def. 3.1) where $\overline{m} = m_1, \ldots, m_n$ and $\overline{B} = B_1, \ldots, B_n$ are non-empty tuples of the same lenght of messages and participants such that the participants in $\overline{B}$ are pairwise distinct and all distinct from A. Intuitively, our refinable action come equipped with an *interface* that constraints legit refinements. By the next definition, the constraints are such that whatever protocol G is used to refine the action has a unique initiator A and ensures that eventually each B_i receives the message m_i.

Definition 3.8 [Refines relation [20,21]] A g-choreography G *refines* $A \xrightarrow{\overline{m}} \overline{B}$ (with $\overline{m} = m_1, \ldots, m_n$ and $\overline{B} = B_1, \ldots, B_n$), if

(i) $\llbracket G \rrbracket = \mathcal{E} \neq \bot$;

(ii) $\mathrm{sbj}(\min(\mathcal{E})) = \{A\}$, by which we say that A is the (unique) *initiator* of G;

(iii) for all $x \in \mathcal{C}_{\max}(\mathcal{E})$ and $1 \leq h \leq n$ there exists $C \in \mathcal{P}(G)$ such that $C B_h ? m_h \in \max(x \restriction B_h)$.

We write G ref $A \xrightarrow{\overline{m}} \overline{B}$ when G refines $A \xrightarrow{\overline{m}} \overline{B}$ and say that $A \xrightarrow{\overline{m}} \overline{B}$ is *ground-refinable* if there exists some ground G such that G ref $A \xrightarrow{\overline{m}} \overline{B}$.

In words, a g-choreography G refines $A \xrightarrow{\overline{m}} \overline{B}$ if G is meaningful, that is well-formed, with a unique participant A initiating the interaction by some output actions, and such that in all branches, namely maximal configurations x of $\llbracket G \rrbracket$, each B_h eventually inputs m_h.

In [20,21] we identify conditions on type judgements (7) that guarantee the existence of ground refinements. In other words, we restrict to typing contexts Π, ϕ, and Λ for which there exists a g-choreography G such that $\Pi \vdash G : \langle \phi, \Lambda \rangle$. This is done by distilling conditions on ϕ and Λ that ensure the existence a g-choreography whose minimal and maximal events are those in ϕ and in Λ, respectively. This guarantees the existence of a well-branched g-choreography characterised by the typing context. Actually, out typing discipline allows us to construct a "canonical" such g-choreography.

4 Framing Our Approach

Generally speaking, refinement consists of a relation between an "abstract" specification S and an "implementation" I. The meaning of 'abstract' and 'implementation' for concurrent systems is a distinctive one. A natural interpretation [41] is that the specification S is *abstract* because it is non-deterministic and I is an implementation when it has *less* non-determinism than S and has some behavioural relation with S (e.g., S and I are weakly bisimilar).

A simple mechanism to move from a specification S towards an implementation I is the *action refinement* mechanism advocated in concurrency theory. This was our source of inspiration. This mechanism envisages modularity in terms of the replacement of an action with a "complex process". A map $r : a \mapsto P_a$ is an *action refinement function* when it assigns a (concurrent) process P_a to each action a. For the moment let us appeal to our intuition and consider processes built out of actions, leaving unspecified the model of concurrency. Intuitively, actions are *atomic* and the refinement map substitutes them with processes having a richer interaction patterns.

With few exceptions (see [4] and references therein) action refinement breaks most of the behavioural relations. More precisely, given an equivalence relation $\sim$ and a refinement function r, a desirable property would be

$$\text{if} \quad S \sim I \quad \text{then} \quad r(S) \sim r(I) \tag{8}$$

where $r(S)$ and $r(I)$ denote the replacement of each action a with $r(a)$ in S and I respectively. Unfortunately (8) does not hold in most of the known equivalences.

The literature offers different approaches to action refinement. Even restricting to refinement of concurrent systems would make exhaustiveness unfeasible. Therefore, we frame our choreographic refinement according to a few categories described in the next paragraphs. We relied on the discussion in [43] and on some seminal papers to identify these categories.

Syntactic & Semantic refinement Action refinement can be *syntactic* or *semantic*. In models where concurrency can be expressed through some syntax, it seems natural to define action refinement as a syntactic operator. For instance, this is a natural approach in process algebraic settings where the seminal work in [1,2,3] suggested the idea of introducing refinement as operators of process algebras. Basically, a specification is a term S derivable from a given grammar built on an alphabet of actions a and a process P is another term (usually derivable from the same grammar barred a possibly different alphabet of actions). Hence, action refinement can be formalised as $S\left[^P/_a\right]$, that is the syntactic replacement of the occurrences of an action a in the term S with the term P.

A pioneering systematic study of semantic action refinement is conducted by van Glabbeck and Goltz [44,45]. This work essentially shows that equivalence relations are usually not preserved under refinement. The relations between syntactic and semantic action refinement have been investigated in [31].

> Our approach clearly falls under the category of syntactic refinement. An interesting observation is that, although ground interactions are assumed atomic in global views, they actually represent asynchronous communications at the local level. Given that the semantics of global views is based on event structures, one could study how our syntactic refinement relates to semantic ones based on event structures in the style of [31]. One could also think of refining local views of choreographies. In this respect, two interesting problems emerge. First, one could study refinements of local views that preserve properties of global views (e.g., well-branchedness). The other problem would be to relate refinements of global views (such as the ones in Section 3) and those of local views.

Selective vs total refinement Refinement approaches may also differ on their capability for refining a model. In some approaches, any action is susceptible of being refined, as for instance in [44,45]. On the contrary, some approaches restrict the kind of elements in a model that can be refined. Formally this boils down to require refinement functions to be total or partial, where the domain of the function determines the elements that are refinable. Such approaches – which we called *selective* in contrast to *total* ones, usually distinguish between *atomic* and *compound* actions. While atomic actions do not admit further refinements, compound ones can be substituted by a combination of compound and atomic actions.

> Our refinement mechanism is selective. Indeed, the use of refinable actions casts in the syntax the elements susceptible of refinements.

Vertical & Horizontal Refinement A somewhat unorthodox approach has been explored in [41] where it is argued that the problem of enforcing the implication (8) "makes sense" only for "horizontal" action refinement. That is, implementations obtained by refining actions with processes built on the same alphabet used in the specification. In other words, the preservation of behavioural equivalences is a desirable requirement if refinements live at the same level of abstraction of the specification.

The perspective changes when considering implementations that live at lower levels of abstraction than their specification. In fact, an important consequence in this case is that one can admit different (incomparable) implementations of the same specifications. Henceforth, the problem above simply disappears. Under this scenario it is more appropriate to consider relations between a specification and its refinements different than equivalences.

85

Following [41], we propose a vertical refinement of global views. The property that we want our refinement to preserve is realisability (here reduced to well-branchedness for simplicity). The use of a typing discipline to guarantee correctness and feasibility of refinements is, as far as we are aware, an original facet of our work.

Forgetful refinements Normally, refinement functions cannot map actions on the empty process. A forgetful refinement is one that forgets (i.e., removes) actions by replacing them with the empty process. As discussed in [43], forgetful refinements are difficult to deal with because the behaviour of a refined model may significantly deviate from the abstract one. For instance, the removal of an action may prune essential behaviours (such as the prevention of certain situations) or even conflicts.

Our refinement mechanism is not forgetful. In fact, our typing discipline imposes to preserve minima and maxima of refinable actions. We observe that forgetful refinement would easily spoil the preservation of well-branchness.

Uniform vs non-uniform refinement A main distinction when dealing with refinement concerns the way in which different occurrences of an action are refined. The preeminent approach is that of refining all occurrences *uniformly*. This is the standard in action refinement: every occurrence of an action is substituted by the same process (see [44,19]). On the contrary, *non-uniform* refinement allows different occurrences of an action to be replaced by different processes, e.g., depending on the context in which the action occurs. For instance, [34] explores that actions can be refined differently if they occur in different sequential agents.

We propose a non-uniform mechanism since different occurrences of a same refinable action $\mathsf{A} \overset{\overline{m}}{\dashrightarrow} \overline{\mathsf{B}}$ can be replaced by different g-choreographies. This is consistent with a "type-based" interpretation. Namely, our refinable actions can be thought of as representing classes of protocols with a given interface, all acceptable as possible refinement.

Interpreted & uninterpreted refinement In general, not every refinement is allowed. *Correctness-preserving* transformations have been advocated since the pioneering work on the systematic construction of software such as those on *step-wise* refinement [24] and on program transformations [30,12]. In a sequential setting, this amounts to require refinement steps not to alter the input-output relation of the specification. This has been formalised in the *refinement calculus* [5], in terms of weakest preconditions or, alternatively with Hoare triples. In the latter case, we say that a is *correctly refined* by $r(a)$ (with r a refinement function), when

$$\forall P, Q : \ P\{a\}Q \implies P\{r(a)\}Q$$

where $P\{a\}Q$ stands for the total correctness of a with respect to precondition P and postcondition Q. Moreover, refinements are required to be congruences, namely a is *correctly refined* by $r(a)$ when

$$\forall P, Q, C[\_] : \ P\{C[a]\}Q \implies P\{C[r(a)]\}Q$$

This notion is in contrast with approaches like the action refinement of [44,45], in which actions are uninterpreted. In fact, the main concern when dealing with action refinement is about the preservation of equivalences, i.e., if $a \sim b$ then $r(a) \sim r(b)$. However, for an action a, in general, it does not hold that $a \sim r(a)$.

> To some extent, our refinement mechanism is interpreted because the refinement have to preserve minima and maxima. Notice that this is a different notion than the one present in the literature. In fact, in our case we do not require equivalences between the g-choreographies replacing refinable actions. We simply demand that replacing g-choreographies respect the minima and maxima of their refinable action.

Inheritance Generally, refinement approaches of concurrent systems require some relations among actions to be inherited in refined models. For instance, causal dependencies should be inherited: if a follows b, then the refined model should ensure that all actions in $r(a)$ follow all actions in $r(b)$; and likewise for conflicts. Inheritance of atomicity is mentioned in [31].

In [44] action refinement is limited to replace events labelled with an action a with an element of a finite (non-empty) pomset [1] $r(a)$. (As observed in [44], the use of flow event structures [9,10] would allow us to generalise to the case where $r(a)$ is an event-structure.) Fixed a refinement function r on the labels of an event structure $\mathcal{E}$, the refined event structure $r(\mathcal{E})$ is obtained by replacing each event e labelled by a by a disjoint copy $\mathcal{E}_e$ of $r(a)$ so that the events in $\mathcal{E}_e$ inherit causality and conflicts of e.

Approaches like the dependency-based action refinement of [41] relax such requirement and allow for the concurrent execution of the independent parts of the implementation of the refined actions.

> The typing discipline that is used in our approach preserves causality and conflicts. Atomicity is not preserved by our refinement mechanism.

5 A Note on Subtyping and Refinement

Subtyping and refinement are often related, albeit independent concepts. In functional programming languages subtyping is a form of polymorphism based on the concept of safe substitution: the type T is a subtype of T' if any expression of type T can be placed in any context expecting an expression of type T', without breaking safety properties that the given system is supposed to guarantee: see e.g. [39, Part III].

Subtyping of sufficiently expressive type systems can be seen as a form of abstract interpretation [28]. Basically, subtypes play the role of finer specifi-

---

[1] Recall that a pomset is an equivalence class of isomorphic conflict-free event structures.

cations of certain subsets of expressions of a given type. This has opened a wide range of research and applications, referred to as the topic of *refinement types* [35].

In the context of communication-centered programming, the new notion of *session types* was proposed in [32] and developed in the subsequent decades building a substantial body of research [22]. Session types have a hybrid syntax, embodying features from ordinary types and from process algebras, and have been designed to specify interaction protocols. In the dyadic scenario, session types are attached to names representing the end-points of a channel shared by a client and a server. The syntactical property of being "dual" of such pairs of types suffices to guarantee error freeness and, in case of certain systems, progress and (forms of) deadlock-freeness [23,18].

The idea to extend subtyping to session types, building over previous work on polymorphic type systems for the π-calculus [40], appears in [29]. This naturally reminds the concept of horizontal protocol refinement: a session type S specifies the interaction protocol on a given channel c; now S is a subtype of another type S' if any communication through c respecting the protocol S will work as well in a context where protocol S' must be respected. This happens when S is more liberal with respect to S' concerning the inputs along c, but more restrictive about the outputs to c, that are caused by internal choices of the process holding c. Shortly, the specification S is more "specific" and less non-deterministic than S': two typical features of specification refinement. Similar ideas as in the theory of session types and subtyping have been investigated with respect to the theory of contracts [14] and of semantical subtyping [15] and various sub-contract relations: see the survey [6]. Subtyping is explicitly treated as a protocol refinement notion in [11].

Session types for dyadic interaction have been generalized to the case of multiparty communication [33]. Global types represent the global view in the picture (1); if a global type is "well formed" then the projections with respect to its participants are ordinary session types, formalising the local view. In this respect global types are quite close to choreographies, although, unlike the latter, global and session types do not allow neither parallel nor sequential composition (in fact, sequential behaviour is attained by action prefixing). This is suggestive when studying formal specifications of protocols at the different levels, but unfortunately there is no generalisation of the theory of subtyping to global types.

More promising are the semantic investigations of multiparty session types based on event structures. Intriguing recent contributions are in [16,17]. Here, global types have been interpreted as prime event structures, while sessions (namely local views of global types) are flow event structure, where the flow ordering needs not to be transitive, reflexive nor, more crucially, to have hereditary an conflict relation. As it explained in [43], these properties yield more liberal refinements, which are not necessarily conflict-free substructures. When compared to our approach it comes out that there are some similarities if we interpret the local views as refinements of global ones. However local sessions are radically different than global types, while our refinable and ground chore-ographies only differ for the respective abstraction levels.

6 Concluding Remarks

We have considered our approach to refinement of choreographies under the lenses of the features of action refinement discussed in the literature. We can summarise this discussion by saying that our refinement mechanism is an interpreted syntactic, vertical, and selective one which preservers dependencies and conflicts and it is neither forgetful nor uniform.

The connection between our choreographies, the typing discipline used in our approach, and global types immediately suggests to extend our framework with subtyping. This is a challenging future direction since, as said in Section 5, defining subtyping on global types is an open problem.

Finally, we discuss an intriguing future direction inspired by Tom's paper [27] discussed in Section 2. Discounting the use of the synchronous nature of interaction adopted, the rather elegant approach in [27] is complementary to ours: we refine the communication pattern of a complex system while in [27] local behaviour of components is refined. This is an appealing idea that could possibly be useful in our context. In fact, the logical refinement in [27] could drive the identification of implementation of refinable actions $A \xrightarrow{\overline{m}} B$. In particular, the refinement of the logical specification of the counter example in [27] is instructive: the proof-obligation yield the conclusion that an "adder" object must be added to a counting system. In our setting this would correspond to the introduction of new participants other than A or those in $\overline{B}$ (or new messages other than those in $\overline{m}$). This would go beyond our current constructive approach in that the canonical g-choreographies built in [20,21] do not introduce components that are not occurring in the refinable action $A \xrightarrow{\overline{m}} B$.

References

[1] Luca Aceto and Matthew Hennessy. Towards action-refinement in process algebras. In *Proceedings of the Fourth Annual Symposium on Logic in Computer Science (LICS '89), Pacific Grove, California, USA, June 5-8, 1989*, pages 138–145. IEEE Computer Society, 1989.

[2] Luca Aceto and Matthew Hennessy. Adding action refinement to a finite process algebra. In Javier Leach Albert, Burkhard Monien, and Mario Rodríguez-Artalejo, editors, *Automata, Languages and Programming, 18th International Colloquium, ICALP91, Madrid, Spain, July 8-12, 1991, Proceedings*, volume 510 of *Lecture Notes in Computer Science*, pages 506–519. Springer, 1991.

[3] Luca Aceto and Matthew Hennessy. Towards action-refinement in process algebras. *Information and Computation*, 103(2):204–269, 1993.

[4] Luca Aceto and Matthew Hennessy. Adding Action Refinement to a Finite Process Algebra. *Information and Computation*, 115:179–247, 1994.

[5] Ralph-Johan R. Back. On correct refinement of programs. *Journal of Computer and System Sciences*, 23(1):49–68, 1981.

[6] Franco Barbanera and Ugo de'Liguoro. Two notions of sub-behaviour for session-based client/server systems: 10 years later. In *PPDP '20: 22nd International Symposium on*

Principles and Practice of Declarative Programming, Bologna, Italy, 9-10 September, 2020, pages 2:1–2:3. ACM, 2020.

[7] Davide Basile, Pierpaolo Degano, Gian-Luigi Ferrari, and Emilio Tuosto. Relating two automata-based models of orchestration and choreography. *JLAMP*, 85(3):425 – 446, 2016.

[8] Egon Börger. Approaches to modeling business processes: a critical analysis of BPMN, workflow patterns and YAWL. *Software and Systems Modeling*, 11(3):305–318, 2012.

[9] Gérard Boudol and Ilaria Castellani. Permutation of transitions: An event structure semantics for CCS and SCCS. In J. W. de Bakker, Willem P. de Roever, and Grzegorz Rozenberg, editors, *Linear Time, Branching Time and Partial Order in Logics and Models for Concurrency, School/Workshop, Noordwijkerhout, The Netherlands, May 30 - June 3, 1988, Proceedings*, volume 354 of *Lecture Notes in Computer Science*, pages 411–427. Springer, 1988.

[10] Gérard Boudol and Ilaria Castellani. Flow models of distributed computations: Three equivalent semantics for CCS. *Information and Computation*, 114(2):247–314, 1994.

[11] Mario Bravetti, Julien Lange, and Gianluigi Zavattaro. Fair refinement for asynchronous session types (extended version). *CoRR*, abs/2101.08181, 2021.

[12] Rod M Burstall and John Darlington. A transformation system for developing recursive programs. *Journal of the ACM (JACM)*, 24(1):44–67, 1977.

[13] Marco Carbone, Fabrizio Montesi, and Hugo Torres Vieira. Choreographies for reactive programming. *CoRR*, abs/1801.08107, 2018.

[14] Giuseppe Castagna, Nils Gesbert, and Luca Padovani. A theory of contracts for web services. In George C. Necula and Philip Wadler, editors, *Proceedings of the 35th ACM SIGPLAN-SIGACT Symposium on Principles of Programming Languages, POPL 2008, San Francisco, California, USA, January 7-12, 2008*, pages 261–272. ACM, 2008.

[15] Giuseppe Castagna, Rocco De Nicola, and Daniele Varacca. Semantic subtyping for the pi-calculus. *Theor. Comput. Sci.*, 398(1-3):217–242, 2008.

[16] Ilaria Castellani, Mariangiola Dezani-Ciancaglini, and Paola Giannini. *Event Structure Semantics for Multiparty Sessions*, pages 340–363. Springer International Publishing, Cham, 2019.

[17] Ilaria Castellani, Mariangiola Dezani-Ciancaglini, and Paola Giannini. Global types and event structure semantics for asynchronous multiparty sessions. *CoRR*, abs/2102.00865, 2021.

[18] Mario Coppo, Mariangiola Dezani-Ciancaglini, Nobuko Yoshida, and Luca Padovani. Global progress for dynamically interleaved multiparty sessions. *Math. Struct. Comput. Sci.*, 26(2):238–302, 2016.

[19] Pierpaolo Degano, Roberto Gorrieri, and Giuseppe Rosolini. A categorical view of process refinement. In *Workshop/School/Symposium of the REX Project (Research and Education in Concurrent Systems)*, pages 138–153. Springer, 1992.

[20] Ugo de'Liguoro, Hernán C. Melgratti, and Emilio Tuosto. Towards refinable choreographies. In Julien Lange, Anastasia Mavridou, Larisa Safina, and Alceste Scalas, editors, *Proceedings 13th Interaction and Concurrency Experience, ICE 2020, Online, 19 June 2020*, volume 324 of *EPTCS*, pages 61–77, 2020.

[21] Ugo de'Liguoro, Hernán C. Melgratti, and Emilio Tuosto. Towards refinable choreographies. *Journal of Logic and Algebraic Methods in Programming*, 2021. Submitted.

[22] Mariangiola Dezani-Ciancaglini and Ugo de'Liguoro. Sessions and session types: An overview. In Cosimo Laneve and Jianwen Su, editors, *Web Services and Formal Methods, 6th International Workshop, WS-FM 2009, Bologna, Italy, September 4-5, 2009, Revised Selected Papers*, volume 6194 of *Lecture Notes in Computer Science*, pages 1–28. Springer, 2009.

[23] Mariangiola Dezani-Ciancaglini, Ugo de'Liguoro, and Nobuko Yoshida. On progress for structured communications. In Gilles Barthe and Cédric Fournet, editors, *Trustworthy Global Computing, Third Symposium, TGC 2007, Sophia-Antipolis, France, November 5-6, 2007, Revised Selected Papers*, volume 4912 of *Lecture Notes in Computer Science*, pages 257–275. Springer, 2007.

90

[24] Edsger W. Dijkstra. Notes on structured programming. In *Structure Programming*, pages 1–82. ACM, January 1972.

[25] Theodosis Dimitrakos and Tom S. E. Maibaum. Notes on refinement, interpolation and uniformity. In *1997 International Conference on Automated Software Engineering, ASE 1997, Lake Tahoe, CA, USA, November 2-5, 1997*, pages 108–116. IEEE Computer Society, 1997.

[26] Zinovy Diskin, Tom S. E. Maibaum, Alan Wassyng, Stephen Wynn-Williams, and Mark Lawford. Assurance via model transformations and their hierarchical refinement. In Andrzej Wasowski, Richard F. Paige, and Øystein Haugen, editors, *Proceedings of the 21th ACM/IEEE International Conference on Model Driven Engineering Languages and Systems, MODELS 2018, Copenhagen, Denmark, October 14-19, 2018*, pages 426–436. ACM, 2018.

[27] José Luiz Fiadeiro and Tom Maibaum. Sometimes "tomorrow" is "sometime". In Dov Gabbay and H. Ohlbach, editors, *Temporal Logica*, volume 827 of *LNAI*, pages 48–66. Springer, 1994.

[28] Timothy S. Freeman and Frank Pfenning. Refinement types for ML. In David S. Wise, editor, *Proceedings of the ACM SIGPLAN'91 Conference on Programming Language Design and Implementation (PLDI), Toronto, Ontario, Canada, June 26-28, 1991*, pages 268–277. ACM, 1991.

[29] Simon J. Gay and Malcolm Hole. Subtyping for session types in the pi calculus. *Acta Informatica*, 42(2-3):191–225, 2005.

[30] Susan L. Gerhart. Correctness-preserving program transformations. In *Proceedings of the 2nd ACM SIGACT-SIGPLAN Symposium on Principles of Programming Languages*, pages 54–66, 1975.

[31] Ursula Goltz, Roberto Gorrieri, and Arend Rensink. On syntactic and semantic action refinement. In Masami Hagiya and John C. Mitchell, editors, *Theoretical Aspects of Computer Software*, pages 385–404. Springer, 1994.

[32] Kohei Honda, Vasco Thudichum Vasconcelos, and Makoto Kubo. Language primitives and type discipline for structured communication-based programming. In Chris Hankin, editor, *Programming Languages and Systems - ESOP'98, 7th European Symposium on Programming, Held as Part of the European Joint Conferences on the Theory and Practice of Software, ETAPS'98, Lisbon, Portugal, March 28 - April 4, 1998, Proceedings*, volume 1381 of *Lecture Notes in Computer Science*, pages 122–138. Springer, 1998.

[33] Kohei Honda, Nobuko Yoshida, and Marco Carbone. Multiparty asynchronous session types. *Journal of the ACM*, 63(1):9:1–9:67, 2016. Extended version of a paper presented at POPL08.

[34] Michaela Huhn. Action refinement and property inheritance in systems of sequential agents. In *International Conference on Concurrency Theory*, pages 639–654. Springer, 1996.

[35] Ranjit Jhala and Niki Vazou. Refinement types: A tutorial. *CoRR*, abs/2010.07763, 2020.

[36] Nickolas Kavantzas, Davide Burdett, Gregory Ritzinger, Tony Fletcher, and Yves Lafon. Web services choreography description language version 1.0. http://www.w3.org/TR/2004/WD-ws-cdl-10-20041217, 2004.

[37] Da-Hai Li and Tom S. E. Maibaum. A top-down step-wise refinement methodology for protocol specification. In Friedrich H. Vogt, editor, *Concurrency 88: International Conference on Concurrency, Hamburg, FRG, October 18-19, 1988, Proceedings*, volume 335 of *Lecture Notes in Computer Science*, pages 197–221. Springer, 1988.

[38] Mogens Nielsen, Gordon D. Plotkin, and Glynn Winskel. Petri nets, event structures and domains, part I. *Theor. Comput. Sci.*, 13:85–108, 1981.

[39] Benjamin C. Pierce. *Types and programming languages*. MIT Press, 2002.

[40] Benjamin C. Pierce and Davide Sangiorgi. Typing and subtyping for mobile processes. *Math. Struct. Comput. Sci.*, 6(5):409–453, 1996.

[41] Arend Rensink and Roberto Gorrieri. Action refinement as an implementation relation. In Michel Bidoit and Max Dauchet, editors, *TAPSOFT '97: Theory and Practice of Software Development*, pages 772–786. Springer, 1997.

[42] Emilio Tuosto and Roberto Guanciale. Semantics of global view of choreographies. *Journal of Logic and Algebraic Methods in Programming*, 95:17 – 40, 2018.

[43] Rob Van Glabbeek and Ursula Goltz. Refinement of actions and equivalence notions for concurrent systems. *Acta Informatica*, 37(4-5):229–327, 2001.

[44] Rob J. van Glabbeek and Ursula Goltz. Equivalence notions for concurrent systems and refinement of actions (extended abstract). In *Mathematical Foundations of Computer Science 1989, MFCS'89, Proceedings*, volume 379 of *Lecture Notes in Computer Science*, pages 237–248. Springer, 1989.

[45] Rob J. van Glabbeek and Ursula Goltz. Equivalences and refinement. In Irène Guessarian, editor, *Semantics of Systems of Concurrent Processes, LITP Spring School on Theoretical Computer Science, La Roche Posay, France, April 23-27, 1990, Proceedings*, volume 469 of *Lecture Notes in Computer Science*, pages 309–333. Springer, 1990.

[46] Niklaus Wirth. Program development by stepwise refinement. In *Pioneers and Their Contributions to Software Engineering*, pages 545–569. Springer, 2001.

πPML: A Product-Centred Formal Language for Business Processes

Germán Regis

Department of Computer Science
University of Río Cuarto, Argentina
`gregis@dc.exa.unrc.edu.ar`

Marcelo Frias

Department of Software Engineering
Instituto Tecnológico de Buenos Aires, Argentina
National Council for Scientific and Technical Research (CONICET), Argentina
`mfrias@itba.edu.ar`

Abstract

The *Product/Process Modelling Language* (PPML) is a formal language for the specification of business processes. As opposed to other business process modelling languages, PPML puts an emphasis on *products* (not only processes), allowing the specifier to describe properties of these, and how processes affect them. In this work, we propose a variant of PPML, called πPML, with a cleaner syntax and a new semantics entirely based on the π-calculus. This semantics takes advantage of the possibility of expressing mobility, and enables us to provide semantics to some constructs of the language which were not formalised previously. Moreover, this semantics will also enable us to perform some analysis activities, by resorting to algorithmic analyses on the π-calculus.

1 Introduction

The constant effort of different organisations in improving their business processes for better efficiency and control has led to the development of languages and methods for business process modelling and analysis [26,5,13]. Currently, there exist a wide variety of business process modelling languages, some of which enjoy a formal semantics (e.g., YAWL [1]), and some which are based on notations with (at least partially) informal semantics (e.g., BPEL, WS-CDL [15], etc.). Most of these have been defined with a significant emphasis on modelling service oriented systems [15]. PPML [16], on the other hand, is a *formal* business process modelling language focusing, not only on processes, but also in the elements affected by them, called *products*. Having the possibility of describing products and their structure is essential in cases in which the information flow of processes and how products evolve in these processes need to be explicitly specified, e.g., for stating invariants, properties describing relationships between different products (or different states of the same product), etc. PPML semantics has traditionally been concentrated on the semantics of *products* and basic processes, but the concrete, detailed formal semantics of process composition has not been tackled previously. In this paper, we propose a variant of PPML, called πPML, with an extended and improved syntax, as well as a new formal semantics for the language. This semantics is based on the π-calculus [18], a formalism sufficiently rich as to enable expressing dynamism and interaction. The resulting language provides, in our opinion, a greater flexibility, compared to other business process modelling formalisms, particularly when describing models in which products are complex, and their description is as important as that of processes, while also achieving a fully formal semantics with significant uses regarding analysis.

1.1 Product/Process Modelling Language

The formalism is based on the methodology presented in [20], in which a system is described in terms of its products and processes, and the relationship between them. Now, what is a product?. What is a process?. To answer these questions, we must first study real world problems involving objects, assembly lines, people, etc., and how to represent these scenarios. We call *entity* to every distinct thing in the (non formalized) real world, and a *referent* will be an entity of interest. The main idea is to use a standard and generic *representation* for the referents in order to give a formal specification of the problem. In the real world, informal problem descriptions may be overflown with irrelevant details, so a good representation must be unambiguous, and only consider the relevant characteristics of the referents.

The referents can be viewed at a *time instant*, or over a *time period*. If we take a snapshot of a referent at a time instant then we obtain its representation as a *product*. If we model the operation of a referent over a period of time then we have its representation as a *process*. Thus, we define a *product* as a passive entity characterised by its *relevant attributes*. These attributes such as size, colour, weight, etc., must be measured; that is, must have a *value* in a corresponding *scale of measurement*. We then define a *process* as a description of an activity which *transforms* an input product into an output product over a period of time.

Sometimes we need to analyse a referent as a *whole* or as *composed of parts*. In the first case, we can obtain a model of the complex referent from an abstract view as a unique thing (product or process). In the second, we specify the referent in a bottom-up mode, putting emphasis in its details, modelling each part in a separate view and merging these parts with some established constructs. Complex products may be modelled using attributes referencing the constituent products. Complex processes (as programs in programming languages), may be modelled in two ways: a bottom-up way (i.e., modelling simpler processes first and composing these later on), or a top-down way (i.e., modelling complex processes abstractly first and later on refining these into more detailed subprocesses). In either case, our referent will, in the end, be modelled in terms of its constituent processes combined in some specific way.

The application of this methodology for business process specification provides us with a way to describe a business process as a collaboration of processes which operate with products. Note that, as opposed to what is normally found in business process modelling notations, we have an explicit, richer and integrated mechanism for specifying products and their characteristics. That is, we can describe, as part of the model, the objects being manipulated by processes and how these objects evolve through the system. We think this is beneficial for modeling a wide range of business processes in which the information of the data processed or shared by the processes need to be detailed and precise.

In order to illustrate these concepts, let us describe a simplified version of (part of) an assembly line in a factory producing motherboards, as depicted in Fig. 1. A motherboard can be characterised as a product that contains a processor and memory banks, where the processor and the memory banks are products characterised by their corresponding relevant attributes such as size, speed, weight, capacity, etc. Note that, for example, the weight of the motherboard can be calculate from the weight of the printed circuit board (an attribute of the motherboard) plus its components weights.

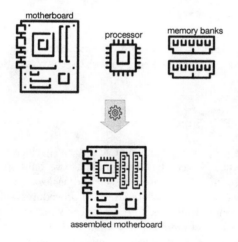

Fig. 1. Motherboards production line process

As stated before, products represent empirical referent objects (i.e., "things" in the modelled world). Products are characterized by their measurable attributes, e.g., length, weight, colour, etc. These characteristics may be *directly* observable or can be *calculated* by functions applied to values of other existing features. The characteristics associated with a product entity must be given in a suitable measurement scale [10]. Initially, let us assume the possible values for the attributes can be either integer or boolean.

```
Product Processor {                        Product Memory {
    int form_factor,                           int Memory_type,
    int mhz,                                   int capacity,
    int mb_cache,                              int mem_weight,
    int weight,                                boolean assembly _test
    boolean assembly_test                  }
}
```

Fig. 2. PPML Products Specification: *Processor* and *Memory*

Products that need to be treated as atomic artefacts, but whose definitions are given in terms of constituent parts are called *structured* products. Their constituents are specified by means of reference attributes, that is, an attribute which type is the constituent product name. To get some constituent attribute value, we refer to it as: *reference_attribute.constituent_attribute*. Figure 3 shows the specification of the Motherboard product.

```
Product Motherboard {
    Processor Proc,
    Memory Mem,
    int socket,
    int memory_type,
    int pcb_weight,
    int mother_weight = pcb_weight + Proc.proc_weight + Mem.mem_weight,
    boolean assemble_test = Proc.assemble_test and Mem.assemble_test
}
```

Fig. 3. PPML Structured Product Specification: *Motherboard*

In Figure 4 we propose a formal syntax for the specification of atomic and structured products. Notice that for simplicity we only adopt as measures (values) for the product's attributes *integer* and *boolean* types.

Regarding processes, they model real world procedures which transform an input product into an output one. In order to carry out these transformations, each process has a *virtual machine* that interprets its basic commands. Intuitively, a virtual machine is an object system with routines representing basic actions that it is capable of performing.

As for products, processes may be *atomic* or *structured*. The last ones are defined in terms of subprocesses.

A process specification contains the *input product* with its required conditions, i.e., some properties of its attributes that must be satisfied in order to perform the process, the *output product* with it's ensured properties, and the *invariant condition* that must be preserved by the transformation.

A special consideration is required for those situations in which a process inputs or outputs more than one product. For such scenarios we formally in-

Product	$\rightarrow$	'Product' Product_name '{' Product_body '}'
Product_body	$\rightarrow$	Product_refs ',' Product_atts | Product_atts
Product_refs	$\rightarrow$	Product_ref ',' Product_refs | Product_ref
Product_atts	$\rightarrow$	Product_att ',' Product_atts | Product_att
Product_ref	$\rightarrow$	Product_ref_name Product_ref_ID
Product_att	$\rightarrow$	Product_direct_att | Product_derived_att
Product_direct_att	$\rightarrow$	Product_att_type Product_att_ID
Product_derived_att	$\rightarrow$	Product_att_type Product_att_ID '=' Expression
Product_att_type	$\rightarrow$	'int' | 'boolean'
Expression	$\rightarrow$	Expression Binary_op Expression | Unary_op Expression
		| Product_att_ID | Product_ref_name'.'Product_att_ID
		| '('Expression')' | NAT_const | BOOLEAN_const
Binary_op	$\rightarrow$	'+' | '-' | '*' | '/' | '==' | 'and' | 'or' | '&&' | '||'
Unary_op	$\rightarrow$	'-' | 'not' | '!'

Fig. 4. BNF for the syntax of atomic and structured products.

troduce *compound* products. Compound products are artifacts of the language in the sense that they do not have a real world counterpart. They can either be a *tuple* of products (Cartesian product of products) or a *choice* product (disjoint union of products). We propose the following syntax for the compound products:

$$[Product\_name_1 : Product\_ID_1, ..., Product\_name_n : Product\_ID_n]$$

for tuple products where each *Product_ID* is the projection on this element; and

$$< Product\_name_1, ..., Product\_name_n : Product\_ID >$$

for choice products where *Product_ID* is the projection of the current product. In order to determine the current product name held on a choice product, we have the function *Product_name*. Note that the *choice* products are useful when a process awaits *some* of several products in a non deterministic way.

In order to illustrate a *process* definition, let us model part of the motherboard production line, namely the process that takes a motherboard without processor and a processor, and returns the partially assembled motherboard resulting from seating the processor in its corresponding socket in the motherboard. As shown in Fig. 5, the input product is a composite product, consisting of a motherboard without processor, and a processor. The initial condition requires the compatibility of motherboard sockets and the processor form factor, and the motherboard's processor socket being empty. The invariant for this process specifies that the processor cannot be assembled in parallel with the memory banks. The output product is the original motherboard with its newly assembled processor.

In Fig. 1.1 we propose a formal syntax for specifying atomic process in terms of its *input* and *output* products, the *requires* and *invariant* expressions which state the conditions to be satisfied initially and during the process task respec-

```
Process assem_1 {
  input: [Motherboard Mother_in, Processor Proc_in]
  output: MotherBoard Mother_out
  invariant: Mother_in.HasMemory == false
  requires: Mother_in.Processor_Socket == Proc_in.Processor_Socket
            && Mother_in.HasProcessor=false,
  ensures: Mother_out == Mother_in && Mother_in.MProcessor == Proc_in
            && Mother_in.hasProcessor == true
}
```

Fig. 5. Process that assembles a motherboard and a processor

tively. Finally, the *ensures* expression describes the input/output relation, i.e., how the process produces the output products from the input ones.

Process	$\rightarrow$	'Process' Process_name '{' Process_body '}'
Process_body	$\rightarrow$	'input:' Input_def ',' 'output:' Output_def
		'invariant:' Invariant_def ',' 'requires:' Requires_def
		'ensures:' Ensure_def
Input_def	$\rightarrow$	Product_ref | Composite_product_ref
Output_def	$\rightarrow$	Product_ref | Composite_product_ref
Invariant_def	$\rightarrow$	Expression
Requires_def	$\rightarrow$	Expression
Ensure_def	$\rightarrow$	Expression

Fig. 6. BNF for the syntax of atomic processes.

When modelling complex empirical referents, it is often the case that one needs mechanisms for *abstraction* and *encapsulation* in order to deal with complexity. This is the usual situation when one decides to model processes in a bottom-up way, i.e., modelling simpler processes first and composing these later on, as well as in top-down approaches, i.e., modelling complex processes abstractly first and later on refining these into more detailed subprocesses. PPML [3] provides facilities for dealing with abstraction and encapsulation, particularly the notion of *framework process*. Framework processes are defined via process combinators. These are the following: Let p_1 and p_2 be two processes, $i(p)$ and $o(p)$ two functions that returns the corresponding input and output products of a process p.

- *Sequential combination*: Denoted as $p_1; p_2$, sequentially combines two processes into a new one. The input product and the requires condition of the sequentially combined process are those corresponding to process p_1. The output product and the ensures condition are the output product and ensures condition of p_2. The new invariant specifies that p_1's invariant holds until its ensures condition becomes true, and after that, once p_2's requires condition becomes true, its invariant holds until its ensures condition becomes true.

- *Semaphore combination*: The semaphore composition of p_1 and p_2, denoted

98

by $p_1;_s p_2$, is defined as for the sequential composition, but the invariant is strengthened in the sense that s (semaphore condition) must be true in order to start the second process.

- *Conditional combination*: The conditional composition of p_1 and p_2, denoted by $p_1 + p_2$, is defined in the following way: the input product of p is the choice compound product $\langle i(p_1), i(p_2) \rangle$ and its output is $\langle o(p_1), o(p_2) \rangle$. The "requires" and "ensures" conditions are the exclusive disjuncts of the corresponding "requires" and "ensures" conditions of the constituent processes. The new invariant requires that, when one of the processes is ready to start, it is executed and, when it finishes, the whole framework process reaches the final state.

- *Parallel combination*: The parallel composition p of $p1$ and $p2$, denoted by $p1|p2$, is defined as follows: The input of p is the cartesian compound product $[i(p1), i(p2)]$ and its output $[o(p1), o(p2)]$. The required and ensured conditions are the conjunctions of the corresponding required and ensured conditions of the constituents processes. The new invariant requires that, when the two processes are ready to start, they are executed in parallel. Further, when one of them finishes, it must wait for the other process to reach its final state.

Notice that in case of the Conditional and Parallel combinations, we need a way to synchronize and build the corresponding compound product in order to feed these framework processes. To overcome these situations, PPML provides the concept of *gate*. These are artefacts of the method in the sense that they do not appear explicitly in empirical referents. Gates have two integrated behaviours, one of them is to manipulate products in order to build (compose or decompose) inputs for processes. The other behaviour is to be a tool for processes synchronization. Note that the gates only can manipulate existing products, i.e., they cannot create new atomic or structured products.

PPML provides two basic gates, namely *multiplexer* and *demultiplexer* gates. The former are useful when a process depends on the execution of previous parallel processes, i.e., on their completion or on their output products. The latter are useful when two or more processes await some part of the output product from a previous process. As an example, for Parallel combination $(p_1|p_2)$, we have:

- A demultiplexer gate that receives the compound product $[i(p_1, i(p_2))]$ and its outputs are $i(p_1)$ and $i(p_2)$. These outputs will be the corresponding inputs of the constituent processes.

- A multiplexer gate that receives as inputs the output products of each parallel process, i.e. $o(p_1)$ and $o(p_2)$, and builds, as its output, the compound product $[o(p_1), o(p_2)]$.

1.2   Pi-calculus

The π-calculus [18] is a process algebra that can be used to describe mobile systems, i.e. systems in which the communication and structure of their elements evolve over time. The short introduction to the π-calculus we include, follows the lines of [23]. Systems are specified in the π-calculus by resorting to *agents* (processes) and *names*, where names are used to refer to communication channels between processes, but they can also refer, for instance, to processes themselves. Each name has a scope. Agents use names to interact, and their evolution is modelled through the actions they execute. The capabilities for actions are expressed by means of (four varieties of) *prefixes*:

$$\pi ::= \quad \bar{x}\langle y\rangle \mid x(y) \mid \tau \mid [x=y]\pi \; .$$

Prefix $\bar{x}\langle y\rangle.P$ *sends* name y via the name x, and afterwatds proceeds as P. Its dual prefix $x(y).P$, *receives* any name through x, and binds it to name y, and afterwards proceeds as P. To specify an unobservable (for instance an internal) action we use $\tau.P$ which evolves (unobservably) to P. Finally, $[x=y]\pi.P$ is the *conditional* prefix that evolves to $\pi.P$ depending on the equality of x and y, i.e., if they are the same name.

The agents and the *summations* of the π-calculus are defined via the productions

$$\begin{array}{rcl} P & ::= & M \mid P_1 \mid P_2 \mid \mathbf{new}\, zP \mid A(x_1,\ldots,x_n) \\ M & ::= & \mathbf{0} \mid \pi.P \mid M_1 + M_2, \end{array}$$

where the composition $P_1|P_2$ is the parallel execution of P_1 and P_2, $\mathbf{new}zP$ is the scope restriction of the name z to P (which implies the generation of a new, unique and fresh name z to be used exclusively by P). $A(x_1,\ldots,x_n)$ is the parametric recursion over the set of agent identifiers, and M is one of the following:

- $\mathbf{0}$ is the agent that does nothing,

- $\pi.P$ can only exercise π, and afterwards proceeds as agent P,

- $M_1 + M_2$ is the exclusive choice between M_1 and M_2. Once a capability of M_1 has been exercised, the capabilities of M_2 cannot be exercised, and viceversa.

An extension of π-calculus is the *polyadic* π-calculus, that allows actions to send and receive more than one name, e.g.,

$$\bar{x}\langle y_1 y_2\rangle.P_1 \mid x(z_1 z_2).P_2 \quad \longrightarrow \quad P_1 \mid P_2\{{}^{y_1,y_2}/_{z_1,z_2}\}$$

which means that after the communication between P_1 and P_2 via channel x P_1 and P_2 continue in parallel, but in P_2 each occurrence of z_i is substituted by y_i. Along the paper we use abbreviations like $\sum_{i=1}^{m}(M_i) = M_1+,\ldots,+M_m$ for summation of m choices and $\prod_{i=1}^{m}(P_i) = P_1|\ldots|P_m$ for multiple parallel compositions.

2 A π-Calculus semantics for πPML

A semantics for πPML comprises a semantics for products and a semantics for processes. The most interesting part from a technical point of view is the semantics of products, which requires a π-calculus encoding of a kind of state based variable.

2.1 Products

As seen before, products in PPML have attributes. These attributes have a measurement scale, i.e., a type in which they take their values. In this section we follow the syntax for recursive characterization of parametric processes from [17]. For each attribute of a product we want to capture its notion of state, i.e., the correspondence between their identification and value. This situation can be specified by considering for each attribute a channel to access its value. We assume a *nil* name as the universal value to represent undefined attributes. The process creating an instance of a product is specified by the following expression:

$$PROD_I(prod_{id}, val\_att_1, \ldots, val\_att_n) \stackrel{\text{def}}{=}$$

$$\overline{prod_{id}}\langle att_1, \ldots, att_n \rangle . PROD_I(prod_{id}, val\_att_1, \ldots, val\_att_n) \, +$$

$$\sum_{i=1}^{n} att_i(n\_val_i).PROD_I(prod_{id}, val\_att_1, \ldots, [^{n\_val_i}/val\_att_i], \ldots, val\_att_n) +$$

$$\sum_{i=1}^{n} \overline{att_i}\langle val\_att_i \rangle . PROD_I(prod_{id}, val\_att_1, \ldots, val\_att_n)$$

The above definition expresses, first, the interface communication. When a process links with the reference name of a product instance, it receives the reference names of its attributes to access them. Then, with these attribute reference names, the process can read or write the values of each attribute of the instance. The read and write access to the attributes values is modelled with the corresponding read and write operation to each attribute's reference name. In case of calculated attributes, the write access is not available. Note that we can specify uninitialized product's instances with the expression $PROD_I(prod_{id}) \stackrel{\text{def}}{=} PROD_I(prod_{id}, nil, \ldots, nil)$, i.e., a new instance is generated by setting all its attributes to the *nil* value.

As an example, let us consider the *Processor* product presented in Figure 2. $PROCESSOR_I$ specifies the behaviour of a processor instance:

$PROCESSOR_{id}(id, val_{ffactor}, val_{mhz}, val_{mcache}, val_{weight}, val_{a\_test}) =$

$\overline{id}\langle ffactor, mhz, mcache, weight, a\_test \rangle$.

$\qquad\qquad PROCESSOR_{id}(id, val_{ffactor}, val_{mhz}, val_{mcache}, val_{weight}, val_{a\_test}) +$

$ffactor(n\_val).PROCESSOR_{id}(id, n\_val, val_{mhz}, val_{mcache}, val_{weight}, val_{atest}) +$

$mhz(n\_val).PROCESSOR_{id}(id, val_{ffactor}, n\_val, val_{mcache}, val_{weight}, val_{a\_test}) +$

$mcache(n\_val).PROCESSOR_{id}(id, val_{ffactor}, val_{mhz}, n\_val, val_{weight}, val_{a\_test}) +$

$weight(n\_val).PROCESSOR_{id}(id, val_{ffactor}, val_{mhz}, val_{mcache}, n\_val, val_{a\_test}) +$

$a\_test(n\_val).PROCESSOR_{id}(id, val_{ffactor}, val_{mhz}, val_{mcache}, val_{weight}, n\_val) +$

$\overline{ffactor}\langle val_{ffactor} \rangle . PROCESSOR_I(id, val_{ffactor}, val_{mhz}, val_{mcache}, val_{weight}, val_{a\_test}) +$

$\overline{mhz}\langle val_{mhz} \rangle . PROCESSOR_I(id, val_{ffactor}, val_{mhz}, val_{mcache}, val_{weight}, val_{a\_test}) +$

$\overline{mcache}\langle val_{mcache} \rangle . PROCESSOR_I(id, val_{ffactor}, val_{mhz}, val_{mcache}, val_{weight}, val_{a\_test}) +$

$\overline{weight}\langle val_{weight} \rangle . PROCESSOR_I(id, val_{ffactor}, val_{mhz}, val_{mcache}, val_{weight}, val_{a\_test}) +$

$\overline{a\_test}\langle val_{a\_test} \rangle . PROCESSOR_I(id, val_{ffactor}, val_{mhz}, val_{mcache}, val_{weight}, val_{a\_test})$.

For structured products, the attributes that reference their components (i.e., the constituent products), will have as values the *ids* that identify the corresponding component instance. As an example, we can give a simplified specification for the motherboard as:

$$MB_{id}(id, val_{proc\_id}, val_{mem\_id}, val_{socket}, val_{m\_type}) \stackrel{\text{def}}{=}$$
$$\overline{id}\langle proc\_id, mem\_id, socket, m\_type \rangle \; .$$
$$MB_{id}(id, val_{proc\_id}, val_{mem\_id}, val_{socket}, val_{m\_type}) +$$
$$proc\_id(n\_val).MB_{id}(id, n\_val, val_{mem\_id}, val_{socket}, val_{m\_type}) +$$
$$\cdots$$
$$\overline{m\_type}\langle val_{m\_type} \rangle.MB_{id}(id, val_{proc\_id}, val_{mem\_id}, val_{socket}, val_{m\_type}) \; .$$

where $proc\_id$ and mem_id are the attributes corresponding to component parts of the structured product.

2.2 Processes

For each atomic process, the following expression captures its semantics:

$$P_{name}(in, out) = in\langle i_p \rangle.REQ(i_p).DO(i_p, o_p).\overline{out}\langle o_p \rangle.P_{name}(in, out) \; .$$

This expression characterises an atomic process with input and output channels used to receive an send products. It comprises two distinguished agents, *REQ* and *DO*. The *REQ* agent checks the required conditions for the input product. The *DO* agent processes the input product to obtain the output one with the ensured specification. Finally, the process writes the output product into the send channel and becomes available again for a new execution.

Let us consider as example the process presented in the Figure 5. This part of the assembly line takes an unassembled motherboard, a processor and assembles them. The following definition specifies it behaviour. Process P_{assem} has two channels $assem_{in}$ and $assem_{out}$ used to receive and return the products that it manipulates, i.e., its input and output products. Then, the process waits for its input products, namely, a motherboard and a processor. Once the products arrive, the requirements REQ_{assem} are verified. If the requirements are satisfied, the process assembles the motherboard with the processor by accessing their corresponding attributes and updating them as needed. Finally, the assembled motherboard is communicated through the output channel as a result.

$$P_{assem}(assem_{in}, assem_{out}) \stackrel{\text{def}}{=} in\langle mb \rangle.in\langle proc \rangle.REQ_{assem}(mb, proc).$$
$$DO_{assem}(mb, proc.\overline{out}\langle mb \rangle.P_{assem}(assem_{in}, assem_{out})$$
$$REQ_{assem}(mb, proc) \stackrel{\text{def}}{=} mb(\ldots, mb_{socket}, \ldots).proc(\ldots, proc_{ffactor}, \ldots).$$
$$mb_{socket}(s).proc_{ffactor}(f).[s = f].0$$
$$DO_{assem}(mb, proc) \stackrel{\text{def}}{=}$$
$$mb(\ldots, mb_{proc\_id}, \ldots).proc(proc_{id}, \ldots).\overline{mb_{proc\_id}}(proc_{id}).0$$

Framework processes are obtained by combining basic processes using π-calculus process composition operators (e.g., sequential, conditional, parallel compositions). As example, let P_1, P_2 be the π-calculus specification of two atomic processes, for the *sequential* (*parallel*) combination the π-calculus expression $P_1.P_2$ ($P_1|P_2$) captures the desired behaviour, respectively.

In order to give a whole picture of the assembly line specification, we can define a *SYSTEM* as the parallel composition of the products instances with the framework process that can assemble the process and the memory with the motherboard and then test them.

$$SYSTEM \stackrel{\text{def}}{=} (PROCESSOR_1|MODERBOARD_1|MEMORY_1|(P_{assem}|M_{assem}).Mb_{test}.$$

3 Related Works and Conclusions

Various approaches for the formalisation of business processes exist [27,24,19,28,12,9], and even formalisations based on the π-calculus have been proposed (e.g., [22]). Our approach to business process specification, as opposed to other approaches we are aware of, enables for a rich, state-based, specification of *products*. The formal semantics based on the π-calculus that we briefly described in this paper, provides new opportunities for automated analyses on specifications, e.g., verifying properties using model checkers for the π-calculus, and analysing simplifications/minimisations of processes via different notions of bisimulation.

There exists several tools and techniques for the analysis of π-calculus specifications. The Mobility Workbench [25] provides as its main feature the possibility of open bisimulation. In [29] a partial model checker for the π-calculus is presented which uses an expressive value-passing logic as the property language. Two different approach for π-calculus analysis are presented in [21], the first one is a tool to help the exploration of the state-space of a model; the other approach provides a tool for properties verification by a translation to the Promela language and afterwards using the Spin model checker [14]. Another technique to verify properties of π-calculus models is shown in [2]; in this work the systems described in distributed π-calculus are translated into a rewriting logic which is executable on the Maude software platform [7]. In [4], Applied Pi Calculus and the tool ProVerif are proposed to verify Security Protocols. Close to this work, the use of Process Algebras for modeling and analyzing concurrent systems are explored in [11,8,6].

Our language πPML is strongly based on its predecessor PPML. We have ignored, for the moment, the real-time components of the language, and concentrated in simplifying and structuring the language's syntax and semantics. As a consequence, we obtained a language whose semantics is fully based on the π-calculus, and where some aspects of the language which were previously understood only informally, are now fully formalised.

References

[1] Michael Adams, Andreas V. Hense, and Arthur H. M. ter Hofstede. YAWL: an open source business process management system from science for science. *SoftwareX*, 12:100576, 2020.

[2] Bogdan Aman and Gabriel Ciobanu. Analyzing distributed pi-calculus systems by using the rewriting engine maude. In Kamel Barkaoui, Hanifa Boucheneb, Ali Mili, and Sofiène Tahar, editors, *Verification and Evaluation of Computer and Communication Systems - 11th International Conference, VECoS 2017, Montreal, QC, Canada, August 24-25, 2017, Proceedings*, volume 10466 of *Lecture Notes in Computer Science*, pages 155–170. Springer, 2017.

[3] Gabriel Baum, Marcelo F. Frias, and T. S. E. Maibaum. A logic for real-time systems specification, its algebraic semantics, and equational calculus. In Armando Martin Haeberer, editor, *Algebraic Methodology and Software Technology, 7th International Conference, AMAST '98, Amazonia, Brasil, January 4-8, 1999, Proceedings*, volume 1548 of *Lecture Notes in Computer Science*, pages 91–105. Springer, 1998.

[4] Bruno Blanchet. Modeling and verifying security protocols with the applied pi calculus and proverif. *Found. Trends Priv. Secur.*, 1(1-2):1–135, 2016.

[5] Hadrien Bride, Olga Kouchnarenko, and Fabien Peureux. Reduction of workflow nets for generalised soundness verification. In Ahmed Bouajjani and David Monniaux, editors, *Verification, Model Checking, and Abstract Interpretation - 18th International Conference, VMCAI 2017, Paris, France, January 15-17, 2017, Proceedings*, volume 10145 of *Lecture Notes in Computer Science*, pages 91–111. Springer, 2017.

[6] Olav Bunte, Jan Friso Groote, Jeroen J. A. Keiren, Maurice Laveaux, Thomas Neele, Erik P. de Vink, Wieger Wesselink, Anton Wijs, and Tim A. C. Willemse. The mcrl2 toolset for analysing concurrent systems - improvements in expressivity and usability. In Tomás Vojnar and Lijun Zhang, editors, *Tools and Algorithms for the Construction and Analysis of Systems - 25th International Conference, TACAS 2019, Held as Part of the European Joint Conferences on Theory and Practice of Software, ETAPS 2019, Prague, Czech Republic, April 6-11, 2019, Proceedings, Part II*, volume 11428 of *Lecture Notes in Computer Science*, pages 21–39. Springer, 2019.

[7] Manuel Clavel, Francisco Durán, Steven Eker, Santiago Escobar, Patrick Lincoln, Narciso Martí-Oliet, and Carolyn L. Talcott. Two decades of maude. In Narciso Martí-Oliet, Peter Csaba Ölveczky, and Carolyn L. Talcott, editors, *Logic, Rewriting, and Concurrency - Essays dedicated to José Meseguer on the Occasion of His 65th Birthday*, volume 9200 of *Lecture Notes in Computer Science*, pages 232–254. Springer, 2015.

[8] Rance Cleaveland and Steve Sims. Generic tools for verifying concurrent systems. *Sci. Comput. Program.*, 42(1):39–47, 2002.

[9] Juliana de Melo Bezerra and Celso Massaki Hirata. A polyadic pi-calculus approach for the formal specification of UML-RT. *Adv. Softw. Eng.*, 2009:656810:1–656810:26, 2009.

[10] Norman E. Fenton and James Bieman. *Software metrics - A Rigorous and Practical Approach, Third Edition*. CRC Press, 2014.

[11] Thomas Gibson-Robinson, Philip J. Armstrong, Alexandre Boulgakov, and A. W. Roscoe. FDR3: a parallel refinement checker for CSP. *Int. J. Softw. Tools Technol. Transf.*, 18(2):149–167, 2016.

[12] Nicolas Guelfi and Amel Mammar. A formal semantics of timed activity diagrams and its PROMELA translation. In *12th Asia-Pacific Software Engineering Conference (APSEC 2005), 15-17 December 2005, Taipei, Taiwan*, pages 283–290. IEEE Computer Society, 2005.

[13] Xudong He, Qin Liu, Shuang Chen, Chin-Tser Huang, Dejun Wang, and Bo Meng. Analyzing security protocol web implementations based on model extraction with applied PI calculus. *IEEE Access*, 8:26623–26636, 2020.

[14] Gerard J. Holzmann. *The SPIN Model Checker - primer and reference manual*. Addison-Wesley, 2004.

[15] Rania Khalaf, Nirmal Mukhi, Francisco Curbera, and Sanjiva Weerawarana. The business process execution language for web services. In Marlon Dumas, Wil M. P. van der Aalst, and Arthur H. M. ter Hofstede, editors, *Process-Aware Information Systems: Bridging People and Software Through Process Technology*, pages 317–342. Wiley, 2005.

[16] T. S. E. Maibaum. An overview of the mensurae language: Specifying business processes. In *Rigorous Object-Oriented Methods, ROOM 2000, York, UK, 17 January 2000*, Workshops in Computing. BCS, 2000.

[17] Robin Milner. The polyadic pi-calculus: A tutorial. *LFCS report ECS-LFCS-91-180*, 1991, 1991.

[18] Robin Milner. *Communicating and mobile systems - the Pi-calculus*. Cambridge University Press, 1999.

[19] Shoichi Morimoto. A survey of formal verification for business process modeling. In Marian Bubak, G. Dick van Albada, Jack J. Dongarra, and Peter M. A. Sloot, editors, *Computational Science - ICCS 2008, 8th International Conference, Kraków, Poland, June 23-25, 2008, Proceedings, Part II*, volume 5102 of *Lecture Notes in Computer Science*, pages 514–522. Springer, 2008.

[20] Margaret Myers and Agnes Kaposi. *A First Systems Book: Technology and Management (Second Edition)*. FACIT: Formal approaches to computing and information technology. Imperial College Press; 2nd Revised ed., 2004.

[21] Frédéric Peschanski. Verifying mobile systems: Take two - stateful observations of pi-calculus processes. In *Communicating Process Architectures 2017 & 2018*, volume 70 of *Concurrent Systems Engineering Series*, pages 501 – 524. IOS Press, 2019.

[22] Frank Puhlmann and Mathias Weske. A look around the corner: The pi-calculus. *Trans. Petri Nets Other Model. Concurr.*, 2:64–78, 2009.

[23] Davide Sangiorgi and David Walker. *The Pi-Calculus - a theory of mobile processes*. Cambridge University Press, 2001.

[24] Wil M. P. van der Aalst and Christian Stahl. *Modeling Business Processes - A Petri Net-Oriented Approach*. Cooperative Information Systems series. MIT Press, 2011.

[25] Björn Victor and Faron Moller. The Mobility Workbench — a tool for the π-calculus. In David Dill, editor, *CAV'94: Computer Aided Verification*, volume 818 of *Lecture Notes in Computer Science*, pages 428–440. Springer-Verlag, 1994.

[26] Yuepeng Wang, Shuvendu K. Lahiri, Shuo Chen, Rong Pan, Isil Dillig, Cody Born, Immad Naseer, and Kostas Ferles. Formal verification of workflow policies for smart contracts in azure blockchain. In Supratik Chakraborty and Jorge A. Navas, editors, *Verified Software. Theories, Tools, and Experiments - 11th International Conference, VSTTE 2019, New York City, NY, USA, July 13-14, 2019, Revised Selected Papers*, volume 12031 of *Lecture Notes in Computer Science*, pages 87–106. Springer, 2019.

[27] Mathias Weske. *Business Process Management - Concepts, Languages, Architectures, Third Edition*. Springer, 2019.

[28] Peter Y. H. Wong and Jeremy Gibbons. Formalisations and applications of BPMN. *Sci. Comput. Program.*, 76(8):633–650, 2011.

105

[29] Ping Yang, Samik Basu, and C. R. Ramakrishnan. Parameterized verification of pi-calculus systems. In Holger Hermanns and Jens Palsberg, editors, *Tools and Algorithms for the Construction and Analysis of Systems, 12th International Conference, TACAS 2006 Held as Part of the Joint European Conferences on Theory and Practice of Software, ETAPS 2006, Vienna, Austria, March 25 - April 2, 2006, Proceedings*, volume 3920 of *Lecture Notes in Computer Science*, pages 42–57. Springer, 2006.

Logic and Formal Methods in Model-Driven Engineering

Kevin Lano

Department of Informatics
King's College London, UK
kevin.lano@kcl.ac.uk

Abstract

Model-driven engineering (MDE) has become the most widely-adopted form of formal software development. The use of models, especially models expressed in the UML language, and of automated code generation from models, have become mainstream software engineering techniques.

In this paper we look at the origins and evolution of MDE and trace the influence of traditional formal methods work and methods integration research in these origins during the 1990's, and in the later development of MDE up to the present.

1   Introduction

The successful adoption of model-driven engineering (MDE) by many sectors of the software industry represents perhaps the widest commitment to formally-based methods to date. Whilst traditional formal methods such as Z, VDM and B have been adopted mainly within the safety-critical systems domain, particularly in transport, MDE has been used in a wide variety of applications including business systems, telecoms, finance and software modernisation [18,31,79].

A principal reason for the success of MDE has been the international standardisation of the UML notation since 1997 by the OMG [64], and related standards such as those for the QVT model transformation notation [68]. The OCL textual specification notation of UML [65] has been more generally usable by software practitioners, compared to the more purely mathematical notations of traditional formal methods.

The success of MDE should not obscure the many defects which still exist in UML, OCL and related notations, due to lack of sufficient formality in their semantics. Throughout the development and revision process of the UML standards there have been two countervailing trends: (i) towards more rigorous foundations; (ii) towards pragmatic ease of use by practitioners and alignment to mainstream OO programming and design concepts.

In this paper I want to describe some of the influences which led to the concepts of MDE, and especially the influence of formal methods research on

107

the UML and OCL and upon their formalisation. I will also describe the continuing contribution of formal methods and mathematical logic to MDE research.

2 Object-oriented Formal Methods and Methods Integration

The first formal methods, Z, B and VDM, were developed prior to the widespread adoption of object-oriented programming languages (initially, C++ and Smalltalk). The specification structures of the formal languages were instead aligned to those of procedural programming languages, especially Ada. B and VDM specifications were organised around modules and procedures at different levels of abstraction, whilst Z adopted a more purely mathematical structuring of *schemas* and schema combination operators.

Once object-orientation became more established as a strong trend in software research and development practice, there were efforts in the formal methods research community to re-align formal languages to OO concepts. One motivation for this work was a perception that the existing structuring mechanisms of formal languages were ineffective for the specification of large-scale systems, and the belief that object-oriented structuring would be more successful at organising such specifications. It was identified that the traditional formal methods were only *object-based* at most: they supported the definition of the state of a single object, and operations on that state (only somewhat loosely associated with the state, in the case of Z), but not object-oriented in the sense of allowing multiple objects to exist and be dynamically created, and where objects belong to classes which can be organised in a class hierarchy, with object behaviour depending upon the definitions of their most-specific class.

In the Z world these initiatives to introduce object-oriented concepts resulted in languages such as Object-Z and Z++ [37,74]. For VDM, the extended VDM++ language was developed [43], and a variety of other OO formal languages were also proposed, as described in [39]. In the B world, styles of specification were adopted whereby B modules could represent collections and systems of objects, instead of single objects [41,73]. However, inheritance remained difficult to represent in a satisfactory manner. There was also a strand of research work linking formal methods to structured design notations such as SSADM. With the advent of diagrammatic object-oriented methods such as OMT [71] and the Booch method [7], researchers looked for ways by which formal and semi-formal object-oriented methods could be usefully combined. This area of work was known as *methods integration*.

By the early 90's there was considerable interest by both academia and industry researchers in the area of OO methods and their enhancement by formal approaches, and one result was the formation in 1992 of an industry-led UK research forum called EROS (Extensible Requirements for Object Specification). This was organised by industrial researchers from Logica, LBMS, Hewlett Packard and other companies. The forum held regular meetings addressing specific issues in object-oriented specification, and organised public workshops.

While the development of Object-Z, Z++, VDM++ and other object-oriented formal methods continued, there were also initiatives in creating entirely new rigorous OO methods which used diagrammatic models, but which also had a precise underlying semantics. The three principal approaches of this kind were Syntropy [12], Catalysis [82] and Fusion [3]. The developers of the Catalysis and Fusion methods were members of EROS. Syntropy (created by Cook and Daniels in 1994) was the first OO analysis and design method (OOAD) to integrate formal and graphical specification, it used a Z-style notation to specify constraints on objects, and provided precise rules for refinement. The Syntropy specification notation can be considered the forerunner of OCL, also devised by Cook, using a more conventional program expression style notation [35,78].

In the US, there was also interest in methods integration, and there was initial work by Robert France and others on combining rigorous approaches with OO methods [3]. The advent of UML and its adoption by the OMG meant that other OOADs such as Syntropy and Fusion became sidelined in comparison with UML, and the focus of research moved into considering UML application and improvement, especially at a semantic level [27,35,13].

3 Semantic underpinnings for rigorous object-oriented modelling

A number of fundamental issues in object-oriented specification were addressed by researchers over this period using different formalisms.

It was increasingly realised that the distinctive issues for formal OO semantics related to the *composition* of object behaviour and the inter-relations between different models (such as class diagrams and state machines). In addition, the semantics of *encapsulation* in the OO context, and of subclassing/inheritance with dynamic binding of object behaviour were also critical.

3.1   Object composition

Individual objects in isolation could be specified using conventional means (indeed a standard Z specification could be viewed as a specification of such an object). Difficulties arise however when assemblies of interacting objects are present and their behaviours need to be combined in a consistent manner. This became the focus of the research group at Imperial College, based upon the *object calculus* formalism of Maibaum and Fiadeiro [23,22].

The core concepts of the object calculus are (i) the use of sets S of attribute symbols and A of action symbols to represent the data and operations of a component or object x; (ii) the use of axioms Γ in linear temporal logic over S and A to specify the behaviour of x; (iii) an encapsulation or locality principle which expresses that if no action of x takes place in a time step, then the attributes of x do not change in value:

$$\bigvee_{\alpha \in A} \alpha \vee \bigwedge_{a \in S} a = Xa$$

109

where X is the temporal symbol denoting the next state.

Such a characterisation of an object leaves open the possibility of many objects existing and interacting simultaneously, possibly executing actions concurrently, but with clearly separated data. The theories Ω_C of individual objects of a class C consist of triples (S_C, A_C, Γ_C) of attributes, actions and logical properties of C objects. These can be combined via theory morphisms into theories Λ_C of the class C, representing the family of objects of C, and in turn such class theories can be combined into theories of modules or subsystems consisting of several classes. A *theory morphism*

$$\sigma : (S_1, A_1, \Gamma_1) \to (S_2, A_2, \Gamma_2)$$

maps attribute symbols of the first component to attribute symbols of the second, and action symbols of the first to action symbols of the second, in such a way that each translation of an axiom of Γ_1 is provable from the second theory:

$$\varphi \in \Gamma_1 \;\Rightarrow\; \Gamma_2 \vdash \sigma(\varphi)$$

In particular, the locality axiom of the first component is provable in interpreted form in the second. A category of components with arrows as theory morphisms can be defined [22]. This category has co-limits, which provides a mathematical construction of composite components.

This work led to an approach in which successive levels of composition within an OO system were represented by compositions of theories representing individual classes, classes related by associations, and packages [42,5,6,33]. Within a class theory, different objects are distinguished by object identifiers, and each attribute and action of the class theory is parameterised by an object identifier: $a(x)$ and $\alpha(x)$, which can be rendered as $x.a$ and $x.\alpha$ in a more conventional OO notation. The locality axiom applies for each individual object:

$$\forall x : \overline{C} \cdot \bigvee_{\alpha \in A} \alpha(x) \vee \bigwedge_{a \in S} a(x) = Xa(x)$$

where $\overline{C}$ is the set of instances of class C.

Hence the OO structuring of a system in terms of its parts is reflected in a corresponding composition structure of the theories of the parts into a theory of the whole system. The object calculus formalism also provided a modular proof mechanism for the composed theories [24].

3.2   Object encapsulation and extension

The concept of encapsulation of the data and behaviour of a software component, in order to support reuse and reasoning about the component, long predated object-orientation. The principle of *information hiding* [70], and the idea of an *abstract data type* with a mathematical specification and possibly many different implementations, were key influences in the design of the original version of Ada (Ada 83). Ada modules are separated into a module specification which provides the public interface of the module, and a module body which contains the implementation details. Even the more primitive C language used the same approach: code modules $m.c$ were expected to be provided with a separate header interface file $m.h$, which declared what functions were available in $m.c$, but omitting detail of implementations. The benefit of such mechanisms is that components can be reused on the basis of their specifications, independently of their implementations. One of the most extensive applications of reuse in practice was the C mathematical and systems libraries, which could be used by any C programmer, in most cases without knowledge of the detail of their implementations. However the semantics of the library specifications were only expressed in natural language in the documentation of the libraries.

The B formal language also adopted an Ada-like encapsulation and abstraction mechanism, with a system specification defined in terms of module specification components, which provide an interface of operations and a high-level definition of data for modules. Separate refinement and implementation components then provide more explicit and lower-level versions of modules, ultimately down to a level which can be directly implemented in code.

In the procedural language versions of encapsulation, the module implementations are hidden from users of the module – who use it by means of its specification and only know (in principle at least) information that is made public in or associated with this specification. For this to work successfully, the module implementation must be semantically consistent with its specification, via some *refinement relation*. This is usually implicit in a programming language, or is limited only to parameter type information (C header definitions of operations only give such typing information). In B, the refinement relation is formalised and must be defined in the refinement/implementation components which refine a specification. The refinement concept leads to the covariant/contravariant rule for operations: a refined version opR of an operation specification opS must be defined for at least the same set of inputs as opS, but can accept more inputs (ie., its domain could be wider). However, on the output side, opR must produce no output which could not be observed for opS, on a given input in the domain of opS. Ie., opR can be more determinate than opS, and produce outputs of more specific types than opS.

The Eiffel programming language [63] was the first OO language to include semantic specifications of behaviour: operations can have pre and post -conditions, with the rule that an operation can have equivalent or stronger post-conditions in a subclass than in the superclass, and equivalent or weaker pre-conditions.

As described in Section 3.1, the object calculus formulation of object semantics defines a form of encapsulation whereby object state can only be changed by actions belonging to the same object. A pre-post specification of action behaviour has the form:

$$Pre_\alpha \wedge \alpha \;\Rightarrow\; X(Post_\alpha)$$

If a theory morphism σ interprets α by an action β, and attributes by same-named attributes, the interpreted pre-post axiom for α must be provable from

111

that for β in the new theory:

$$Pre_\beta \wedge \beta \Rightarrow X(Post_\beta) \ \vdash \ Pre_\alpha \wedge \beta \Rightarrow X(Post_\alpha)$$

This will be the case when

$$Pre_\alpha \ \Rightarrow \ Pre_\beta$$

and

$$Post_\beta \ \Rightarrow \ Post_\alpha$$

This is the contra/covariant rule of refinement.

An extended concept of refinement, enabling abstract actions to be decomposed into a series of concrete actions, was also developed in the object calculus [25].

3.3 Subclassing and inheritance

The semantic interpretation of inheritance, and the interaction of inheritance with information hiding and refinement, was an area of particular difficulty in formalising object-oriented specification.

A simple view of subclassing regarded the set of existing objects $\overline{D}$ of a subclass D of a class C as a subset of the set $\overline{C}$ of objects of C (also referred to as the *extent* of C). By transitivity of $\subseteq$, the same should hold for any descendant D of C. However, D objects may have more operations and additional behaviour compared to C objects, so cannot be regarded as C objects from a behavioural perspective. D is also not a refinement of C, because only certain of the instances of C are also D instances. Thus operations of C inherited by D have restricted domains in their D versions.

A key behavioural principle, now known as the *Liskov substitutability principle* was formulated in [62]: that if D is a subclass of C, users of an instance $x : C$ cannot distinguish if they are actually using a D instance by executing methods of C. In addition, methods of D cannot introduce state changes in D instances which could not be observed in C instances. The motivation for this is that if an object $x : D$ is shared between two clients, one with a declaration of $x : C$ and one with a declaration $x : D$, the second client cannot perform actions which would violate the expectations of the first regarding x.

This principle is closely related to the object calculus locality axiom. Considering the object theory $\Omega_C = (S_C, A_C, \Gamma_C)$ of a superclass C of a class D, Ω_C can be embedded into the subclass object theory $\Omega_D = (S_D, A_D, \Gamma_D)$: S_C is a subset of S_D, A_C is a subset of A_D, so a morphism $\sigma : \Omega_C \to \Omega_D$ can be defined as an identity on these symbols. The requirement that the locality axiom of C is preserved by D amounts to requiring that

$$\bigvee_{\alpha \in A_C} \alpha \vee \bigwedge_{a \in S_C} a = Xa$$

is provable in Ω_D, ie., new actions of D either do not change the state of C, or they co-occur with actions of C. In either case the change to the attributes of C is consistent with the behaviour defined in Ω_C.

3.4 Polymorphism and dynamic binding

As noted above, subclasses are not refinements of a superclass, even though their objects should be behaviourally compatible with objects of the superclass. Moreover, the behaviour of an action can vary from one subclass to another, and be dynamically selectable depending upon which class an object belongs to.

One approach to formalise such semantics is to consider the class theory Λ_C of a superclass C as being an extension of the co-limit of its subclass theories Λ_{C1}, ..., Λ_{Cn}, where the Ci are all the direct subclasses of C.

For each action α of C, there are action symbols $\alpha(x)$ in Λ_{Ci}, for each $x \in \overline{Ci}$. There will be a pre-post specification

$$x \in \overline{Ci} \wedge Pre_i(x) \wedge \alpha(x) \ \Rightarrow \ X(Post_i(x))$$

in Λ_{Ci} for each Ci. Therefore these axioms are also valid in Λ_C, which contains disjointness axioms of the form:

$$\overline{Ci} \cap \overline{Cj} = \varnothing$$

for $i \neq j$. Additionally, the axiom $\overline{Ci} \subseteq \overline{C}$ is valid in Λ_C for each i. Taken together, these properties give the semantics of $\alpha(x)$ for C as a conditional choice between the behaviours of $\alpha(x)$ in each subclass Ci, depending upon the subclass which x belongs to.

4 Influence of formal methods and semantics work on UML

Between 1994 and 1997 the initial proposals and first version of the UML were developed, with version 1.0 of UML being principally based on the combination of the respective OOAD methods of James Rumbaugh, Grady Booch and Ivar Jacobson (OMT [71], Booch [7] and Objectory [32]). A formal textual language, OCL, was also incorporated into UML version 1.0. As discussed in Section 2, OCL was based on formal specification concepts originating in Z and Syntropy. However, unlike Z or B, it did not possess a fully-defined mathematical semantics, and this has led to ongoing issues in the semantics of OCL and languages using OCL, such as UML and QVT.

In the research community, the EROS forum was superseded by the pUML "Precise UML" group, which worked specifically on providing rigorous underpinnings for the new unified method. This was an internationally-based group including researchers from Imperial College, York University, and researchers from the US and Europe, such as Robert France and Bernhard Rumpe. The key publication by pUML was the paper "The UML as a Formal Modelling Notation" [27] which also appeared in the first UML conference (the UML conference later became the MODELS conference series). The paper proposed a semantic framework for UML, including a formalisation of OCL, and adopted the structured theories approach pioneered by Tom Maibaum's group. The paper was ranked at the 2008 MODELS conference as the most influential paper from the 1998 UML conference.

113

The pUML group also organised the ROOM "Rigorous object-oriented methods" series of workshops, which considered specific issues in UML, OCL and software modelling. Some of the first research on model transformations originated from pUML [46]. The pUML group participated in the UML revision process, and made the case for more rigorous semantics in the foundations of UML. A particular contribution was the concept of metamodelling as a means of systematically defining the architecture of UML [19,11].

4.1 Extensions of the object-oriented paradigm

The work of Maibaum's group was further extended into the domain of reactive and real-time systems [45,48], enabling the theory-composition semantics to be applied to UML specifications of such systems. It was also extended to a wider range of UML modelling notations [49].

5 The development of UML and MDE

The period from 2000 to 2009 saw substantial revision of UML (version 2.0 was released in 2005 after a revision process lasting 6 years) and the initiation of the model-driven architecture (MDA) and concepts of model-driven engineering (MDE). Research specialised and diversified, with specialised conferences on MDE topics such as model transformations, and new journals, such as Software and Systems Modeling (SoSyM), initiated and edited by members of pUML.

5.1 UML development and semantics

The UML as standardised in Versions 1.1 (1997), 1.3 (2000), 1.4 (2001) and 1.5 (2003) incorporated some of the semantic insights from researchers, in particular the OCL notation and the use of "package merging" to implement (meta)model composition at a syntactic level. However, lack of semantics in OCL and the UML, and lack of flexibility in the UML definition, became significant concerns amongst UML users. The UML definition documents used OCL to specify model validity constraints (for example, that the two ends of an association cannot both be aggregations), but only specified model semantics in natural language. Additionally, variation points were permitted for alternative semantics, because of the need to accommodate different application domains and software environments. Thus it was impossible to determine the intended semantics of a given model.

A range of different semantics approaches were applied to parts of UML, such as translation to Object-Z [34], operational semantics [61] and metamodelling based semantics [20]. Research into UML semantics uncovered extensive semantic problems [28], especially with statemachines [21] and with the metamodel constraints of the UML languages [4].

A particular concern was the lack of flexibility in UML concepts, with some aspects of UML closely based on specific programming language approaches (eg., C++ for inheritance concepts), making it difficult to adapt for different software applications. The pUML group were involved in proposals for re-organising UML as a family of specification languages to address these is-

114

sues [10], however these proposals were not incorporated into UML, and UML
2.0 (2005) maintained the same unitary language approach as previous versions. Instead, the pUML proposals formed a starting point for the concept of
"domain-specific languages" (DSLs) [14,26], which has become one of the most
significant approaches within MDE in the last decade. DSLs provide a specific
language to define a particular system aspect at a high level. They are usually
small languages and consist of a metamodel, concrete syntax, and tools for
writing models in the DSL and for synthesising other artifacts (such as code)
from the DSL models [29]. DSLs were in alignment with the increasing trend
of the software industry towards lightweight development approaches and agile
methods.

An important step forward in UML semantics was the integrated operational semantics of [9], which provided a systematic formalisation of large parts
of UML 2, using a compositional approach. Other work on UML semantics by
pUML members included the axiomatic semantics of class diagrams [53], state
machines [52] and interactions [51].

6 Developments in UML and MDE to the present

UML versions 2.4 (2011) and 2.5 (2017) addressed some of the flaws in the
previous versions of the standard, but retained the concept of UML as a single
language with a loose semantics encompassing many different application areas
and permitting many alternative interpretations. The facility of UML *profiles*
was used to provide specialised and extended UML notations and semantics for
particular areas (such as MARTE for real-time systems, or fUML for executable
UML).

MDE became a widespread and mainstream software practice, although
the most substantial industrial uptake of MDE was focussed in domains (such
as automotive systems or safety-critical systems) where the additional costs
of MDE could be justified by long-term benefits [31,79]. MDE became incorporated as a permitted approach in software standards such as DO-178C
(Aerospace). MDE was also adopted to reduce the costs of mobile application
development, using a DSL approach and automated code generation [30,77,59].

Two areas of particularly active research were DSLs and model transformations (MT). These are fundamental components of an MDE approach: DSLs
enable the definition of models of specific system aspects, whilst transformations enable the transformation and analysis of models, including the mapping
of design models to code, or the migration of models to evolved or alternative
metamodels [72]. Conceptually, transformations could be regarded as language
interpretation morphisms. As specification languages, MT languages have the
distinctive property that they relate elements of two (or more) different models.
In particular, given specific source elements, they need to lookup (or *resolve*)
the target elements which these elements have been mapped to.

The OMG issued a RFP for a model transformation language which could be
used within the MDA [66]. The research group of Maibaum and Lano at King's
College London [75], [76], and associated pUML researchers [2], were centrally

involved in the development of the transformation concepts which eventually were incorporated into the QVT standard, issued in 2005 [67]. The QVT-R language of the standard adopts a logical style of specification based upon relationships between source and target models, specified in OCL. Element resolution is achieved by relation tests: $R(s, t)$ is true if source element s has been related to target element t via relation R.

The QVT standard and the research which led to it also inspired alternative transformation languages, such as ATL [17] and ETL [36], also based on OCL or OCL-like foundations, however ETL also includes procedural elements similar to those of the QVT-O language of [67]. An alternative MT approach, more directly based on OCL, was proposed in [54]. Transformation research expanded considerably after the publication of the QVT standard, with specialised conferences (ICMT and TTC) and novel transformation languages being proposed.

As with the UML and OCL standards, questions arose regarding the semantics of QVT-R, which revealed many subtle aspects due to the aim of the language to support bidirectional transformations (bx) and incremental execution, propagating changes from source to target models. Logic-based semantic foundations for QVT-R were proposed [58,8]. A revision of the standard was published in 2013 [68], and a list of resolved and outstanding semantic issues are at [69].

Transformation verification was a major concern of transformation developers, and such verification required rigorous semantic foundations for MT languages, and for the models which transformations operate on – in order to be able to prove that a transformation preserves or refines/abstracts the meaning of a model. A transformation verification framework, based on an MT semantics integrated with the axiomatic semantics of UML [53] was defined in [57]. Other approaches to MT verification are described in [1].

The development of OCL has continued, however the current standard remains version 2.4 [65], which has several flaws and inconsistencies (for example, different parts of the document take different views on whether the *OclAny* type is a universal type or simply the most general object type) [80]. The need for extension of OCL to include aspects such as map types and function types has become evident [81,60], but such extensions will require resolution of OCL semantic issues (for instance, a universal type is evidently inconsistent with the ability to define general function types).

The category-theory concepts of the object calculus have also been used for specifying model management and other MDE processes [15,16].

Conclusions

In this survey of the history of MDE and the UML, we have highlighted the important influence of formal methods research on the origins and development of MDE. The work of individual researchers and research teams in formal logical approaches contributed fundamental insights into the semantics of object-oriented systems. This was an important counterweight to more pragmatically-oriented influences on UML and MDE, enabling rigorous foundations to be es-

116

tablished for MDE and hence facilitating the application of MDE in domains of high-integrity systems.

References

[1] L. Ab Rahim, J. Whittle, *A survey of approaches for verifying model transformations*, Sosym, vol. 14, 2015.

[2] D. Akehurst, S. Kent, O. Patrascoiu, *A relational approach to defining and implementing transformations between metamodels*, SoSyM vol. 2, no. 4, 2003, pp. 215–239.

[3] B. Bates, J.-M. Bruel, R. France, M. Larrondo-Petrie, *Formalising Fusion Object-oriented analysis models*, FMOODS 1996, IFIP.

[4] H. Bauerdick, M. Gogolla, F. Gutsche, *Detecting OCL traps in the UML 2.0 superstructure*, UML '04, Springer-Verlag LNCS vol. 3273, 2004.

[5] J.C. Bicarregui, K.C. Lano, T.S.E. Maibaum, *Objects, Associations and Subsystems: a hierarchical approach to encapsulation*, ECOOP 97, Springer Verlag LNCS, 1997, pp. 324–343.

[6] J.C. Bicarregui, K.C. Lano, T.S.E. Maibaum, *Formalising Object-Oriented Models in the Object Calculus*, ECOOP 97 Workshop on "Precise Semantics for Object-Oriented Modeling Techniques". ECOOP 97 workshop reader, Springer-Verlag LNCS vol. 1357, 1997, pp. 155–160.

[7] G. Booch, *Object-oriented design with applications*, Benjamin/Cummings Publishing, Redwood City, 1991.

[8] J. Bradfield, P. Stevens, *Enforcing QVT-R with mu-calculus and games*, FASE '13, LNCS, 2013.

[9] M. Broy, M. Cengarle, H. Gronniger, B. Rumpe, *Definition of the system model*, in UML 2 semantics and applications, K. Lano (ed), Wiley, 2009.

[10] T. Clark, A. Evans, S. Kent, S. Brodsky, S. Cook, *A feasibility study in re-architecting UML as a family of languages using a precise OO meta-modeling approach*, pUML 2000.

[11] T. Clark, A. Evans, S. Kent, *The metamodelling language calculus: foundation semantics for UML*, FASE '01, 2001, pp. 17-31.

[12] S. Cook, J. Daniels, *Designing object systems: object-oriented modelling with Syntropy*, Prentice Hall, 1994.

[13] S. Cook, A. Kleppe, R. Mitchell, B. Rumpe, J. Warmer, A. Wills, *The Amsterdam manifesto on OCL*, in Modelling with the OCL, T. Clark and J. Warmer (eds), Springer-Verlag, 2002, pp. 115–149.

[14] S. Cook, *Domain-specific modeling and model driven architecture*, MDA Journal, 2004.

[15] Z. Diskin, T. Maibaum, *Category theory and model-driven engineering: from formal semantics to design patterns and beyond*, Model-driven engineering of information systems, 2014.

[16] Z. Diskin, T. Maibaum, K. Czarnecki, *Towards category theory foundations for model management*, internal report, University of Waterloo, 2014.

[17] Eclipse, *ATL user guide*, eclipse.org, 2019.

[18] U. Eliasson, et al., *Agile MDE in mechatronic systems – An industrial case study*, MODELS 2014, LNCS vol. 8767, Springer, 2014.

[19] A. S. Evans and R. B. France and K. Lano and B. Rumpe, *Meta-modelling semantics of UML*, in Behavioural Specifications for Businesses and Systems, Kluwer, Editor: Haim Kilov, Chapter 4, 1999.

[20] A. Evans, S. Kent, *Core metamodelling semantics of UML: the pUML approach*, UML '99 proceedings, Springer-Verlag, 1999, pp. 140–155.

[21] H. Fecher, J. Schonborn, M. Kyas, W-P de Roever, *29 new unclarities in the semantics of UML 2.0 state machines*, ICFEM '05, Springer-Verlag LNCS vol. 3785, 2005, pp. 52–65.

[22] J. Fiadeiro, T. Maibaum, *Temporal theories as modularisation units for concurrent system specification*, FACS 4(3), pp. 239–272, 1992.

117

[23] J. Fiadeiro, T. Maibaum, *Describing, structuring and implementing objects*, Foundations of object-oriented languages, LNCS vol. 489, 1991.

[24] J. Fiadeiro, T. Maibaum, *Verifying for reuse: foundations of object-oriented system verification*,

[25] J. Fiadeiro, T. Maibaum, *Sometimes "tomorrow" is "sometime": action refinement in a temporal logic of objects*, in D. Gabbay, H. Ohlbach (eds), *Temporal Logic*, LNAI vol. 827, Springer-Verlag, 1994, pp. 48–66.

[26] M. Fowler, *Domain-specific languages*, Pearson Education, 2010.

[27] R. France, A. Evans, K. Lano, B. Rumpe, *The UML as a Formal Modelling Notation*, Computer Standards and Interfaces 19 (1998), 325–334, 1998. Also in the UML '98 conference.

[28] M. Gogolla, O. Radfelder, M. Richters, *A UML semantics FAQ: the view from Bremen*, University of Bremen, 1999.

[29] J. Greenfield, K. Short, S. Cook, S. Kent, *Software Factories*, Wiley, 2004.

[30] H. Heitkotter, T. Majchrzak, H. Kuchen, *Cross-platform MDD of mobile applications with MD^2*, SAC 2013, ACM Press, 2013.

[31] J. Hutchinson, J. Whittle, M. Rouncefield, S. Kristoffersen, *Empirical assessment of MDE in industry*, ICSE 11, ACM, 2011.

[32] I. Jacobson, *Object-oriented software engineering: a use case driven approach*, Addison-Wesley, 1992.

[33] S. Kent, K. Lano, J. Bicarregui, A. Hamie, J. Howse, *Component Composition in Business and System Modelling*, OOPSLA 97 workshop on Specification of Behavioural Semantics.

[34] S. Kim, D. Carrington, *A formal denotational semantics of UML in Object-Z*, L'Objet, 7(3), 2001, pp. 323–362.

[35] A. Kleppe, J. Warmer, S. Cook, *Informal formality? The OCL and its application in the UML metamodel*, UML '98 conference, Springer-Verlag, 1999, pp. 148–161.

[36] D. Kolovos, R. Paige, F. Polack, *The Epsilon Transformation Language*, ICMT 2008.

[37] K. Lano, Z^{++}: *An Object-oriented Extension to Z*, Z User Meeting '90, Nicholls J. (Ed.), Springer-Verlag Workshops in Computer Science, 1991, pp. 151–172.

[38] K. Lano, H. Haughton, *Standards and Techniques for Object-oriented Formal Specification*, Software Engineering Standards Symposium, IEEE Press, 1993.

[39] K. Lano, H. Haughton (Eds.), *Object-oriented Specification Case Studies*, Prentice Hall series in Object-orientation, October 1993, ISBN 0-13-097015-8, 236 pages.

[40] K. Lano, *Formal Object-oriented Development*, Springer-Verlag, September 1995, 422 pages.

[41] K. Lano, *The B language and method*, Springer-Verlag, 1996.

[42] K. Lano, *Enhancing Object-Oriented Methods with Formal Notations*, TAPOS, Vol. 2, No. 4, pp. 247–268, 1996.

[43] K. Lano, S. Goldsack, *Integrated Formal and Object-oriented Methods: The VDM^{++} Approach*, 2nd Methods Integration Workshop, Leeds Metropolitan University, April 1996.

[44] K. Lano, J. Bicarregui, *Refinement Through Pictures: Formalising Syntropy Refinement Concepts*, BCS FACS/EROS workshop on "Making Object-oriented Methods More Rigorous", 1997.

[45] K. Lano, *Logical Specification of Reactive and Real-Time Systems*, Journal of Logic and Computation, Vol. 8, No. 5, pp 679–711, 1998.

[46] K. Lano, J. Bicarregui, *UML Refinement and Abstraction Transformations*, ROOM 2 workshop, Bradford University, May 1998.

[47] K. Lano, R. France, J.-M. Bruel, *A Semantic Comparison of Fusion and Syntropy*, The Computer Journal, Vol. 43, No. 6, 2000, pp. 451–468.

[48] K. Lano, J. Bicarregui, T. Maibaum, J. Fiadeiro, *Composition of Reactive System Components*, Foundations of Component-Based Systems, G. T. Leavens, M. Sitaraman, editors. Cambridge University Press, 2000.

[49] K. Lano, J. Bicarregui, and A. Evans, *Structured Axiomatic Semantics for UML Models*, ROOM 2000 Proceedings, Electronic Workshops in Computer Science, Springer-Verlag, 2000.

[50] K. Lano, *Catalogue of model transformations*, http://nms.kcl.ac.uk/kevin.lano/tcat.pdf, 2005.

[51] K. Lano, *Formal specification using interaction diagrams*, SEFM '07, 2007.

[52] K. Lano, D. Clark, *Direct Semantics of Extended State Machines*, Journal of Object Technology, 6(9), pp. 35–51, 2007.

[53] K. Lano, *A compositional semantics of UML-RSDS*, SoSyM 8(1), 2009, pp. 85–116.

[54] K. Lano, S. Kolahdouz-Rahimi, *Specification and Verification of Model Transformations using UML-RSDS*, IFM 2010, LNCS vol. 6396, pp. 199–214, 2010.

[55] K. Lano, S. Kolahdouz-Rahimi, *Constraint-based specification of model transformations*, Journal of Systems and Software, vol. 88, no. 2, February 2013, pp. 412–436.

[56] K. Lano, S. Kolahdouz-Rahimi, *Model-transformation Design Patterns*, IEEE Transactions in Software Engineering, vol 40, 2014.

[57] K. Lano et al., *A framework for MT verification*, FACS, 2014.

[58] K. Lano, S. Kolahdouz-Rahimi, *Implementing QVT-R via semantic interpretation in UML-RSDS*, SoSyM, 2020.

[59] K. Lano et al., *Synthesis of mobile applications using AgileUML*, ISEC 2021.

[60] K. Lano, S. Kolahdouz-Rahimi, *Extending OCL with map and function types*, FSEN 2021.

[61] J. Lilius, I. Porres Paltor, *The semantics of UML state machines*, technical report, Turku center for computer science, Turku, Finland, 1999.

[62] B. Liskov, J. Wing, *A behavioral notion of subtyping*, ACM Trans. Program. Lang. Syst. 16(6), 1994, pp. 1811–1841.

[63] B. Meyer, *Eiffel: the language*, Prentice Hall, 1992.

[64] OMG, *Unified Modeling Language*, specification version 2.5.1, December 2017, https://www.omg.org/spec/UML.

[65] OMG, *Object Constraint Language 2.4 Specification*, 2014.

[66] OMG, *MOF 2.0 Query/Views/Transformations RFP*, ad/2002-04-10, 2002.

[67] OMG, *MOF QVT final adopted specification*, ptc/05-11-01, 2005.

[68] OMG, *MOF2 Query/View/Transformation v1.3*, 2016.

[69] OMG, MOF Query/View/Transformation – Open issues, https://issues.omg.org/issues/lists/qvt-rtf, Dec 2019.

[70] D. Parnas, *On criteria to be used in decomposing systems into modules*, Communications of the ACM, 14(1), 1972, pp. 221–227.

[71] J. Rumbaugh, M. Blaha, W. Premerlani, F. Eddy, W. Lorensen et al., *Object-oriented modeling and design*, Prentice-Hall, 1991.

[72] S. Sendall, W. Kozaczynski, *Model transformation: the heart and soul of model driven software development*, IEEE Software, 20(5), 2003, pp. 42–45.

[73] R. Shore, *Object-oriented modelling in B*, 1st Conference on the B method, Nantes, France, 1996.

[74] S. Stepney, R. Barden, D. Cooper, *Object orientation in Z*, Workshops in Computing, Springer-Verlag, 1992.

[75] L. Tratt, T. Clark, *Revised submission for MOF 2.0 Query/Views/Transformations RFP*, Version 1.1, 18/08/2003.

[76] L. Tratt, *Model transformations and tool integration*, SoSym, vol. 4, no. 2, 2005.

[77] S. Vaupel, G. Taentzer, R. Gerlach, M. Guckert, *Model-driven development of mobile applications*, Sosym, Feb. 2018.

[78] J. Warmer, J. Hogg, S. Cook, B. Selic, *Experience with Formal Specification of CMM and UML*, Object-oriented Technologies, Springer-Verlag 1998, pp. 216–220.

[79] J. Whittle, J. Hutchinson, M. Roucefield, *The state of practice in Model-driven Engineering*, IEEE Software, May/June 2014, pp. 79–85.

[80] E. Willink, *OCL omissions and contradictions*, OMG ADTF, 2012.

[81] E. Willink, *Reflections on OCL 2*, Journal of Object Technology, Vol. 19, No. 3, 2020.

[82] A. Wills, D. De Souza, *Objects, components and frameworks with UML: the Catalysis approach*, Addison-Wesley, 1998.

A Personal Perspective on Logic and Category Theory in the Foundations of Software Engineering

Paulo Alencar

David R. Cheriton School of Computer Science
University of Waterloo, Canada
`palencar@uwaterloo.ca`

Abstract

This paper presents a personal account of how Tom Maibaum has influenced my research and scholarship through his contributions to logic and category theory in the foundations of software engineering. The essay will describe his influence in terms of logics for describing software specification based on actions and advances in object-oriented specifications based on category theory.

1 Introduction

This Festschrift aims to recognize Tom Maibaum's many contributions to the computer sciences, and I am humbled and honored to participate in this worthy initiative by providing an account of his influence on my research journey. As a pioneer in the foundations of software engineering, Tom's phenomenal contributions to novel formal approaches to support the engineering of software systems had a significant impact on this scholarly field and in my personal research. In this context, I present a personal perspective from someone who has known Tom Maibaum for over thirty years.

The essay will be divided into two parts, the first describing his influence in terms of logics for describing software specification based on actions and the second discussing advances in object-oriented specifications based on category theory.

2 Logical Approach for Software Architectural Description Changes

In the late 1980s, when I was a doctoral student at the Pontifical Catholic University of Rio de Janeiro (PUC-Rio), under the supervision of Professor Carlos Lucena, I was introduced to this professor from the Imperial College who was working with one of his doctoral students, Samit Khosla, on a variant of action logic for software specification. This was the first time I met Tom, and I was immediately impressed by the depth and insightfulness of his approaches and explanations. I had known him previously only through his books (or handbooks) on computer program specification and logic [31,1].

I was also very impressed with how fast and insightful novel ideas came to him. I remember that in one of his visits to PUC-Rio, when he was the external member of a doctoral committee, he came back after the first break and told us he had found a solution for the thesis problem that had been investigated. Then, he went on and amazed us with an elegant solution that had not been found by the student.

2.1 Deontic Action Logic

The solution Tom introduced in cooperation with Samit was a formal framework for the specification of dynamic computer-based systems [23,24]. The framework was presented as a number of formal logics used to model concepts such as actions, permission and obligation.

I quote (loosely) what Samit stated in some excerpts from [23]:

"As the basis of our framework we propose and motivate the idea of a system being modelled in terms of a collection of global, perhaps incomplete, information states called scenarios and a notion of action for describing movement between these scenarios. We employ a novel modal extension of many sorted first order logic for this. In order to model the behaviour of a system we extend this by introducing the deontic concepts of permissible and obligatory action (and subsequently property) this then allows us to state when actions may and must happen as opposed to just describing the effects of such actions. Two further perhaps less central extensions are also incorporated: action combinators and agents. The former is used to describe more complex actions such as non deterministically and parallel composed actions and the later is used to associate actions with the things (agents) which perform them. The introduction of action combinators and agents also serves to illustrate the advantages and benefits of separating behaviour from action description.

The major issue which is discussed is the discrimination and relationship between the way in which a systems behaviour is described and the way in which mechanisms that allow a system to "change" (and hence make possible desired behaviour) are modelled. A clean and smooth formal integration of these two related concepts is the major contribution of this dissertation.

The core logic of the proposed logical framework was based on a logic called (Sorted First Order Action Logic) that can be used to model the structural aspects of a system's requirements. Syntactically, this logic involves several elements: sorts, constant symbols, action names, predicate symbols, function symbols, equality symbols, variables, quantifiers, logical operators and punctuation symbols.

Based on the sorted logic core and following the definition of the first logic, a conservative extension (that is, one which preserves all the logical properties of the logic being extended) to SFOAL is then introduced to deal with the prescription of actions. This new logic, referred to as DAL (Deontic Action Logic) captures two deontic notions, permissions and obligations, that express when an action may occur, in which case the action is permitted, and when an action must occur, in which case it is obliged, to occur. Syntactically, DAL has the following elements: a sort Act for actions and also a sort S(Act) for finite sequences of actions, variables of sort S(Act), predicate symbols, P of type Act (for permissions), O of type Act for obligations, function symbols, logical constant and connectives, among other elements.

In this way, being an extension of SFOAL, DAL supports the specification of both descriptive and prescriptive aspects of actions. Consider, for example, the following simple example provided by Samit [23] involving the action of opening a window:

i. When a window is closed, opening that window results in it being open.

ii. When a window is open, opening it results in it remaining open.

iii. If it is sunny it is permitted to open the window.

iv. If it is raining it is prohibited to open the window.

The first two of these statements provide a description of what it means to open a window when the window is closed and when the window is open. These statements can be expressed as the following expressions:

i. $Closed(W) \rightarrow [Open(W)]\ Opened(W)$

ii. $Opened(W) \rightarrow [Open(W)]\ Opened(W)$

iii. $Sunny \rightarrow P(Open(W))$

iv. $Raining \rightarrow \neg\ P(Open(W))$

As illustrated, DAL can support the concepts of actions and describe and prescribe actions and allows the separation the definition of the actions (i-ii) and the prescriptions on their use (iii-iv). In this way, the information that prescribes the behaviour of the action does not interfere with the description of opening the window. As it will be described in the next sub-section, the ability to formally specify descriptive and prescriptive behaviours is fundamental to capturing the evolutionary aspects of software architecture."

Tom's collaboration with Samit had been part of an Alvey funded project called FOREST (standing for Formal Requirement Specification Techniques) and many ideas described in [23] and [24] were the basis for a formal specification logic called MAL (Modal Action Logic) [22].

2.2 An Approach to Software Architecture Specification

When I first met Tom I was working on a formal specification of architectural descriptions and their evolution as part of my thesis. I was particularly impressed with the expressive power of the Deontic Action Logic (DAL), and this led to the work on a formal description of evolving software system architectures. I quote (loosely) from [6]:

"A discussion of the evolution of software system configurations should have some formal basis in order to make the concepts applicable in a broad environment. Formal definitions should be provided for a number of notions associated with this topic including the notions of software system architecture, the restrictions of the software system configurations and the mechanisms used to control the evolution of the structural and functional descriptions. The basis for the logical formalism is a formal description of the transitions that might occur in the software change process, the purpose of the formalism being to allow deductions to be made about the validity of such transitions. Transitions are represented as actions with deontic notions to allow the statement of "permission" and "obligation". Actions apply to a state model of a change process scenario. This model describes some of the essential features of a configuration management system, that is, versions, and module and subsystem families. Predicates are defined for this model essentially as invariants describing, for example, the relationship between a concrete interface and an abstract interface. We argue the generality of the logical formalism by illustrating its applicability to the expression of change processes in general software descriptions.

We proposed in this work a logical approach to evolving software systems which can be viewed as a programming-in-the-large transformation process applied to architectural descriptions of software systems [26,6]. First, we introduced a generalized formal description of the software system architectures from the viewpoint of evolving software systems. The semantics of the change process of the software configuration states (taken as software system architectural descriptions) is presented through a logical approach that involves theories representing these states and their changes when affected by actions. A deontic/modal (action) extension of the many-sorted first-order logic is used to capture the changes and their prescriptions. We also indicate a deductive reasoning method to show the step-by-step evolution of the software system descriptions. The method is based on a general tableau using constant domain first-order action logic with arbitrary (constant and nonconstant) actions and some deontic features. This proof method is a realization of the semantics of the change process of evolving software system configurations. We show how the logical formalism allows us to describe and reason about changes in the structure, the interface and the functional aspects of the components of architectural descriptions of the software systems. In the proposed approach the alterations of software descriptions can be viewed as programming-in-large transformations stated by means of the descriptive/prescriptive (deontic) features of actions."

I quote from [26,6] with some changes for purposes of abbreviation:

"The logical approach we adopted allows us to distinguish explicitly between the descriptive and the prescriptive aspects of the high-level software system descriptions. Furthermore, the introduction of a modal connective in order to represent action descriptions gives us certain advantages over other approaches. Two significant advantages are the possibility to state action prescriptions as pre- and post-conditions and the possibility to reason deductively about properties of actions without needing to refer to meta-rules. As an example of the first case, the iterated modalities, i.e. an action description relative to the execution of another action, is given by:

$$[\alpha][\beta]\phi$$

Here, the pre-condition states that α is the last action that is executed and thus we can formulate action descriptions in relation to the information about actions that were previously executed. In our case, the actions α and β denote software system description changes. The possibility to reason deductively about action descriptions and prescriptions will be used in the investigation about the consequences and the acceptability of particular changes. Another advantage is the possibility to construct more complex actions from more primitive ones. Another relevant feature is the possibility to represent negative information about actions as, for example, "it is not the case that an action α results in a property ϕ" does not allow us to conclude that such action a results in the property $\neg\phi$.

Note also that in the present approach the pre-condition is only used to identify the context in which the action is executed. In order to state when actions may and must occur, we use the deontic concepts of permitted/obliged actions.

The change process for the description of software system architectures is a sequence of software system architectural descriptions. First, we begin with an initial description SS_0 of the software system architecture which evolves by the execution of a particular change r_0 to a description SS_1. This intermediate software description then evolves to descriptions SS_i, $(i = 2, 3, \dots)$ through the execution of the successive changes r_i, $(i = 2, 3, \dots)$, until an actual software system description is reached.

Each software architectural description SS_k $(k = 1, \dots)$ can be seen as a configuration state of the software system. These configuration states will later be defined as software structure graphs, being represented by acyclic directed graphs in which the leaf nodes are modular families and the internal nodes are subsystem families [29,28]. The purpose here is to describe how the software system components and their different configurations can be specified so that they can be maintained."

A software architectural description is defined as the tuple

$$SS = <SG, SR, SV, SI, SC>$$

where

a) SG is a structure graph;

b) SR extends SG with resource-related information;

c) SV extends SG with version-related information;

d) SI extends SG with interface-related information;

e) SC extends SG with configuration-related information.

We represented the above simplified software architectural description in the logical approach as theory presentation corresponding to a particular description, denoted by D, which is given by:

$$D = < L_D, A_D >$$

where L_D denotes the extra-logical language of the theory and includes the specific sorts related to the architectural description and the names of the chosen predicates and functions and A_D denotes the set of axioms for the architectural description stated in the language L_D.

The language L_D has the following extra-logical symbols:

(a) A finite set T of sorts related to the entities stated in the software architectural descriptions, and particularly including the following sorts:
1. nf : names of the subsystem and module families;
2. nr : resources described in the interfaces of the components of the description;
3. nv : versions that belong to the module families;
4. nc : configurations that belong to the subsystem families;
5. ni : implementations related to each of the module versions;
6. ns : selectors for the configuration components that are defined by $ns = nc \cup nv \cup \{null\}$ where null is a special value which will have its meaning explained later;
7. nt : type of the resources included in the software architectural description;
8. cr : names of the subsystem and module family creators.

(b) Extra-logical constant symbols:
For each sort $\tau \in T$ there exists a set (possibly empty) of constant symbols, each of which we say to be of sort τ.

(c) Action names:
For each $n > 0$ and each n-tuple $< \tau_1, \ldots, \tau_n >$ such that $\tau_i \in T$, $i = 1, \ldots, n$, there exists a set (possibly empty) of action names of arity n that belong to the sort Act, each of which we say to be of type $< \tau_1, \ldots, \tau_n >$. The action names will be given in the next sections when we treat the alterations of the software architectural descriptions from the logic-deductive viewpoint.

(d) Predicate extra-logical symbols:
For each $n > 0$ and each n-tuple $< \tau_1, \ldots, \tau_n >$ such that $\tau_i \in T$, $i = 1, \ldots, n$, there exists a set (possibly empty) of n-arity predicates each of which we say to be of type $< \tau_1, \ldots, \tau_n >$. The following predicates and their associated types are included in the language L_D:
1. module_family : <nf, cr>;
2. subsystem_family : <nf, cr>;
3. object_provides : <nf, nr>;
4. object_requires : <nf, nr>;
5. module_version : <nf, nv, ni>;

6. subsystem_configurations : <nf, nc>:
7. configuration_components : <nf, nc, nf, ns>;
8. version_provides : <nf, nv, nr, nt>;
9. version_requires : <nf, nv, nr, nt>;

(e) Functional extra-logical symbols:
For each $n > 0$ and for each $n+1$-tuple $< \tau_1, \ldots, \tau_{n+1} >$ such that $\tau_i \in T$, $i = 1, \ldots, n$, there exists a set (possibly empty) of n-arity function symbols each of which we say to be of type $< \tau_1, \ldots, \tau_{n+1} >$.

(f) Equality symbols: for some sorts $\tau \in T$ (possibly all) there exists a special predicate symbol $=_\tau$ of sort $< \tau, \tau >$ which represents equality between objects of the sort τ.

(g) Variables: the usual infinite set of distinct variables for each sort τ.

The first two predicates presented above in item (d) are used to state the known different objects of a configuration at a particular time. These objects can be modules or subsystems. The predicates 3 and 4 state the resources required and provided by a particular object of the configuration. The predicate 5 is used to state the versions of each module family and the name of the particular source file that characterizes each version or implementation of the family. In order to express the fact that each family of subsystems is a set of configurations we use the predicate 6 to list all the names of configurations of a particular subsystem. The components of a given configuration, that can be either modules of other configurations, are given explicitly by the predicate 7, in which when the name of the component is the name of a subsystem family, the content of selector is the name of the configuration that belongs to the family and when the name of the component is the name of a module family, the name stated by selector is the name of a version of this family. In other words, selector is used to indicate which particular version of a module or subsystem family has been selected to participate in a certain configuration. The component that does not have such a version receives the value null as the content of selector. The predicates 8 and 9 are used to provide the details of the representation of the required and provided resources since each version of an object (module or subsystem) has its own representation for each named resource in the module family interface. These predicates contain type attributes of programming language resources. Note that in principle, the subsystems do not need to provide the detailed representations of the resources in its specification since these representations can be derived when necessary from the component source files of versions that provide the resources.

A particular set A_{D1} of axioms provided as an example stated in the language L_D is given next. The set of axioms A_{D1} for the representation of a simplified example of a software architectural system with a unique subsystem family SF and two module families $MF1$ and $MF2$ is given by:

I. $subsystem\_family(SF, patrick)$
    $object\_provides(SF, a)$
    $object\_provides(SF, b)$
    $object\_requires(SF, c)$
    $object\_requires(SF, d)$
    $subsystem\_configurations(SF, C1)$
    $subsystem\_configurations(SF, C2)$
    $configuration\_components(SF, C1, MF1, M1.1)$
    $configuration\_components(SF, C1, MF2, M2.1)$
    $configuration\_components(SF, C2, MF1, M1.2)$
    $configuration\_components(SF, C2, MF2, M2.2)$

II. $module\_family(MFl, johnston)$
    $object\_provides(MF1, a)$
    $object\_provides(MF1, f)$
    $object\_requires(MF1, d)$
    $object\_requires(MF1, b)$
    $module\_version(MF1, M1.1, I1.1)$
    $module\_version(MF1, M1.2, 11.2)$
    $version\_provides(MF1, M1.1, a, t1)$
    $version\_provides(MF1, M1.1, f, t2)$
    $version\_requires(MF1, MI.1, b, t3)$
    $version\_requires(MF1, M1.1, d, t4)$
    $version\_provides(MF1, M1.2, a, tS)$
    $version\_provides(MF1, M1.2, f, t1)$
    $version\_requires(MF1, M1.2, b, t3)$
    $version\_requires(MF1, M1.2, d, t4)$

III. $module\_family(MF2, thorne)$
    $object\_provides(MF2, b)$
    $object\_requires(MF2, c)$
    $object\_requires(MF2, f)$
    $module\_version(MF2, M2.1, I2.1)$
    $module\_version(MF2, M2.2, I2.2)$
    $version\_provides(MF2, M2.1, b, t6)$
    $version\_requires(MF2, M2.1, c, t7)$
    $version\_requires(MF2, M2.1, f, t8)$
    $version\_provides(MF2, M2.2, b, t6)$
    $version\_requires(MF2, M2.2, c, t7)$
    $version\_requires(MF2, M2.2, f, tS)$

The meaning of these axioms is obvious since all the predicates and their respective sorts have been previously described.

The generality of the logical formalism that has been adopted can also be seen if we consider the following "pattern" of change of general software descriptions denoted by SS_0. Assume that this description can be represented as an axiom set A_{D1} in some language L_D. Add to this set A_{D1} the integrity restrictions of the description to obtain the set A_{D2}. Now add to the set A_{D2} a set of axioms describing the actions $\alpha_1, \ldots, \alpha_n$ that can alter the description and the description of the actions that check if the description obeys the integrity conditions. Finally, add to the resulting set of axioms a set of axioms which state if each action may or must be executed in an arbitrary scenario of the change process. Assuming that Σ denotes a sequence of actions it is straightforward to define an operator "[[ ]]" to treat sequences of actions instead of a single action. Then the changes to the description because of the execution of the sequence of actions can be stated as:

$$[[\Sigma]] \; new\_descriptions$$

Assuming that Θ denotes a sequence of actions to check if the integrity conditions hold, we also have:

$$\psi \rightarrow [[\Theta]] \; \phi$$

where ψ is the conjunction of the integrity restrictions and ϕ denotes the result of the checking procedure. It is therefore clear that we can query in a general way if after the description is changed by a sequence of actions ("batch case") whether the description obeys some intended (integrity) properties:

$$[[\Sigma]][[\Theta]] \; \phi$$

Note that because of the expressive power of the logical formalism, other "patterns" of change can be specified. For example, assume that we want to know if a change obeys its integrity conditions only in some critical circumstances and let this case be properly characterized by Δ. Then, instead of the previous query we have:

$$\Delta \rightarrow [[\Sigma]][[\Theta]] \; \phi$$

We have developed an automated deduction-method through which the evolution of the software systems architectures are treated. This method can be seen as a realization of the proposed semantics for the change process of the architectural descriptions, such that the alterations of the descriptions can be evaluated in a logic-deductive context. It is a general tableau-based proof method for constant domain first-order action logic with arbitrary (constant and non-constant) actions. This method ultimately leads to a tableau-based theorem prover by which reasoning about structural, interconnection module dependencies and functional changes can be performed. The method is general in the sense that the various action modalities that characterize the different action-logic systems can be treated by considering equal inference rules for these various action modalities and a unification algorithm which can be specialized by changing some of its conditions in order to describe the corresponding conditions on the accessibility relation in Kripke semantics.

Using this approach, regarding reasoning about software system changes, suppose we want to verify if the inclusion of a certain resource in a given configuration implies the preservation of one of the conditions for well-formedness. This is a query involving action descriptions. What we want to prove is the validity of the following formula:

$$[Include\_pr(g, MF1)][Check\_wf(C1)]Wf(C1)$$

In the same way, we can investigate if a particular module version vn continues belonging to a module family on after some structural change is performed in the module on or in vn. In order to be permitted to execute an action to investigate if the family membership condition denoted by

$$family\_membership\_cond(vn, on)$$

is valid in a given state of the structural description of the software system, we require that both the module version vn and the module family on are explicitly given in the software description. Thus, we have:

$$\exists c/creator \exists fn/file\_name$$
$$module\_family(on, c) \wedge module\_version(on, vn, fn)$$
$$\rightarrow per(membership\_test(vn, on))$$

With this, we can execute in a certain state of the structural software description an action $membership\_test(vn, on)$ that investigates the validity of the family membership condition:

$$family\_membership\_cond(vn, on) \rightarrow$$
$$[membership\_test(vn, on)]family\_member(vn, on)$$

As a further generalisation, we can also investigate if after the execution of a desired arbitrary structural change α to the software system description and then the execution of the action to test module family membership, we obtain that vn is a member of the module family on or not. It is the same as testing the validity of:

$$[\alpha]\,[membership\_test(vn, on)]family\_member(vn, on)$$

In the more general case, we can test the validity of the formula:

$$[[\Sigma]]\,[membership\_test(vn, on)]family\_member(vn, on)$$

where Σ is an action sequence that denotes structural changes of the system description ("batch case"). We only require here that all the actions α that belong to the sequence have their descriptions explicitly given. In a similar way we can investigate how structural changes of the software description affect their other relevant properties."

In conclusion, I have summarized in the previous paragraphs how, inspired in DAL and Tom's work on logics for system specification, we have introduced a generalised formal description of software system architectures from the viewpoint of evolving software systems [26,6]. I quote (loosely) from these articles:

"This description used the notion of software structure graphs as the software configuration states and the notion of development sequences of states. Valid software configuration states were defined through some special conditions that were used to control the evolution of the software structure graphs from the structural and functional points of view.

The semantics of the change process of the software configuration states was given by a logical approach that involves theories representing software configurations and their changes when affected by actions in a framework which also includes deontic features of the actions. The description of the logical framework also shows how structural, interconnection and functional changes occur. This involves encoding in the logical formalism the conditions for valid software configuration alterations that were formally described. In this sense, we have to guarantee that the configurations remain valid after the software system is altered. The modules of a particular configuration, for example, make some hypotheses about each other and a particular configuration makes sense essentially if its component modules do not make erroneous hypotheses about the resources that they require from other modules. Furthermore, we have shown how software configuration change actions can be described and used in a deductive way to demonstrate if a desired change to a particular software configuration state is convenient or not. The reasoning method can be seen as a realization of the semantics for the software configuration change process. We described the role of the prescriptive aspects of actions and show that in the adopted logical framework the alterations of high-level software descriptions can be viewed as programming-in-the-large transformations that have both a descriptive and a prescriptive aspect. The functional aspect of configuration changes was treated by the interaction between a constructed theorem prover for the deontic action logic metalanguage and an available programming logic prover.

Queries concerning the desirability of particular changes to software configuration states can have their efficiency enhanced from the standpoint of practical applications if we consider, for example, the possibility of partitioning the whole software configuration theory in modular segments. Each segment describes a particular aspect of the theory (e.g. structural or resource-directed) and each query is submitted to the prover together with its associated modular segment.

Nevertheless, we are more interested in modelling the whole change process and therefore our formal logical framework can be seen essentially as formal specifications for software configuration applications."

This is only an illustration of Tom's influence in my research work. However, his influence is much broader and has impacted so many researchers and collaborators. I also want to mention that this research [26] was selected as the best research work in an open national competition in 1995 and, as a result, Carlos Lucena and I were awarded a first prize of US $40,000 by Compaq.

3 Logical Theory of Interfaces and Objects based on Category Theory

In the late 1990s and early 2000s, some of Tom's papers came to my attention that introduced a novel way to describe component specifications and their formal composition based on category theory [27,14,11,13,15,17,18,21,16,12,7,20].

3.1 A Categorical Approach to Software Specification

Tom and Dr. Luis Fiadeiro developed in a series of articles the idea that modular and incremental development of complex systems could be viewed as interconnections of interacting components based on temporal logic and category theory.

I quote (loosely) from [11]:

"... We introduce the local aspects of object descriptions. First of all, we introduce the notion of object signature which is the core concept in this formalization effort. It is around the notion of signature that the notion of locality (data abstraction, encapsulation of a set of attributes) - itself, in our opinion, the core concept of object orientation - must be understood and formalized. Next, the notion of object description is introduced as a collection of formulae in a logic that includes positional (modal) operators to describe the effects of the events on the attributes, and two (deontic) predicates of permission and obligation with which the behavioural aspects are modeled. Finally, we briefly address the notions of safety and liveness.

Then, ... we show how we can put descriptions together in order to form the description of more complex objects. First, we show how to define a category of object descriptions that is finitely cocomplete. Then, we show how interaction between objects can be expressed through diagrams. And, finally, we show how the colimit of a diagram describes the joint behaviour of the objects in the diagram taking into account their interaction."

3.2 A Logical Theory of Interfaces and Objects

This approach to specify objects and seeing object-oriented systems as interconnections of interacting components based on temporal logic and category theory, has led us to develop a formal theory of interfaces and objects based on logic [4], where interfaces are objects with added properties. We introduced a logic-based specification framework that provides a formal basis to specify and reason about interfaces and objects. In the proposed formal theory, the basic concerns are captured by objects, while the special purpose concerns are related to the interfaces.

According to this view, interfaces can be external, that is, between objects and the outside world, or internal, between two objects. The formal theory was based on the Abstract Design Views1 (ADV) [8,9,5], a design model that clearly addresses separation of concerns through the use of interfaces (ADVs) and their associated objects. The objects are called Abstract Design Objects (ADOs). The development of a theory of interfaces and objects is relevant because it supports separation of concerns, promotes reuse, modifiability, flexibility, and evolution.

I quote (loosely) from [4]:

"... We present one possible approach to formalizing interfaces, their related objects, and the views-a relationship. The approach relies on Fiadeiro and Maibaum's categorical framework [11,13] as a first step. The categorical framework is a formal approach to describing and interconnecting objects. In this framework, each component of the system is described by a temporal logic theory [30,10] and the whole system (or a composite component) results from the interconnection of the components by means of categories. We limit our discussion of this framework to the basic principles required to support our theory of objects and interfaces.

We use the categorical framework for describing and interconnecting objects in order to illustrate how the characteristics of interfaces and their relationship with other objects in the system can be incorporated into a logic-based formalism. This framework was chosen as the formal underlying description because of the use of tools, such as logic. Such formalisms are not dependent on any particular specification language. Thus, other formal specification languages or similar approaches can include the theory of interfaces of objects.

In the categorical framework, the specifications of the viewer and viewed objects are built from signatures. A signature can be seen as the language of the specification of the objects. An ADV/ADO signature SG is a tuple <DT, AT, AC>, where DT = <S, F>is an usual abstract data type signature, i.e., S is a set of sorts and F is an S* × S-indexed family of sets of function symbols; AT is an S* × S-indexed family of sets of attribute symbols; and AC is an S*-indexed family of sets of action symbols.

The DT part describes the data context for the object. A viewer object can, for example, use Booleans, natural numbers, or sequences of characters. If a natural number is to be included as a sort that belongs to DT, then a set of functions that operate on them is also provided. The AT part consists of a set of attribute symbols and describes the time-dependent part of the specification. It represents the data that can change as time passes through the actions or methods of the objects. The AT part models the state of the object. The AC part consists of a set of action symbols and includes the data used to define the effects of the actions (or methods) on the attributes.

From a given signature SG_C of an object C, we can inductively construct the set of well-formed formulae relative to the component C. Thus, for any signature SG (for an ADV or an ADO), we first construct the SG-terms. An SG-formula is a term built from SG-terms, the quantifiers $\forall$ and $\exists$, and some temporal logic operators.

Regarding terms and formulae of ADV/ADO signatures, given a signature SG = <DT, AT, AC>, terms (t_s), atomic formulae (ϕ_{atom}) and well-formed formulae (ϕ) are defined as follows, for every sort $s \in S$:

132

$$t_s ::= c \mid x_s \mid a(t_{s_1}, \ldots, t_{s_n}) \mid f(t_s, \ldots, t_{s_n}) \mid \mathbf{X}\, t_s$$

$$\phi_{atom} ::= (t_s =_s t_s) \mid g(t_{s_1}, \ldots, t_{s_n}) \mid \boxed{BEG}$$

$$\phi ::= \phi_{atom} \mid (\neg\phi) \mid (\phi \Rightarrow \phi) \mid (\mathbf{X}\phi) \mid (\mathbf{F}\phi) \mid (\mathbf{G}\phi) \mid (\phi\mathbf{U}\phi) \mid (\forall x_s \phi) \mid (\exists x_s \phi),$$

where the symbols c, x_s, a, f, and g denote constants, variables of sort s, attributes, functions, and actions, respectively. The special temporal logic operators used previously are $\boxed{BEG}$ (denoting the initial state), $\mathbf{X}$ or $\bigcirc$ ($\mathbf{X}\phi$ holds in a state when ϕ holds in the next state), $\mathbf{F}$ or $\Diamond$ ($\mathbf{F}\phi$ holds in some future state), $\mathbf{G}$ or $\Box$ ($\mathbf{G}\phi$ holds for all the future states), and $\mathbf{U}$ ($\phi\mathbf{U}\psi$ holds when ψ will hold sometime in the future and ϕ holds between now and then).

The ADV and ADO descriptions are defined as theory presentations in temporal logic: a signature SG and a set of axioms AX. Thus, we have a language (vocabulary) given by the signature SG, a way of forming SG-expressions using that vocabulary, and the properties associated with an ADV or an ADO that can be defined by some of these expressions. In general, the temporal logic axioms that specify the behaviour of the viewer and viewed objects include axioms related to a) change: condition $\wedge$ action $\Rightarrow$ attribute = value, b) safety: condition $\wedge$ action $\Rightarrow$ condition, and c) liveness: condition $\Rightarrow$ $\mathbf{F}$ action..

An ADV/ADO description is a pair D = <SG, AX>, where SG is an object signature and AX is a (finite) set of SG-formulae (the axioms of the description). As an example, suppose we have a viewed object that contains only one value attribute (a natural number). However, we wish to present this number both as a column and as a pie chart, where the pie chart is divided in two parts that can be characterized by a single angle. This object description is presented in Fig. 1. Notice that this viewed object, which we call ViewedValue, has one attribute called Value and two actions (or methods) called "Reset" and "Set". "Reset" changes the value to zero and "Set" changes the value to a particular number. The value is restricted to natural numbers less or equal to 1,000 and, in the beginning, the value is zero. The viewer object, called Viewer$_A$, that presents Value as a column with a maximum height of 5 cm (when the value is 1,000) is also shown in Fig. 1. There are two types of axioms triggered by DrawColumnReset and DrawColumnSet. The first type of axiom is used to change an attribute of the Viewer$_A$ object (in this case, the attribute Height). The second type is used to trigger the actions of the ViewedValue object that will update the state (Value) of the viewed object; they are used to cope with the fact that whenever the state of the view (Viewer$_A$) changes the associated state of the object (ViewedValue) must also change. The term ForADO in the header of Viewer$_A$ denotes that Viewer$_A$ is an ADV related to ViewedValue.

Since the scope of an action is local to the component, a locality axiom is added to each theory describing a given component object. The locality requirement is captured by the following axiom: For every signature:

```
ADO ViewedValue
    Attributes
        Value: NAT;
    Actions
        Reset:  Set(NAT);
    Axioms n : NAT
        (o1) G(Value ≤ 1000);
        (o2)  BEG  ⇒ Value = 0;
        (o3) Reset ⇒ X Value = 0;
        (o4) Set(n) ⇒ X Value = n;
End ViewedValue


ADV Viewer_A ForADO ViewedValue
    DataFunctions
        HeightToValue: NAT ⟶ NAT;
        HeightToValue(h) = 200 × h;
    Attributes
        Height: NAT;
    Actions
        DrawColumnReset;  DrawColumnSet(NAT);
        Reset_A;  Set_A(NAT);
    Axioms h, n : NAT
        (a1) G(Height ≤ 5);
        (a2)  BEG  ⇒ Height = 0;
        (a3) DrawColumnReset ⇒ X Height = 0;
        (a4) DrawColumnReset ⇒ Reset_A;
        (a5) DrawColumnSet(h) ⇒ X Height = h;
        (a6) DrawColumnSet(h) ⇒ Set_A(HeightToValue(h));
        (a7) Reset_A ⇒ DrawColumnReset;
        (a8) Set_A(n) ⇒ DrawColumnSet(HeightToValue⁻¹(n));
End Viewer_A
```

Fig. 1. The ViewedValue and Viewer$_A$ objects [4]

$$Locus_{SG} : \left(\left(\bigvee_{g \in AC} (\exists x_g) g(x_g) \right) \right.$$
$$\left. \wedge \left(\bigwedge_{a \in AT} (\forall x_a)(\mathbf{X}a(x_a) = a(x_a)) \right) \right),$$

This axiom means that either one of the actions $g \in AC$ of the ADV/ADO is performed or else all the attributes $a \in AT$ will remain invariant. As an example, the local requirement of the object ViewedValue is given by:

$$Reset \vee \exists x.Set(x) \vee \mathbf{X}Value = Value.$$

Theory presentations are related through morphisms. A morphism of

ADV/ADO theory presentations: $\sigma :< SG_1, \mathbf{AX}_1 > \longrightarrow < SG_2, \mathbf{AX}_2 >$ is an ADV/ADO signature morphism $\sigma : SG_1 \longrightarrow SG_2$ such that:

$$(\mathbf{AX}_2 \Rightarrow_{SG_2} \sigma(\phi)) \text{ holds for every } \phi \in \mathbf{AX}_1$$
$$(\mathbf{AX}_2 \Rightarrow_{SG_2} \sigma(Locus_{SG_1})),$$

where the formula in the righthand side of the implication is the translation of the locality requirement. A signature morphism is used in the previous definition to relate the language of two different object signatures. Essentially, this morphism identifies the data, the attributes, and the actions of the two different signatures. A morphism between signatures $\sigma :< DT, AT, AC > \longrightarrow < DT', AT', AC' >$ is defined by a trio of the total functions $\sigma_{DT} : DT \longrightarrow DT', \sigma_{AT} : AT \longrightarrow AT'$, and $\sigma_{AC} : AC \longrightarrow AC'$. However, for brevity, we can state that a morphism is given $\sigma : SG \longrightarrow SG'$.

In addition, a morphism between theory presentations (or a description morphism) is a signature morphism that defines a theorem-preserving translation between the two theory presentations and preserves the translation of the locality axiom. These morphisms can be used to express a system as an interconnection of its parts, that is, as a diagram. This diagram is a directed multigraph in which the nodes are labeled by ADV/ADO specifications and the edges by the specification morphisms. We can reduce a diagram of specifications to a single specification by taking the co-limit of a diagram. Informally, the co-limit of a diagram is the disjoint union of all specifications (attributes, actions, and axioms), together with the identification of some attributes and action symbols that receive the same name. For example, if two attributes a_1 and a_2 have been identified, they receive the same name a in the resulting colimit. Technically, the co-limit of a diagram is constructed by first taking the disjoint union (coproduct) of all the specifications in the diagram and, then, the quotient of this coproduct via the equivalence relation generated by the morphisms in the diagram.

As an example, we introduce the object Boolean-Flag shown in Fig. 2 and show how this object can interact with ViewedValue . BooleanFlag contains a Boolean attribute Flag and three actions: one to reset the Flag to true, another to reset the Flag to false, and a third one to set the flag to true if a given natural number is less than or equal to 500 or set the flag to false if the natural number is greater than 500.

Now, assuming the object descriptions for BooleanFlag and ViewedValue, we can make these two objects interact by creating a Channel object that contains two actions: Act1 and Act2 and two morphisms between this object and ViewedValue and BooleanFlag, respectively. The description of Channel and the two morphisms M1 and M2 are shown in Fig. 3.

The morphisms which establish the interconnection identify the actions on which the objects ViewedValue and BooleanFlag synchronize. Thus, the role of the morphisms $M1$ and $M2$ is to indicate that Reset and ResetTrue and Set and SetTrueOrFalse must correspond to the same action in the object that will describe the combination. Notice, for example, that both the actions *Reset* and

```
ADO BooleanFlag
    Attributes
        Flag: BOOL;
    Actions
        ResetTrue; ResetFalse;  SetTrueOrFalse(NAT);
    Axioms n : NAT
        (f1) | BEG | ⇒ Flag = true;
        (f2) ResetTrue ⇒ X Flag = true;
        (f3) ResetFalse ⇒ X Flag = false;
        (f4) SetTrueOrFalse(n) ⇒ ((n ≤ 500) ∧ X Flag = true) ∨ ((n > 500) ∧ X Flag = false);
End BooleanFlag
```

Fig. 2. The BooleanFlag object.

```
Channel
    Attributes: ∅ ;
    Actions: Act1, Act2(NAT);
    Axioms: ∅ ;
End Channel


M1: Channel ⟶ ViewedValue
        Attributes: ∅ ;
        Actions
            Act1 ⟼ Reset
            Act2(NAT) ⟼ Set(NAT)
End M1


M2: Channel ⟶ BooleanFlag
        Attributes: ∅ ;
        Actions
            Act1 ⟼ ResetTrue
            Act2(NAT) ⟼ SetTrueOrFalse(NAT)
End M2
```

Fig. 3. The Channel object and the morphisms M1 and M2.

ResetTrue are mapped to the action *Act1* of Channel through the morphisms M1 and M2 (Fig. 3). In this way, each action symbol in the signature of an object (such as *Reset* or *SetNAT* of ViewedValue) provides a port to which another object (in this case, *BooleanFlag*) may be linked for communication. When attributes are also mapped, the appropriate correspondence between attributes is also established. When we compute the pushout of the diagram

$$ViewedValue \xleftarrow{M1} Channel \xrightarrow{M2} BooleanFlag.$$

the resulting object description of Composite is shown in Fig. 4. We are adopting the following convention: Symbols are renamed by prefixing their

136

```
Composite
    Attributes
        I.Value: NAT;
        J.Flag: BOOL;
    Actions
        ResetIJ;  SetIJ(NAT);
        J.ResetFalse;
    Axioms n : NAT
        (c1)  G(I.Value ≤ 1000);
        (c2)  BEG  ⇒ I.Value = 0;
        (c3)  BEG  ⇒ J.Flag = true;
        (c4)  ResetIJ ⇒ X I.Value = 0;
        (c5)  ResetIJ ⇒ X J.Flag = true;
        (c6)  J.ResetFalse ⇒ X J.Flag = false;
        (c7)  SetIJ(n) ⇒ X I.Value = n;
        (c8)  SetIJ(n) ⇒ ((n ≤ 500) ∧ X J.Flag = true) ∨ ((n > 500) ∧ X J.Flag = false);
        (c9)  (ResetIJ ∨ ∃x. SetIJ(x)) ∨ (X I.Value=I.Value);
        (c10) (ResetIJ ∨ J.ResetFalse ∨ ∃y. SetIJ(y)) ∨ (X J.Flag=J.Flag);
End Composite
```

Fig. 4. The Composite object for the ViewValue and BooleanFlag example.

names in the components with the name of the morphism separated by a dot. In the case of our example, we are naming I and J the two morphisms linking the nodes labeled ViewedValue and BooleanFlag to Composite, respectively. Thus, we obtain as the attribute symbols of Composite the translation of the attributes of ViewedValue and BooleanFlag along the corresponding morphism: I.Value and J.Flag. In this way, the attributes and actions that take no part in the interaction between ViewedValue and BooleanFlag stay the same but are prefixed by I or J in order to avoid conflicts of names.

In addition, the theory allows us to reason about the dynamic and structural formal characterizations of views. As a result, the theory enables designers to perform relevant analysis activities while modeling with separation of concerns in mind. We notice that, in general, this approach allows reasoning about many different types of properties, such as those that involve state change, and safety and liveness properties. The theory can be used to derive dynamic and structural properties of the interface objects and the views-a relationship. In particular, we use the theory to derive global properties of interfaces that capture special concerns such as user interface concerns from the local properties of their related objects. We can also derive global properties of interface objects (ADVs) that capture a special concern from the local properties of their related objects. Global properties of the combined interface objects and related objects can be derived in a modular way.

We have presented one possible approach that uses Fiadeiro and Maibaum's categories of temporal logic theories [13] to formalize interfaces, objects, and the views-a relationship. The temporal logic theories represent objects and the fact that the theories form a category allows us to combine objects in the tradition of

[20]. The categorical framework was chosen as the underlying formal technique because it is based on tools (such as logic) that are not dependent on any particular specification language. Our approach can be modified to use other specification languages. The categorical framework used as the underlying formalism for the expression of the theory of interfaces and objects was also used for other purposes, such as the validation of fault-tolerant systems."

3.3 Extension Morphisms and Aspects

In 2006, Tom, Nazareno Aguirre and I worked on extension morphisms for Community [3]. An application of invasive superposition morphisms between components in the architectural design language CommUnity was proposed. This kind of morphisms enable enhancing components to implement certain aspects, in the sense of aspect-oriented software development [25,19]. We have also worked towards defining aspect modularity in a high-level program design language [2].

We quote (loosely) from [30]:

"We have studied a special kind of invasive superposition for the characterisation of extensions between designs in the CommUnity architecture design language. This kind of morphism, that we have defined with special concern regarding the substitutability principle (an essential property associated with sound component extension), allows us to complement the refinement and (regulative) superposition morphisms of CommUnity, and obtain a suitable formal framework to characterize certain aspects, in the sense of aspect-oriented software development.

We have argued that some useful aspects require extensions of the components, as well as in the connectors, and therefore the introduced extension morphisms are necessary. As well, having the possibility of extending components provides us a way of balancing the distribution of augmented behaviour in the connectors and the components, which would otherwise be put exclusively on the connector side (typically by means of higher-order connectors).

We illustrated the need for extension morphisms by means of a simple case study based on the communication of two components via an unreliable channel. We then augmented the behaviour of this original system with a fault tolerance aspect for making the communication reliable, which required the extension of components, as well as the use of higher-order connectors. This small case study also allowed us to illustrate the relationships and combined use of extension, superposition and refinement morphisms.

As we mentioned before, this problem has also arisen in the context of object-oriented design and programming, attempting to define various forms of inheritance, resulting in proposals attempting to characterize the concept of substitutability. We believe that this proposal provides a more solid foundation for substitutivity, one that is better structured and more amenable to analysis. The definition of extension in CommUnity that we introduced has been partly motivated by the definitions and proof obligations used to define the structuring mechanisms in B , that justifies the notion of substitutivity and provides a structuring principle for augmenting components by breaking the encapsulation of the component."

4 Conclusion

I had the pleasure to meet Tom Maibaum many times throughout the years, in places such as Pontifical Catholic University (Rio), Brazil, Imperial College (London), United Kingdom, McMaster University (Hamilton), Canada, and at many conferences such as the International Conference on Software Engineering. I am very grateful for his generous advice and wisdom, and for the time he spent with me, discussing research ideas, discovering novel research directions, and showing that novelty is always possible in science.

It becomes clear that throughout my research journey, Tom and I had some things in common, including a love for logic, a hunger for new ideas, and a passion for football (soccer). I am grateful that, since I met him in the late 1980s, I have been able to take advantage of his encouragement, insights, and a constant source of inspiration. It has been a privilege to have access to him and his work, and to witness over the years his research passion, drive, and vision.

He has been a pioneer in the field of computer sciences, having earned the respect and admiration of all of us who had the privilege of working with him. He also has certainly enriched the intellectual life of thousands of researchers and students. When it comes to the future, we still look forward to hearing about his latest ideas.

Acknowledgments

Thanks go to Donald Cowan and Ivens Portugal for editorial comments.

References

[1] Samson Abramsky, Dov Gabbay, and T Maibaurn. Handbook of logic in computer science. 5 volumes, 1992.

[2] N. Aguirre, P. Alencar, and T. Maibaum. Aspect modularity in a high-level program design language. In *Proceedings of the CASCON Workshop on Aspect Oriented Software Development*. IBM, 2005.

[3] N. Aguirre, T. Maibaum, and P. Alencar. Extension morphisms for community. *Lecture Notes in Computer Science (LNCS)*, 4060:173–193, 2006.

[4] P.S.C. Alencar, D.D. Cowan, and C.J.P. Lucena. A logical theory of interfaces and objects. *IEEE Transactions on Software Engineering*, 28(6):548–575, 2002.

[5] P.S.C. Alencar, D.D. Cowan, C.J.P. Lucena, and L.C.M. Nova. Formal specification of reusable interface objects. In *ACM SIGSOFT Symposium on Software Reusability - SSR*, pages 88–96. ACM, New York, 1995.

[6] P.S.C. Alencar and C.J.P. De Lucena. A logical framework for evolving software systems. *Formal Aspects of Computing*, 8(1):3–46, 1996.

[7] J.C. Bicarregui, K.C. Lano, and T.S.E. Maibaum. Objects, associations and subsystems: A hierarchical approach to encapsulation. *Lecture Notes in Computer Science (LNCS)*, 1241:324–343, 1997.

[8] D.D. Cowan and C.J.P. Lucena. Abstract data views: An interface specification concept to enhance design for reuse. *IEEE Transactions on Software Engineering*, 21(3):229–243, 1995.

[9] Donald D. Cowan, Roberto Ierusalimschy, Carlos Jose Pereira de Lucena, and Terry M. Stepien. Abstract data views. *Structured Programming*, 14(1):1, 1993.

[10] Emersonm E. Temporal and modal logic. In *Handbook of Theoretical Computer Science*, pages 995–1072. Elsevier, 1990.

[11] J. Fiadeiro and T. Maibaum. Describing, structuring and implementing objects. *Lecture Notes in Computer Science (LNCS))*, 489:274–310, 1990.

[12] J. Fiadeiro and T. Maibaum. Temporal reasoning over deontic specifications. *Journal of Logic and Computation*, 1(3):357–395, 1991.

[13] J. Fiadeiro and T. Maibaum. Temporal theories as modularisation units for concurrent system specification. *Formal Aspects of Computing*, 4(3):239–272, 1992.

[14] J.L. Fiadeiro. *Categories for software engineering.* Springer Berlin Heidelberg, 2005.

[15] J.L. Fiadeiro and T. Maibaum. Verifying for reuse: Foundations of object-oriented system verification. *Theory and Formal Methods*, pages 235–257, 1995.

[16] J.L. Fiadeiro and T. Maibaum. Categorical semantics of parallel program design. *Science of Computer Programming*, 28(2-3):111–138, 1997.

[17] Jose Luiz Fiadeiro and Tom Maibaum. Interconnecting formalisms: Supporting modularity, reuse and incrementality. In *Proceedings of the ACM SIGSOFT Symposium on the Foundations of Software Engineering*, pages 72–80. ACM, New York, NY, United States, 1995.

[18] José Luiz Fiadeiro and Tom Maibaum. A mathematical toolbox for the software architect. In *Proceedings of the 8th International Workshop on Software Specification and Design*, pages 46–55. IEEE, 1996.

[19] Robert E. Filman, Tzilla Elrad, Siobhán Clarke, and Mehmet Akşit. *Aspect-Oriented Software Development.* Addison-Wesley, 2004.

[20] J.A. Goguen. Reusing and interconnecting software components. *Computer*, 19(2):16–28, 1986.

[21] SJ Goldsack and SJH Kent. Design structures for object-based systems. In *Formal Methods and Object Technology*, pages 183–204. Springer, 1996.

[22] S.J.H. Kent, T.S.E. Maibaum, and W.J. Quick. Specifying deontic behaviour in modal action logic. Technical Report FOREST Deliverable Report WP1.R2, University of London, 1992.

[23] S Khosla. *System Specification: A Deontic Approach.* PhD thesis, Department of Computing, Imperial College of Science and Technology, University of London, 1989.

[24] S. Khosla and T.S.E. Maibaum. The prescription and description of state based systems. *Lecture Notes in Computer Science (LNCS)*, 398:243–294, 1989.

[25] G. Kiczales, J. Lamping, A. Mendhekar, C. Maeda, C. Lopes, J.-M. Loingtier, and J. Irwin. Aspect-oriented programming. *(LNCS)*, 1241:220–242, 1997.

[26] C.J.P. Lucena and P.S.C. Alencar. A formal description of evolving software systems architectures. *Science of Computer Programming*, 24(1):41–61, 1995.

[27] Saunders MacLane. *Categories for The Working Mathematician.* Springer, 1971.

[28] K. Narayanaswamy and W. Scacchi. A database foundation to support software system evolution. *The Journal of Systems and Software*, 7(1):37–49, 1987.

[29] K. Narayanaswamy and W. Scacchi. Maintaining configurations of evolving software systems. *IEEE Transactions on Software Engineering*, SE-13(3):324–334, 1987.

[30] Amir Pnueli and Zohar Manna. The temporal logic of reactive and concurrent systems. 1991.

[31] M.T. W Ladys Law and T.S.E. Maibaum. The specification of computer programs. *Addison-Wesley*, 1987.

140

Assurance of Assurance

Bridging the Great Assurance Divide with Modus Ponens and Cartesian Closed Categories

Zinovy Diskin

McMaster Centre for Software Certification
McMaster University, Canada
`diskinz@mcmaster.ca`

Abstract

The main problem of assuring a major dependability claim (safety, security, reliability) about a complex system is that it can easily be refuted by presenting an instance of failure whereas proving the claim is true needs, in general, *infinite* resources (either computational or temporal or both). Nevertheless, the writers of an assurance case (AC) have to present an explicit argument that a system is acceptable for its intended use based on the *finite* number of different checks (analyses, simulations, tests) that the system has passed; the paper refers to this challenge as to the Great Assurance Divide. In the centre of the paper is a simple observation that the logical side of building an assurance argument (i.e., the inference engine as such) can be made trivial and formal by reducing the argument to a series of steps based on an appropriately formulated side assumptions and Modus Ponens. It is the system of side assumptions, which encapsulates all the uncertainty and challenge of overcoming the Great Divide, so that everything interesting in an AC is to be found in the claims about the product and side assumptions about its type, which together allow the inference engine to work and derive the top claim from the basic evidence facts.

The simple inference outlined above is actually based on substitutions (of special constructs into general patterns, instances into types, values for variables) and can thus be formalized with typed lambda calculus or with its algebraic equivalent: Cartesian closed categories (CCCs). The latter provides a truly straightforward formalization for a widely used Claim-Argument-Evidence framework for assurance: claims are mapped to objects, arguments to arrows, evidence to elements (i.e., arrows from the terminal object—the truth), and the argument flow is the arrow composition. The paper also shows how two industrial approaches to assurance, one is based on providing evidence required by the corresponding standard and the other is based on an on-site AC, can be formally specified and be seen as two poles on an axis of possible intermediate standardization approaches. The formal framework is carefully motivated and illustrated with an example, and several practical suggestions implied by the framework are discussed.

Dedicated to Tom Maibaum, Scientist and Engineer

Foreword. I have had a privilege to work with Tom Maibaum for over ten years in several projects with non-trivial scientific and (always non-trivial) industrial content. Their immediate focus was on applying Model Driven Engineering ideas and techniques to industrial problems, but the subjects of our discussions ranged from pure mathematics (from lamenting about a beautiful but forgotten notion of clone in universal algebra to Beth and Craig theorems in model theory to Kleisli mappings in category theory) to computer science (from "Is their a real content in the institution theory?" to Mealy machines to concurrency and modal logic) to foundations of software engineering (from institutions to Kleisli mappings to model transformations) to social and psychological aspects of science and engineering including category theory (e.g., it was Tom who discovered an English translation of a not very well-known Piage's work [18]). A recurrent topic of our talks was Engineering as a scientific and social phenomenon, and specifically the magic of design and magical cookbooks of engineering patterns (Tom often referred to Vincenti's book [26] in this regard), and deep differences between Engineering-as-Craft (EasC) and Engineering-as-Technology (EasT), which (in my view) means knowledge transferability and preferring technological rather than ad hoc heuristic approaches to problems including complex ones. An effort of expert engineers and mathematicians should be aimed at downgrading complex problems to routine ones, and the better they do their job, the more simple a complex problem becomes.

Safety assurance was the last project in which we collaborated with Tom but he retired at an early stage of the project. It seems to be an ideal topic for a paper dedicated to Tom as assurance is inherently a system engineering problem encompassing a multitude of techno-social issues from design magic to the logic of certification and legal binding to public attention (to, say, autonomous driving), and this spectrum well reflects the widths of Tom's research interests; indeed, assurance has been on Tom's research radar for many years (and still is [12]). In addition, since Tom left the project several years ago, an essential progress is achieved so that he may be interested to read about some of the results, the more so that a rigorous approach to assurance based on mathematics and logic well corresponds to Tom's manner of approach to complex problems (although the ideas developed in the paper diverge from Tom's own approach he had been developing with his students before the retirement). Finally, assurance in its current state, and especially a sheer popularity of the GSN notation, present an interesting socio-cultural-psychological phenomenon to think about, and the genre of an essay allows the author to write more subjectively and colloquially than is usual for academic writing (and we all know that Tom never hesitated to use strong words for pseudo-science and pseudo-artifacts when discussing them internally).

1 Introduction

Let X be a system (an air plane, a vehicle, a robot, a video-conferencing system, a vaccine, ...), or a new feature to be added to such a system (e.g., an Air plane Collision Avoidance System, Lane Keep Assist system in a vehicle, a new interface to a video-conferencing system, or a new vaccine transportation system, ...), whose safety, security, reliability or other critical property is to be reliably assured in order to allow using this system in the everyday life. [1]
An *assurance case (AC)* is a document providing evidence and an argument based on it that the dependability claim about X holds, which X's manufacturer/producer has to submit to a certifying authority (the *regulator*) to obtain a permission to produce and market X. The regulator is typically a federal or international agency, but sometimes the producer and the regulator are two teams in the same company playing the corresponding roles. Irrespective to the organizational side, the regulator must intensely try to find breaches in the case and defeat it. In practice, the process often turns out to be iterative but its final result is necessarily Boolean: either the assurance case is approved and the system is accepted for production and use, or the case is defeated and rejected.

The remarkable certainty of an AC assessment suggests a rigorous logical perspective on the assurance business, and consulting the most rigorous part of this perspective—mathematical logic—may, perhaps, be instructive. Specifically, the main title of the paper paraphrases the title of a classical book on mathematical logic by Rasiowa and Sikorski *The Mathematics of Metamathematics* [19]. The term *meta-mathematics* refers to the following aspect of the story: mathematicians normally prove their theorems without too much reflection on how to formalize the logical side of their reasoning procedures, while mathematical logic focuses exactly on the formal structure and rules of a mathematician's everyday reasoning and thus could be called meta-mathematics. The latter, in its turn, is just yet another domain to which mathematical modelling could be applied, hence, Rasiowa & Sikorski's book title. Somewhat similarly, engineers build dependable systems based on their expertize and experience, design patterns, standards, and established engineering processes and practices without too much reflections on why those standards and processes ensure dependability (safety, security, reliability) of the system. This latter concern is the subject matter of assurance, which thus could be seen as sort of *meta-engineering*. By treating the parallels between the titles formally, one would conclude that "Assurance of assurance" means "Engineering of meta-engineering", which obviously contradicts the subtitle as there is seemingly nothing engineering in the logical rule called Modus Ponens nor in Cartesian

---

[1] If F is a new feature to be added to X, then what is to be assured (for, say, safety assurance) is the claim $\mathsf{Safe}(X + F)$, which is not followed from $\mathsf{Safe}(X)$ and $\mathsf{Safe}(F)$; the latter claim cannot even be correctly defined. This aspect of assurance is often referred to as *non-compositionality*.

closed categories (CCCs) providing a very general algebraic version of the rule. Here is where the main intrigue of the paper comes into play.

The main problem of assuring a major dependability claim about a complex system is that it can easily be refuted by presenting an instance of failure whereas proving the claim is true needs, in general, *infinite* resources (either computational or temporal or both). Nevertheless, the writers of an AC have to present an explicit argument that a system is acceptable for its intended use based on the *finite* number of different checks (analyses, simulations, tests) that the system has passed—this is the Great Assurance Divide mentioned in the subtitle. Such "great divides" are a subject matter of inductive logic, one of the most mysterious lands in the general logical landscape, which is sometimes attempted to be domesticated with rather exotic logical gadgets like, e.g., the Toulmin Schema [23] but remains either informal or very trickery formalized. In contrast, the present paper is based on a simple observation that the logical side of building an assurance argument (i.e., the inference engine as such) can be made trivial and formal by reducing the argument to a series of steps based on an appropriately formulated assumptions (called *side assumptions*) and Modus Ponens. It is the system of side assumptions, which encapsulates all the uncertainty and challenge of overcoming the Great Divide, so that everything interesting in an AC is to be found in the claims about the product and side assumptions about its type, which together allow the inference engine to work and derive the top claim from the basic evidence facts. This trick makes the inference fully formal and truly trivial: the heart of assurance is in the design of the argument flow rather than in logical figures; the former actually implies the latter. In this way, Modus Ponens and CCCs may ease the psychological pressure of incomprehensible inductive logic on the AC writer, and free him from fears of falling into an inductive logic trap that undermines and breaks the argument.

Moreover, a typical AC is full of general-vs-specific interplays of different types and shapes. Although an AC is normally written for a concrete system X, the argument usually begins with general reasoning valid for a type of systems including X, then proceeds to its subtypes and types of X's subsystems and further on so that an exact X's specificity is actually reached somewhere in the middle or even further down in the AC's path across the Great Divide from inductive to verifiable. On this path, the AC routinely substitutes concrete constructs into general patterns, concrete instances into types, concrete values into functions, and often in a graduate stepwise way if a pattern/function/type depend on multiple variables. Managing this array of substitutions is mainly the matter of accurate "substitutional bureaucracy", which may become a problem on the scale of thousands of substituted and substitutable elements and patterns, which calls for an intelligent automatic support. To be effective and reliable (recall that we are talking about assurance), such automation is to be certified and hence be based on correct specificational foundations. Fortunately, the latter are well-known in logic under the name of typed lambda calculus, and CCCs is nothing but an algebraic version of the latter (and Modus Ponens and its general version called Deduction Theorem become major devices of substitution management in CCCs). Thus, the two actors of the subtitle can help to free the AC writer from a massive array of mechanizable checks and allow her to focus on a truly intelligent and challenging task of building a reasonable argument hierarchy. If we extend the meaning of Great Divide to include also the divide between the general and the specific, and consider MP and CCC as a way to bridge the joint divide, then the title of the paper could be read as "How to use MP and CCC to facilitate engineering of meta-engineering".

Our plan for the paper is as follows.[2] We begin with discussion of inductive logic in Sect.2,1 and explain our approach to its encapsulation with side assumptions and MP. This results in the notion of Main assurance schema (Sect.2.2), which allows us to specify the difference between the two main industrial approaches to assurance: one is based on providing the evidence required by the corresponding standard, and the other is based on an on-site written AC. Section 3 refines Main schema by replacing the black-boxed Main argument with an argument tree (or inference tree) considered as a process with two sets of ports: the *main* set of entry ports is for product's properties (i.e., for the evidence that the product possesses these properties), and the *side* set of entry ports is for side assumptions about the product type and the world, and their interaction (i.e., for the evidence supporting side assumptions). We will also discuss *staged completion* (i.e., different ways of substituting/feeding evidence into the tree) and how it can be used for standardizing ACs. Section 4 provides an algebraic formalization of a major Claim-Argument-Evidence assurance framework (CAE, [1]) in terms of CCCs. It is remarkable that assurance lends itself to the CCC treatment directly rather than through the lambda calculus: CCC appears as a straightforward CAE formalization in a very natural way. Abstract considerations in Sect. 3 and 4 are illustrated with a concrete example of an AC placed in Appendix. It is not meant to imply that reading the example is optional – actually it plays an important role of clarifying and instantiating general patterns developed in the paper; placing it aside of the main content flow suggests consulting the example from any place of the paper after Sect.2. Section 5 briefly surveys the related work and concludes.

2   A bird's eye view of assurance

---

[2] Here and further in the paper, I will write 'the author' when expressing my subjective opinions, and 'we' when the reader is invited to join the author in considering a construct or discussing a subject.

145

2.1 A raven's eye view of inductive logic.

It is well known that assurance logic is inherently inductive: a dependability claim (that the system is safe, secure, bug-free, etc) can easily be refuted by showing an instance of the claim's violation but cannot formally be proved—we can only provide more or less convincing evidence that it is true. The more evidence we can provide, the more solid is our belief that the claim is trustworthy, hence the name *inductive* for logic addressing reasoning about such issues.

Consider the following classical example of an inductive logic claim:

$$\text{"All ravens are black"} \quad \text{(C1)}$$

We can believe in it but hardly can formally prove it as the quantifier "all" requires an infinite amount of checks. In fact, it is an empirical statement of very high trustworthiness until on some beautiful day somebody in Australia would find an orange raven. In terms of inductive logic, this fact would be called a *defeater* to claim (C1). Finding a defeater to an inductive claim is a small catastrophe but logically speaking, nothing terrible happened. The scope of claim (C1) was simply extended beyond its limits, for example, the claim had initially been based on exhaustive observations in, say, Europe and then unjustifiably but unintentionally extended on the whole world. This way or reasoning can be modelled by the following implication

$$(\forall x \in \mathsf{RavenEu})\mathsf{Black}(x) \Rightarrow (\forall x \in \mathsf{RavenWorld})\mathsf{Black}(x) \quad \text{(C2)}$$

which is obviously erroneous as soon as we have subsetting between the two sorts $\mathsf{RavenEu} \subsetneq \mathsf{RavenWorld}$, and neither of reasonable logical systems would have an inference rule allowing us to infer implication (C2). The point, however, is that implications like (C2) are typical for practically any engineering domain: a program is bug-free (in the world) if it was exhaustively tested and all bugs are fixed (the test suite plays the role of "Europe"); a bridge is safe (in the world) if it is safe according to analytical analyses and simulations done during its design (the bridge's "Europe"); a car is safe (in the world) if it is safe according to analyses, simulations and field testing, etc. We can specify such statements in a uniform way by the following logical formula:

$$(\forall t \in \mathcal{T}est)\mathsf{Check}(S, t) \Rightarrow \mathbf{C}_{main}^{\boldsymbol{w}}(S) \quad \text{(C3)}$$

where $\mathbf{C}_{main}^{\boldsymbol{w}}$ is a dependability claim (safety, security, bug-freeness) about system S (a bridge, a car, a video-conferencing software, a program) and $\boldsymbol{w}$ refers to a set of intended uses of the system ("the world"), whereas $\mathcal{T}est$ encompasses a set of analyses, tests, simulations, field tests and other checks to be done during system's design to ensure system's safety in the world and Check is a binary predicate claiming that system S has successfully passed test t. [3]

---

[3] Implication (C3) is also an instance of (C3) if by S we will understand the entire raven population and claim (C1) as property $\mathbf{C}_{main}^{\boldsymbol{w}}$ of the entire S.

Implication (C3) relates two different worlds. Its premise is a conjunction (indexed by t) of verifiable claims that engineers can control and check, whereas its consequence is an inductive statement about the real world; we will refer to this obstacle inherited in assurance as the *Great Assurance Divide(Gad)* or *Great gap* depending on the context. Spanning the gap and assuring the (global) trustworthiness of the top claim based on the success of local checks is a highly non-trivial enterprise; it can be only be done for special cases as, in general, it is logically false. In fact, it is a special property of the test suite $\mathcal{T}est$ that success of all checks imposed by $\mathcal{T}est$ on the system S can be interpreted as a solid evidence for the top claim. In practice, the test suite is designed in a top-bottom way: starting from the top claim $\mathbf{C}^{\mathbf{w}}_{\text{main}}$, we go down to a set of requirements to subsystems and further on to their components so that if these requirements are satisfied (which is to be demonstrated by checks from $\mathcal{T}est$), then the top claim is satisfied too. We will sometimes use notation $\mathcal{T}est[\mathbf{C}^{\mathbf{w}}_{\text{main}}]$ to explicate the dependency from the top claim.

2.2 An eagle's eye view of assurance argument

Now we need to pay attention to details.

2.2.1 Assurance schema.

To make formula (C3) logically accurate, we need to specify sorts/types for variables and constants, first of all, the type of systems $\mathcal{S}ys$ for S. It is necessary not just to satisfy a logical bureaucracy requirement but also because the system type may directly affect its assurance. When we say that a car or an aircraft is a system S and consider their safety, by a system we actually mean a triple (P, E, O) with P the product as such, E the environment and O the operator (e.g., the driver for a car and the crew for an aircraft together with the air dispatcher for some cases) whose interaction determines the system's behaviour. A small aircraft (product P_1) for interstate flights differs from a big transcontinental aircraft P_2 not just because the products P_1 and P_2 are different but because their environments and operators differ too so that we have two very different systems $S_1 = (P_1, E_1, O_1)$ and $S_2(P_2, E_2, O_2)$. Similarly, when we consider safety of a heavy traffic road bridge, we actually mean safety of a pair $S = (P, E)$ with P the bridge as such and E the environment in which it works (traffic, loads, winds, weather conditions). Even for such simple (sub)systems as wire ropes (which consist of several wires helically wounded over a central wire), assuring their safety depends on the embracing system (the environment) that uses the wire rope, e.g., according to a wire rope manual [25], the required safety factor for a wire rope in a hoist is recommended to be set to 5 while for a wire rope in an elevator the required safety factor is twice more (which is similar to using safety integrity levels (SILs) in functional assurance). Thus, the type $\mathcal{S}ys$ of a system S is a parameter of assurance analyses

147

of S.

The discussion above can be summarized by introducing, first, a type $\mathcal{P}rod$ of *products* and a type $\mathcal{W}orld$ of *worlds*, where a world is either a pair $W = (E, O)$ or just E if there is no operator in assurance considerations. Then the type of systems is $\mathcal{S}ys \subset \mathcal{P}rod \times \mathcal{W}orld$ and the top claim is a predicate over systems, $\mathbf{C} \subset \mathcal{S}ys \subset \mathcal{P}rod \times \mathcal{W}orld$, i.e., actually a binary predicate. If some world is fixed (denoted by $\boldsymbol{w}$ to be read "our world"), then type $\mathcal{S}ys$ becomes a unary subtype $\mathcal{S}ys(\_, \boldsymbol{w}) \subset \mathcal{P}rod$, and correspondingly the top claim becomes a property of products $\mathbf{C}^{\boldsymbol{w}}_{\text{main}} \subset \mathcal{S}ys(\_, \boldsymbol{w}) \subset \mathcal{P}rod$. We can eliminate type $\mathcal{S}ys$ by replacing $\mathcal{S}ys(\_, \boldsymbol{w})$ by an indexed type $\mathcal{P}rod^{\boldsymbol{w}}$ and considering the top claim an indexed unary predicate over this type, $\mathbf{C}^{\boldsymbol{w}}_{\text{main}} \subset \mathcal{P}rod^{\boldsymbol{w}}$.

Based on the above, we can rewrite (C3) as follows:

$$(\forall P \in \mathcal{P}rod^{\boldsymbol{w}}) \quad \bigwedge_{t \in \mathcal{T}est} \mathsf{Check}(P, t) \Rightarrow \mathbf{C}^{\boldsymbol{w}}_{\text{main}}(P) \quad (\text{MainAssumption}, \mathbf{A}^{\boldsymbol{w}}_{\text{main}})$$

where the universal quantification acts on the entire implication. We will call this implication the *Main Assumption* of our assurance logic. Note that the Main Assumption is a property of the triple $(\mathcal{P}rod^{\boldsymbol{w}}, \mathcal{T}est, \mathbf{C}^{\boldsymbol{w}}_{\text{main}})$ (to show this we will sometimes write $\mathbf{A}^{\boldsymbol{w}}_{\text{main}} = \mathbf{A}^{\boldsymbol{w}}_{\text{main}}(\mathcal{P}rod^{\boldsymbol{w}}, \mathcal{T}est, \mathbf{C}^{\boldsymbol{w}}_{\text{main}}))$, and this property asserts that for any product of the type given by the first member of the triple, the second member is adequate to the task of assuring the trustworthiness of the third member. The first member of the triple is not less important than the other two: the type-check $P \in \mathcal{P}rod^{\boldsymbol{w}}$ is a major control that the system of checks $\mathcal{T}est$ is properly designed so that the failure of this type-check instantly invalidates the entire implication.

Now suppose that for a given concrete product $thisP \in \mathcal{P}rod^{\boldsymbol{w}}$, we have obtained evidence that it successfully passes all checks:

$$thisP \in \mathcal{P}rod^{\boldsymbol{w}} \text{ and } \bigwedge_{t \in \mathcal{T}est} \mathsf{Check}(thisP, t) \quad (\text{Main Evidence}, \mathbf{E}_{\text{prod}})$$

Detailed notation, $\mathbf{E}_{\text{prod}} = \mathbf{E}_{\text{prod}}(thisP, \mathcal{P}rod^{\boldsymbol{w}}, \mathcal{T}est)$, shows the artifacts evidence $\mathbf{E}_{\text{prod}}$ depends on.

Now we can derive the top claim for product $thisP$ by the following inference tree:

$$Spec \dfrac{\mathbf{A}^{\boldsymbol{w}}_{\text{main}}(\mathcal{P}rod^{\boldsymbol{w}}, \mathcal{T}est, \mathbf{C}^{\boldsymbol{w}}_{\text{main}})}{\bigwedge_{t \in \mathcal{T}est} \mathsf{Check}(thisP, t) \Rightarrow \mathbf{C}^{\boldsymbol{w}}_{\text{main}}(thisP)}$$

$$ModusPonens \dfrac{}{\mathbf{C}^{\boldsymbol{w}}_{\text{main}}(thisP)} \qquad \bigwedge_{t \in \mathcal{T}est} \mathsf{Check}(thisP, t)$$

(Main Argument, $\mathbf{Arg}_{\text{main}}$)

where the horizontal line says that the claim below it is derived from the claims above it by applying an inference rule whose name is attached to the line (on the left). The first step in the tree is an application of *Specialization* rule: as the premise $\mathbf{A}^{\boldsymbol{w}}_{\mathsf{main}}$ is a universally quantified statement that holds for any $P \in \mathscr{P}rod^{\boldsymbol{w}}$, this statement holds for any particular instance, e.g., for $thisP \in \mathscr{P}rod^{\boldsymbol{w}}$.[4] The second step is an application of the classical *Modus Ponens*. We will refer to this two-step inference as to the *Main Argument*, $\mathbf{Arg}_{\mathsf{main}}$.

Three main artifacts considered above: Main Assumption $\mathbf{A}^{\boldsymbol{w}}_{\mathsf{main}}$, Main Evidence $\mathbf{E}_{\mathsf{prod}}$, and Main Argument $\mathbf{Arg}_{\mathsf{main}}$, form what we will call *Main (assurance) schema*. The inference above is fully formal within the ordinary predicate calculus, and the assurance schema is fully deductive. The inductive logic is hidden in semantics of these constructs, which is of course a much more challenging side of the story. We leave its investigation for future work while in this paper we will only work with formal syntax and its intuitive informal interpretation as is typical for the assurance literature. Note also that it is the inductive logic side of assurance, which motivated formal definitions of our basic notions.

2.2.2 Why product type checking is non-trivial.

Note (again) the importance of the type-check $thisP \in \mathscr{P}rod^{\boldsymbol{w}}$ in the evidence $\mathbf{E}_{\mathsf{prod}}$ and the entire main schema. The validity of this check may be not so trivial as it may seem. A typical safety standard begins with an accurate description of its scope; here is a quote from [15, Part 1: Vocabulary. Scope]:

ISO 26262 is intended to be applied to safety-related systems that include one or more electrical and/or electronic (E/E) systems and that are installed in series production passenger cars with a maximum gross vehicle mass up to 3 500 kg. ISO 26262 does not address unique E/E systems in special purpose vehicles such as vehicles designed for drivers with disabilities.

It seems to be a sufficiently clear description of type $\mathscr{P}rod^{\boldsymbol{w}}$ to decide for a given car whether it belongs to this type or not, but there are two caveats. Recall that the product type is actually about the interaction between the product and the world (which is shown by the subscript $\boldsymbol{w}$), but the standard does not explicitly specify what interactions are considered under the scope, i.e., what $\boldsymbol{w}$ actually is. It is silently assumed that the scope description given above also provides a sufficiently clear description of the world (say, some interactions are excluded b/c it is about passenger cars rather than trucks, and because special/unique E/E systems and drivers are also not considered). The standard thus says that the interactions with the world under the scope are *typical* interactions between the car, a *typical* driver and a *typical* environment without actual specification

---

[4] This schema was well-known to ancient Greeks: if we know that "All men are mortal" and that "Socrates is a man", then we can apply specialization and conclude that "Socrates is mortal".

of what these three references to being *typical* mean. A clarification of typical interactions appear later on, when the standard discusses a rather elaborated classification of so called operational situations (say, acceleration in a curve on a highway, or changing lane on a rural road, etc), which, in general, mitigates the problem. However, principles of building this classification are not provided and hence its completeness (which is itself a whole story, see e.g., [27]) cannot be properly assesses (not to mention that the scope concerns are better to be addressed in the Scope section).

The second caveat is related to the scope of the notion of a system: a typical situation when a safety case is written is about safety of a feature rather than the entire car (although safety of a feature is safety of a car with this feature — see footnote on p. 3). Consider, for example, a modern car with an Advanced Driver Assist System (ADAS), which is planned to be extended with yet another ADAS subsystem, say, Lane Keep Assist (LKA). Then ADAS appears as a part of the world for the product LKA, and hence definition of the type $\mathit{Prod}^{\boldsymbol{w}}$ for LKA should include some characterization of ADAS. Suppose that this characterization says "An intelligent ADAS system helps the driver to control the vehicle and stabilizes its dynamics", which obviously affects the extent (population) of type $\mathit{Prod}^{\boldsymbol{w}}$ for LKA and the design of the test suite Test as well; to make the dependency explicit, we can write $\mathit{Prod}^{\boldsymbol{w}(\mathrm{ADAS})}$ and $\mathit{Test}^{\mathrm{ADAS}}$. Then the type-check LKA$\in^{?} \mathit{Prod}^{\boldsymbol{w}(\mathrm{ADAS})}$ may be non-trivial as giving the affirmative answer would mean that ADAS is indeed intelligent enough and LKA may rely on its functionalities (which, of course, does not exclude the hazard of the failure of these functionalities but it is another story). A related issue is that the quote above mentions that unique E/E systems are excluded but does not give a precise description of what this uniqueness means. Thus, type checking $\mathit{thisP} \in \mathit{Prod}^{\boldsymbol{w}}$ may indeed be non-trivial and affects the assurance case.

2.3 Two approaches to assurance in the assurance industry: A bird's eye view

There are two main industrial approaches to assurance: one is based on providing standard-dictated evidence and we will call it *evidence-based*, and the other is based on assurance cases developed on site and called *case-based*.

2.3.1 Evidence-based assurance.

The logic of the evidence-based approach can be well explained in the framework described above. Assurance of a product is regulated by a standard playing the role of an all-mighty oracle who says "The Main Assumption $\mathbf{A}_{\mathrm{main}}^{\boldsymbol{w}}(\mathit{Prod}^{\boldsymbol{w}}, \mathit{Test}, \mathbf{C}_{\mathrm{main}}^{\boldsymbol{w}})$ is true because I know it is true based on the previous experience and advice of Supreme Oracle Counsel": a typical example is an avionics standard DO-178C [10] as the oracle and the Federal Aviation Administration (FAA) in US as the Counsel. Then, to get a product $thisP \in \mathcal{P}rod^{w}$ certified, the product manufacturer (referred to as OEM = Original Equipment Manufacturer) needs to provide evidence that $thisP$ has successfully passed all checks in set $\mathcal{T}est$. This evidence is assessed by the regulator and if the latter finds it to be trustworthy, the top claim is considered assured and the product is certified. This clear schema is, however, too rigid if the product is sufficiently novel and there are no standards or other established normative documents that specify the set of checks $\mathcal{T}est$ to be done to ensure the top claim. If we have a well-working framework based on a Main Assumption schema $\mathbf{A}^{w}_{main}(\mathcal{P}rod^{w}, \mathcal{T}est, \mathbf{C}^{w}_{main})$ for a class of products $\mathcal{P}rod^{w}$, and the OEM created a new product of a somewhat similar but actually different type so that $thisP' \notin \mathcal{P}rod^{w}$, then using the test suite $\mathcal{T}est$ for assuring the new product becomes doubtful and dangerous.

2.3.2 Case-based assurance

The case-based approach mitigates the inflexibility of the evidence-based assurance by allowing the OEM to do the following:

(i) design a new test suite $\mathcal{T}est'$ for a new type of products $\mathcal{P}rod'^{w}$ that subsumes the new product $thisP'$;

(ii) develop an assurance argument demonstrating the validity of the new Main Assumption $\mathbf{A}'^{w}_{main}(\mathcal{P}rod'^{w}, \mathcal{T}est', \mathbf{C}^{w}_{main})$;

(iii) present evidence $\mathbf{E}'_{prod}(thisP', \mathcal{P}rod'^{w}, \mathcal{T}est')$ that the new product successfully passes new tests.

Then $\mathbf{C}^{w}_{main}(thisP')$ follows from $\mathbf{A}'^{main}$ and $\mathbf{E}'_{prod}$ as before. The three items mentioned above constitute an assurance case (AC) to be built by the OEM, hence the name of the approach. Formally speaking, an AC as such may only consists of items 2 and 3, but a basic idea behind the AC approach is that it goes in parallel with assurance (safety, security, strength) engineering and indeed, engineers design the test suite $\mathcal{T}est'$ in such a way that it would be possible to prove the claim $\mathbf{A}'^{w}_{main}(\mathcal{P}rod'^{w}, \mathcal{T}est', \mathbf{C}^{w}_{main})$. The authors of the report [20, Sect.3.1] state this idea rather vigorously:

Thinking that assurance cases are written after the fact (after system development) and simply argue, post facto, that what is already done is sufficient, demonstrates a fundamental misunderstanding of assurances cases. The failure of the Nimrod safety case (...) is a cautionary example of this flawed approach.

Thus, $\mathcal{T}est'$ design and the proof of its adequacy to assuring the main assumption $\mathbf{A}'^{w}_{main}$ go in parallel and an AC encompasses all three items 1-3 in the list above.

3 Logic and Structure of an Assurance Case.

In the preceding section, we considered a principle logical schema of spanning the Gad and deriving an inductive top claim from a finite set of checks. The magic is encapsulated in an if-then logical implication called Main assumption (see p. 8). An assurance case (AC) is basically a structure, in which this magical assumption is decomposed into a tree of claims whose level of details and verifiability (more verifiability means less inductivity) is stepwise increasing from the root (the top claim) down to leaves, which are verifiable claims about components of the system. Each decomposition step in this tree is an argument that claims trustworthiness of the step's conclusion from trustworthiness of its premises (children of the conclusion in the tree structure), and is thus a "small" logical implication. Composition of all small implications into one big implication gives us exactly the Main assumption that spans the great divide. In the present section we consider the structure of the tree, implication composition and different ways it can be implemented. We will begin with a background discussion of generic (variables) vs. special (constants) in logical reasoning in Sect.3.1, then proceed to the structure of the argument tree and implication composition in Sect.3.2, and an accurate formalization of the story in the language of Cartesian closed categories (CCC) in Sect. 3.3.

3.1 Background: Generalization and specialization in logical reasoning.

We will briedly discuss why an assurance argument is to be developed for a whole product type $\mathscr{P}rod$ rather than for a single product $this\boldsymbol{P}$ even though the goal of the case is to assure a concrete product of type $\mathscr{P}rod$. The discussion will be naive and intuitive, later in Section 4 we will give a formal version of the story.

Logical reasoning is normally unravelled over a class of objects rather than a single object. For example, if we want to prove a property Y of a product, say, of a pair of integers $this\boldsymbol{P} = (8, 23)$, we would consider this property for a class $\mathscr{P}(Y) \subset \mathsf{Int} \times \mathsf{Int}$ of pairs. and then show that $(8, 23) \in \mathscr{P}(Y)$. For instance, if we want to prove that the difference $(23 - 8)$ is a multiple of 5, we note that it holds for any pair $P = (a, b)$ with $a < b$, $a = 10 \cdot m - 2$ for some m and $b = 10 \cdot n + 3$ for some $n \geq m$ so that $b - a = 10 \cdot (n - m) + 5$, which is a multiple of 5. For more intricate properties, we may need to see 8 as, say, an exponent of 2 and 23 as a prime number, i.e., an object of type $\mathscr{P}(Y) = \{(2^m, p) | m \in \mathsf{Int}, p \in \mathsf{Prime} \subset \mathsf{Int}\}$ and prove the required property for all such pairs so that it holds for $this\boldsymbol{P} = (8, 23)$ too. After all, we can precisely specify (8,23) as that unique pair for which $m = 3$ and p is the least prime number greater than 20 so that $\mathscr{P}(Y)$ is a singleton $\{(8,23)\}$, but reasoning would still go over a generic pair $P = (2^m, p)$ possessing this or that property rather than (8,23) as such—it is the nature of reasoning to work with generic rather than concrete objects.

On the other hand, when we reason about a pair $P = (a, b) \in \mathscr{P}(Y)$ to prove a property Y for pair $\mathit{thisP} = (8, 23)$, we are allowed to use any property Z of P inferable from the membership $P \in \mathscr{P}(Y)$ and thus build an inference tree $\mathbf{T}_Y(a, b)$ resulting in claim $Y(a, b)$, but not anything beyond. That is, using any specific property of pair (a, b) beyond those inferable from $(a, b) \in \mathscr{P}(Y)$ is prohibited because at the end we want to be sure that we can safely substitute (8,23) into the tree $\mathbf{T}_Y(a, b)$ without violation its logical validity and thus obtain $Y(8, 23)$. For example, if while building the tree we have used some property Z^* of pair (a, b) not inferable from its membership in $\mathscr{P}(Y)$, then it may happen that $Z^*(8, 23)$ does not hold and validity of $Y(8, 23)$ is broken.[5] Thus, the genericness of pair (a, b) for which the inference tree $\mathbf{T}_Y(a, b)$ is built is essential, and if this condition is fulfilled, then the *Generalization* rule of predicate calculus allows us to infer a universal statement $\forall (a, b) \in \mathscr{P}(Y) \; Y(a, b)$. After that for any concrete pair $(\mathit{thisa}, \mathit{thisb}) \in \mathsf{Int} \times \mathsf{Int}$, we can apply *Specialization* and conclude $Y(\mathit{thisa}, \mathit{thisb})$.[6]

The story described above is directly applicable to the assurance case methodology. An AC is an inference tree $\mathbf{T}_{\mathbf{C}^w_{\mathrm{main}}}(P)$ built for a generic product $P \in \mathscr{P}\!\mathit{rod}^w$, from which we derive $\mathbf{C}^w_{\mathrm{main}}(\mathit{thisP})$ by applying universal generalization and then specialization and Modus Ponens as explained above.

3.2 Four Stages of Building an Assurance Case.

The first stage of building an AC is to build an inference tree, which step-by-step infers the top claim from verifiable small assumptions about different aspects of product's structure, its interaction with the world and properties of product's components. Such a tree can be seen as a process that takes leaf assumptions at its input ports and produces the top claim after some internal processing; we will interchangeably use terms leafs and input ports. Box 1 in Fig. 1 (the leftmost big rectangle with rounded corners) shows a principle schema: the (initial) tree as such is shown as a big parallelogram, the leaves are claims placed in pink (except one) boxes and they are partitioned into a set of product checks $\mathit{Check}(P)$ (for a generic product P) below the tree and a set of

---

[5] If Z^* is so essential for the proof of $Y(a, b)$ that we cannot overcome its use, then we need to redefine the type to be $\mathscr{P}^*(Y)$ so that Z^* is legally inferable for this new type, but then we need to assure that $(8, 23) \in \mathscr{P}^*(Y)$.

[6] Here we apply yet another well-known logical trick. Symbols a, b, x, y are logical variables that can be interpreted by any integers, whereas symbols thisa, thisb are names referring to concrete integers, say, 8 and 23 if thisa is 8 and thisb is 23. Such variables with a fixed interpretation are called *constants*.

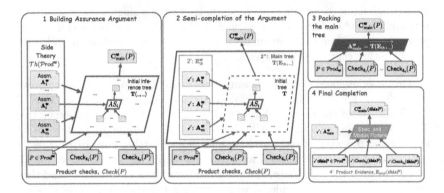

Figure 1. Basic Anatomy of an Assurance Case

side assumptions $\mathit{Theory}(\mathit{Prod}^{\boldsymbol{w}})$ on the left of the tree; the output of the tree is the top claim for P. As explained above in the background, the inference tree is a "compile-time" structure operating variables, product variable P in our case, while symbols $\boldsymbol{w}$, $\boldsymbol{t}_i$, $i = 1, ..., n$ are constants, i.e., refer to a concrete world and concrete tests while variables can be instantiated by concrete objects (e.g., $\mathit{this}\boldsymbol{P}$). An instantiation (at "run-time") makes a claim either true (in which case we would colour that claim in green) or false (then we make it red), but at compile time the truth value is not known yet and we thus paint claims in pink as a colour in-between green and red (one claim is green as it is assumed to be true already at compile time). As variable P refers to a (rather complex) data structure, claims are actually statements about data, and in the UML terms can be called *constraints*; we will also borrow a UML notational habit to place constraints into dog-eared rectangles.

The inference tree consists of multiple inference steps that we also call *argument steps* as is common in the assurance literature. Each such step, AS_i, takes several claims (called its *premises*) as its input and produces a claim (the *conclusion* of the step) at the output as shown inside the big parallelogram; the parallelogram notation for argument steps is borrowed from CAE/GSN notation. In this way, step by step (but there may be several locally concurrent threads) the inference tree produces the top claim $\mathbf{C}^{\boldsymbol{w}}_{\mathrm{main}}(P)$.

Recall the main challenge of building an assurance argument: the input to the tree consists of (close to be) verifiable claims while its output is an inductive claim about future interactions of the product and the world. This distinction is notationally shown by using grey thin frames for inductive claims (e.g., the top one), and thin blue frames for verifiable claims at the bottom: the blue colour suggests something mechanically computable (but thin blue is 1pt thicker than thin grey to make a non-colour distinction). An inference tree can be seen as a device that bridges the great assurance gap in a stepwise way: each argument

154

step AS_i covers a small local fragment but altogether they bridge the great gap. This is actually the idea of requirement decomposition: the top requirement $\mathbf{C}^{\boldsymbol{w}}_{\mathrm{main}}$ to the system is decomposed into requirements to subsystems and further on to their components until we reach the level of verifiable checks. At each argument step AS_i, the magic of passing from "less inductive/more verifiable" premises to the "more inductive" conclusion is achieved by the same formal trick we used for specifying the Main Argument $\mathbf{Arg}_{\mathrm{main}}$ above, to wit: the inference of the conclusion from the premises is formally backed by a special if-then assumption $\mathbf{A}^{\boldsymbol{w}}_i$ (where $\boldsymbol{w}$ is a constant referring to the world as before) called the *side assumption* of step AS_i, which says that if premises are trustworthy then the conclusion is no less trustworthy as well:

$$(\forall P \in \mathit{Prod}^{\boldsymbol{w}}_i) \quad \bigwedge_{\mathsf{C}\in\mathit{Prem}_i} \mathsf{C}(P) \Rightarrow \mathsf{C}^!_i(P) \qquad (AS_i \text{ Assumption, } \mathbf{A}^{\boldsymbol{w}}_i)$$

In this formula, $\mathit{Prod}^{\boldsymbol{w}}_i$ is a local product type for that component of the product whose assurance is considered in the step AS_i so that the bounded variable P refers to the subsystem/component rather than the entire product; finite set Prem_i is the set of premises of step AS_i and $\mathsf{C}^!_i$ is the conclusion of the step. Another phrasing of the local interpretation i is that $\mathbf{A}^{\boldsymbol{w}}_i$ is an assumption about the i-th aspect of interaction between the product and the world (example in the Appendix shows how it works and the reader may take a look at Fig. A.2 right now). It is easy to see that the side assumption together with premises imply the conclusion due to Modus Ponens. This makes each argument step, and the entire tree, fully formal, which is shown by thick blue frames of the parallelograms and arrows from the premises and the side assumptions into the inference engine. Note, however, that although an inference step AS_i is formal, and if even the main (non-side) premises for the step are absolutely true, the trustworthiness of the step's conclusion is not guaranteed unless the side assumption is fully trustworthy. In this way the uncertainty inherent in inductive logic is removed from inference rules and placed into side assumptions.

Some of side assumptions may depend on other side assumptions and together they form a logical theory of the type $\mathit{Prod}^{\boldsymbol{w}}$ referred to as *side theory* or just *theory*, and denoted by $\mathit{Theory}(\mathit{Prod}^{\boldsymbol{w}})$ or $\mathit{Theory}^{\boldsymbol{w}}$. Note that the theory of global type $\mathit{Prod}^{\boldsymbol{w}}$ includes theories of local types $\mathit{Prod}^{\boldsymbol{w}}_i$ but is not their union (nor the type $\mathit{Prod}^{\boldsymbol{w}}$ is the mathematical product of local types $\mathit{Prod}^{\boldsymbol{w}}_i$): there are properties of the whole not reducible to the properties of the components. Importantly, as side assumptions depend on the product type and its component (sub)types rather than on the individual product P as such, their trustworthiness lies deeper than trustworthiness of premise checks from sets Prem_i so that they can be taken true for granted if we write our AC for a new product of the same type, and then we can paint them green at compile time as shown in the figure for assumptions $\mathbf{A}^{\boldsymbol{w}}_1$. However, when we design a sufficiently new product of a new type $\mathit{Prod}'^{\boldsymbol{w}}$, the failure of some assumptions is possible and so they all need to be carefully checked. Hence, a general colour of an assumption during compile time is pink, and to make it green, some evidence is to be provided. This evidence is similar to the main evidence $\mathbf{E}_{\text{prod}}$ with side assumptions playing the roles of tests for the product type (rather than the product):

$$\bigwedge_{\mathbf{A}_i^w \in \mathcal{T}heory} \mathscr{P}rod_i^w \models \mathbf{A}_i^w \qquad \text{(Theory Evidence, } \mathbf{E}_{\text{th}}^w\text{)}$$

where $\models$ is a typical binary relation of satisfiability/compliance of a semantic entity placed on the left of the symbol, and a syntactic entity (requirement, logical formula) on the right of the symbol. In Fig. 1, these checks are shown in Box 2' and together make set $\mathbf{E}_{\text{th}}^w$ referred to as *(side) theory evidence*.

To summarize, each argument step AS_i is an if-if-then statement that derives its conclusion from two sets of premises: main premises about the product and the side premise about the product type. We will call the act of stating trustworthiness of a premise by providing a corresponding evidence a *completion* of the argument step, and each completion removes one of the 'ifs' in the argument; we may see it as substituting/feeding an evidence into the argument. When all ifs are substituted by evidences, the argument step is completed and becomes a trustworthy claim – its conclusion. When all steps are completed, the entire tree is completed and assures its conclusion – the top claim.

The order of replacing leaves by evidences, i.e., feeding evidences into the input ports of the tree, does not affect the trustworthiness of the conclusion and can be considered as implementation details— we will make it precise in Section 4. However, it does matter for practical building of the tree. Clearly, the two types of evidence to be fed into the argument tree are very different: $\mathbf{E}_{\text{th}}^w = \mathbf{E}_{\text{th}}^w(\mathscr{P}rod^w)$ is much more general and rooted deeper in the assurance knowledge than quite concrete and agile $\mathbf{E}_{\text{prod}} = \mathbf{E}_{\text{prod}}(thisP)$. It makes reasonable to feed, first, all (or much of) the theoretical evidence, and then proceed with product evidence. Box 2 in Fig. 1 shows such a schema, in which all theoretical evidence is fed into the tree, which makes it a purely product-dependent if-then statement. If we make such a semi-completed tree a black box with only the leaves and the root visible, we arrive at exactly the Main assumption discussed in Section 2. The operation of converting a tree $\mathbf{T}(\_,\_)$ (where each of the placeholders $\_$ actually denotes a set of ports) into an implicational arrow (a black-box argument) of the form "if the leaves are true, then the root is true", is denoted by $\overrightarrow{\mathbf{T}(\_,\_)}$: it is nothing but composition of all arrows the tree consists of. We will say that a tree is packed into an implication—this is shown in Box 3 of Fig. 1. Finally, by substituting the premises of this implication by the product evidence (i.e., an evidence that the product passed all the required checks), we complete the argument and arrive at the root conclusion—the top claim about the product. The story is formalized in Sect.4

Each step AS_i and the entire procedure are fully mechanical based on spe-

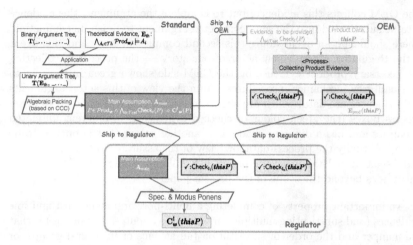

Figure 2. Principle workflow of an evidence-based assurance

cialization and Modus Ponens inference rules (which can be understood algebraically as substitution rules as explained in Sect.4), hence the thick blue frames of the parallelograms. All uncertainty inherent in the inductive logic nature of assurance is absorbed in the side assumptions (thin grey frames), once they are trustworthy, the top claim is no less trustworthy. This statement of mechanizability is, of course, about the final result and validation of building the assurance argument, whereas the very process of building the argument is very far from being mechanizable and is based on experience, intuition, patterns, and other magical gadgets from the engineering toolbox.

3.3 Assurance as a workflow: Staged Completion

The goal of the section is to discuss possible schemas of industrializing assurance in an intermediate way in-between the two currently known approaches to assurance, the two extremes: either the AC is fully built by the Standard (implicitly or explicitly, see [14]) and the OEM is informed about the evidence to be provided, or the AC is fully built on the OEM side. What we are going to discuss is an approach in the Standard and the OEM build their own part of the AC, more accurately, fill-in their own parts of one integral AC.

Let us first map activities in the schema in Fig. 1 onto agents who will do them. This is shown in Fig. 2 with grey rectangles with rounded corners, and grey arrows in-between them show shipment actions. In the next section we will consider a formal underpinning of packing an argument into a shippable form, but intuitively it is clear and was explained above: the argument tree is semi-completed with side theoretical evidence, abstracted as an if-then implication and shipped to the OEM as a specification of what evidence is to be provided.

The OEM collects this evidence, but to complete the argument, this evidence is to be substituted into the semi-completed argument to finish its completion. There should be an agent doing this second completion step, and this agent is the Regulator. Note a new actor of our story — the process of collecting the necessary product evidence on the OEM side shown green in contrast to blue and grey mechanical procedures. From the view of this actor, arguments and evidences are data, which are shown in orange boxes as opposed to green process boxes (the green colour of checked evidence is of different unrelated semantics and has a different shade; it is another colour that happened to be green). Actually the process-dataflow view of the assurance business is crucial and discussed in detail in several papers [9,8,2,3] under the name of Workflow$^+$ but it goes beyond the scope of the present paper.

An important property of completing a multi-port argument with multiple evidences (and substituting multiple variables into a multi-ary function) is that the manner and the order of substitution (all at once or in several groups, or one-by-one sequentially in the order x,y,z,... or z,x,y,... etc) does not matter for the result; in Sect. 4 this is stated formally with *interleaving* equations. Moreover, a partially completed argument can be considered as a syntactically correct argument with a reduced number of entry ports and thus be "shipped" to another actor for doing another part of completion. In other words, completing an argument with evidences can go in stages, and we will refer to it as *staged completion*.

Staged completion opens interesting possibilities for the assurance industry. A standard may build an argument and do its partial completion with side evidence, whereas the OEM finishes the side evidence completion (reworking the corresponding part of the case if necessary) and fully does the product evidence completion. Or, the OEM can be building an AC but delegate some part of it to a standardization body. The staged completion is applicable not only to side-theory evidence, but also to type-checking evidence. For example, the standard may provide evidence (and thus complete the corresponding part of the case) for a broad product type $\mathcal{P}rod^{w}$, while the OEM would narrow it to $\mathcal{P}rod'^{w}$ in its part of the AC. In this way the standard can regulate how much freedom the OEM is allowed to have: the narrower is type $\mathcal{P}rod^{w}$ specified by the standard, the tighter are restrictions on the OEM. In this way, the standard can still provide some reasonable limitations even if the AC is to be built on the OEM side, which may be a useful option in comparison with the current practice that allows the OEM free sailing amongst the reefs of assurance so that all problems are to be catch during assessment.

4 Assurance Algebraically via Cartesian Closed Categories.

This section is basically a rephrasing of a standard categorical logic framework for the typed lambda calculus based on Cartesian closed categories (CCC), but discovering a mapping of assurance to CCC and sorting out details took some non-neglectable time. An excellent presentation of CCC and their relation to lambda calculus can be found in a classical book by Lambek and Scott [17], and our presentation below will although be sufficiently formal but phrased in a narrative style focused on explaining details for non-categorical audience rather than giving well-known formal definitions. Several new definitions relating assurance and CCC are given in formal phrasing to avoid confusion.

4.1 Argumentation in CCC terms

We are going to define a CCC category *Assr*, in which basic assurance notions of a claim, an argument, evidence, and argument flow, can be formally modelled. We will also formally define the notions of a product to be assured, and correspondingly the main evidence and the side evidence for side assumptions.

4.1.1 Argument flow as arrow composition.

Let us begin with a notion of an *argument* graph *Assr*, whose nodes (categoricians say objects) are called *claims* (or assertions, logical statements, or use your favourite term), and arrows are called *arguments* so that an arrow $g: A \to B$ is interpreted as that we have an argument g showing that claim A implies claim B. We will use a shorter geometric terminology and say that an argument g is from A to B. There can be multiple arguments from A to B, which models very naturally the notion of a multi-leg argument [4]. We write *Assr*(A, B) for the set of all arguments from A to B, which, of course, may be empty. If there is at least one argument $g: A \to B$, we say that A *entails* B and write $A \vdash B$.

If there is an argument $g: A \to B$ and an argument $h: B \to C$, then it is natural to assume that we have a composed argument $e; f: A \to C$ so that we will require arrows of any argument graph to be composable. Having in addition $k: C \to D$, it is natural to identify arguments $(g; h); k$ and $g; (h; k)$ as being equal, which makes arrow composition associative. For any claim A there is a trivial identity argument $\mathrm{id}_A: A \to A$ required to satisfy equations $g; \mathrm{id}_B = g$ and $\mathrm{id}_B; h = h$. If all these requirements are satisfied, our argument graph becomes a category. Given a category, say, *Assr*, the set of all its objects will be denoted by $|Assr|$, while by the abuse of notation, *Assr* will also denote the class of all arrows (which is partitioned into *Assr*(A, B), $A, B \in |Assr|$).

159

Now we will add to category **Assr** some logical constructs, which would make it a Cartesian category, i.e., a category with finite products including a terminal object.

We require **Assr** to have a special claim **1** called *truth* such that any claim A entails **1** in a unique way, i.e., $A \vdash \mathbf{1}$ via a unique arrow $!_A : A \to \mathbf{1}$. (Categoricians call **1** a *terminal* objects.)This formalizes the idea that trustworthiness of A cannot exceed trustworthiness of **1** via a unique proof of this assumption.

To have in our logic conjunction, we require category **Assr** to have finite products so that for any pair of claims A, B, we have a claim $A \wedge B$ together with trivial *projection* arguments $\mathsf{pr}_A : A \wedge B \to A$ and $\mathsf{pr}_B : A \wedge B \to B$. Moreover, having a pair of arguments from the same source, $g_i : A \to B_i$, $i = 1, 2$, we postulate the existence of a unique *paired* argument $g = (g_1, g_2) : A \to B_1 \wedge B_2$ such that $g; \mathsf{pr}_i = g_i$. This is referred to as the universal property of conjunction. Sometimes we will use an unusual notation for pairing and write $g_1 \dot{\wedge} g_2$ (note the dot above $\wedge$; the point is that notation $g_1 \wedge g_2$ is standard for tensorial pairing of two g_i with different sources and targets).

4.1.2 Evidence, variables and constants

Availability of argument $!_A : A \to \mathbf{1}$ says nothing interesting about specifically A. In contrast, an argument $e : \mathbf{1} \to A$ says that the trustworthiness of A is not less than the trustworthiness of the truth, i.e., A is true. In the assurance parlance, having such an arrow would be referred to as having some "evidence" of A's trustworthiness, and we will follow this terminology: arrows from **1** are called *evidential* (arrows, arguments) or just *evidence*. The more such arrows into a claim A exists the more evidence of A's trustworthiness we have so that the set **Assr**$(\mathbf{1}, A)$ can be seen as a measure of A's trustworthiness; we will use a "semantically-suggestive" notation and write $[\![A]\!]$ for **Assr**$(\mathbf{1}, A)$. Universality of **1** implies that $[\![\mathbf{1}]\!]$ is a singleton $\{\mathsf{id_1}\}$.

Having an argument $g : A \to B$ and an evidence $e : \mathbf{1} \to A$, we can compose them and obtain an evidence $e; g : \mathbf{1} \to B$; we will refer to this as to a *completion* of argument g. Note that any $g : A \to B$ gives rise to a function $[\![g]\!] : [\![A]\!] \to [\![B]\!]$ by completion, hence notation $g(e)$ for $e; g$. An arrow/argument g can thus be considered in two ways: i) logically, as an implication "if A then B", and ii) procedurally, as a process/function $[\![g]\!]$: "if an evidential datum is placed/fed into the entry port A, the process will produce an evidential datum at the output port B". This duality is known under the name of Howard-Curry isomorphism and have important consequences some of which will be considered below.

It is time to discuss how category **Assr** would appear in the (modelling part of the) world. Suppose we have a class of products $\mathscr{P}$ that we want to assure.

160

Products of this type have various properties, which gives us a class of claims $Claim(\mathcal{P})$ including $\mathbf{1}$ and claim $C_\in$ which formally models the membership in class $\mathcal{P}$. Some claims imply other claims so that we have arguments and their composition, and finally a Cartesian category $\boldsymbol{Assr}_\mathcal{P}$. (Note that $\mathcal{P}$ is not a formal index, it is only a part of a single notational symbol $\boldsymbol{Assr}_\mathcal{P}$ to guide our intuition. In contrast, claim $C_\in$ is a formal object, namely, an object of category $\boldsymbol{Assr}_\mathcal{P}$.) To show that a product from $\mathcal{P}$ does satisfy claim $C \in Claim(\mathcal{P})$, we need to present an evidence $e\colon \mathbf{1} \to C$ and let $\mathbf{E}_\mathcal{P} \subset \boldsymbol{Assr}_\mathcal{P}(\mathbf{1}, \_)$ denotes all such evidences. We can thus model a product as a set of evidences it provides. A formal definition is below, where the script $\mathcal{P}$ is dropped to avoid confusion (but its is useful to keep it in mind).

Definition 4.1 [Assurance categories] *An* assurance category *is a triple* $(\boldsymbol{Assr}, C_\in, C^!)$ *where* $\boldsymbol{Assr}$ *is a (small) Cartesian category whose objects are called* claims *and arrows are* arguments*, and* $C_\in, C^! \in |\boldsymbol{Assr}|$ *are two claims called the* type-check *claim and the* top *claim. Arrows from* $\mathbf{1}$ *are called* evidences *and let* $\mathbf{E}$ *denotes the class* $\boldsymbol{Assr}(\mathbf{1}, \_)$ *of all such.*

Definition 4.2 [Products]*A* product *is a pair* $(this\boldsymbol{P}_0, \mathbf{E}_{this\boldsymbol{P}})$ *of an evidence arrow* $this\boldsymbol{P}_0\colon \mathbf{1} \to C_\in$ *and an evidence set* $\mathbf{E}_{this\boldsymbol{P}} \subset \mathbf{E}$*. The target claims of these arrows are called* product's properties *and let* $\mathcal{P}rop_{this\boldsymbol{P}}$ *denotes the class of all such.*

A typical way of reasoning is to use assumptions, "assume that claim C is true, and then ....", which in our language is specified by arrows $x\colon \mathbf{1} \to C$ that are added to category $\boldsymbol{Assr}$; Lambek and Scott call such arrows *indeterminate*, we will also call them *variables*. It is easy to show (see [17]) how a finite number X of new arrows can freely be added to $\boldsymbol{Assr}$ and make a bigger Cartesian category $\boldsymbol{Assr}[X]$ with the same objects but whose class of evidences is partitioned into product evidences (in the logical parlance called *constants*) and variables, $\boldsymbol{Assr}[X](\mathbf{1}, \_) = \mathbf{E} \cup X$. Note that composition of variables with other arrows give rise to a whole set of new arrows in $\boldsymbol{Assr}[X]$.

An argument employing variables is shown in diagram Fig. 3(a). The black part of the diagram shows an argument $g!$ with $n + 1$ entry ports $C_0, ..., C_n$ to which evidence variables $x_0, ..., x_n$ are connected. The dashed blue upper arc is the multi-pairing of all variables, and the lower blue dashed arrow is the completed argument obtained by composiiton of the arc with $g!$. The black part of the diagram is given, the blue dashed part is derived using operations provided by the Cartesian structure. The so called *functional completeness* of Cartesian categories states that any arrow derived in $\boldsymbol{Assr}[X]$ can also be derived in $\boldsymbol{Assr}$ without variables. The latter way (so called *element-free* reasoning) is favoured by categoricians (and is probably one of the reasons preventing the wide use of category theory despite numerous essential benefits), but reasoning with variables is convenient and is as ancient as mathematics. For example,

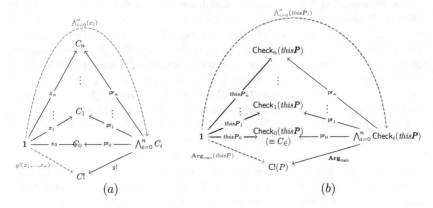

Figure 3. Argument with variables (a) and its completion with evidence (b)

when Euclid had been proving a theorem about triangles and thus drawing a non-specific triangle of a common shape, he had actually been reasoning using a triangle variable in the sense above (see also the work of Makowksy about using variables by ancient Babylonians and another formal view of the subject).

Diagram Fig. 3(b) is an instance of diagram (a), in which claims C_i become concrete claims about some product $thisP$, and variables become evidences provided by the product. Claim $Check_0 P$ is the type-check, and other claims are checks/tests we considered above. Importantly, the family of arrows $thisP_i$ in diagram (b) is a part of the semantics of the notion of product as defined in Def. 4.2 — all this arrows belong to the same $thisP$, hence, the notation. In contrast, diagram (a) can be interpreted in two ways. Either as just an argument with $n+1$ entries connected to $n+1$ pieces of evidence, which could be denoted by, say, $x, y, x, ...$ Or as an argument for a variable product X whose evidence pieces are denoted by x_i; to suggest this second interpretation, it would be better to denote claims by $C_i(X)$ as we did in diagram (b).

Definition 4.3 [Assurance arguments and their completion]*An assurance argument in an assurance category* ($\boldsymbol{Assr}, C_\in, C^!$) *is an arrow $g!$ in category* $\boldsymbol{Assr}[X]$, $X = \{x_0, .., x_n\}$ *as shown in Fig. 3. We say that the argument shows trustworthiness of the top claim for product $thisP$, if all $C_i \in \mathscr{P}rop_{thisP}$ (defined in Def. 4.2) for all $i = 1...n$, and we assume that C_0 is $C_\in$. In other words, we can substitute $thisP$ into the argument and replace variable assumptions by $thisP$ evidences. Then we say that the argument is* completed.

162

4.2 Implication as an Exponent and Modus Ponens

Our argument logic needs, of course, a notion of implication, i.e., an operation that for any pair of claims A, B makes a new claim $A \Rightarrow B$. To make reading some formulas easier and avoid confusion of argument arrows $\rightarrow$ and implications, we will sometimes write the later as an exponent B^A. To make this operation behave as logical implication should behave, we require:

a) the existence of a special argument called *modus ponens*, $\mathsf{mp}_{A,B} \colon A \wedge B^A \rightarrow B$ for each pair (A, B);

b) an operation on arguments called *Currying*: for any arrow $g \colon A \wedge B \rightarrow C$, there is an arrow $\lambda^C_{A,B}(g) \colon A \rightarrow C^B$. As a rule, we will omit sub- and sup-scripts and write $\mathsf{mp} \colon A \wedge B^A \rightarrow B$ and $g^\lambda \colon A \rightarrow C^B$.

c) Operations mp and Currying to satisfy some equations which make the behaviour of the algebraic implication (exponent) exactly similar to the behaviour of the logical implication.

Specifically, it can be shown that in any CCC **Assr**, for any objects A, B, sets **Assr**(A, B) and **Assr**$(\mathbf{1}, B^A)$ are naturally isomorphic: there are mutually inverse bijections

$$\mathsf{pack} \colon \boldsymbol{Assr}(A, B) \rightarrow \boldsymbol{Assr}(\mathbf{1}, B^A) \text{ and } \mathsf{unpack} \colon \boldsymbol{Assr}(\mathbf{1}, B^A) \rightarrow \boldsymbol{Assr}(A, B),$$

(Packing Structure)

which moreover commute with other arguments. In our context, we interpret these operations as follows: the left one "packs" an argument into an evidence that it exists, and the right one unpacks an evidence of existence into a real argument that can be completed with an evidence $e \colon \mathbf{1} \rightarrow A$ by composition. This gives rise to another understanding of packing as creating a definition of an argument, and unpacking as a compilation of the definition into a ready-to-run code. We also have a mete-version of Modus Pones as a (family of) binary operations on evidential arrows:

$$\frac{E \colon \mathbf{1} \rightarrow A \Rightarrow B \qquad e \colon \mathbf{1} \rightarrow A}{\mathsf{MP}^A_B(E, e) := e; \mathsf{unpack}(E) \colon \mathbf{1} \rightarrow B}$$

(Meta ModusPonens)

which take an argument definition and (after unpacking) apply it to an appropriate type of evidence. We write the derived arrow as $\mathsf{unpack}(E)(e)$ or $E_{\mathsf{MP}}(e)$ to be read as "unpack E with Modus Ponens and complete it with e".

A category having conjunction (product) and implication (exponent) specified above is called *Cartesian closed*, hence a standard abbreviation CCC for such categories.

Fig. 4 shows how substitution works in a CCC. Suppose we have an argument g with two entry ports as shown in diagram Fig. 3(a). We can complete the argument by feeding two evidences x, y into its entries (we work with formal/variable evidence arrows x, y but could use concrete product evidences as

163

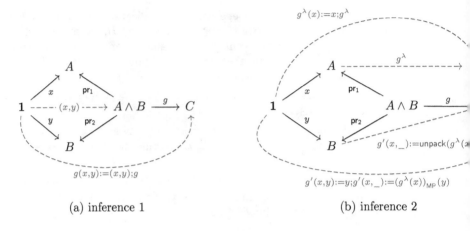

(a) inference 1   (b) inference 2

Figure 4. Substitution in CCC

well), then pair them and obtain evidence (x, y), whose composition with g completes the argument. This is just a binary case of a general Cartesian case in Fig. 3(a). However, in CCC we have a much more interesting story described in diagram Fig. 4(b)

(i) From argument arrow g we can derive arrow g^λ by Currying;

(ii) We apply this arrows to x (i.e., compose it with x) and get an element/evidence $g^\lambda(x)$ of implicational claim $B{\Rightarrow}C$;

(iii) Unpacking $g^\lambda(x)$ gives us an argument from B to C as shown;

(iv) We complete this argument with evidence y and get the lower arc arrow. Steps 3. and 4. can be combined in one Meta-ModusPonens step, hence the second := in the label on the lower arc arrow.

A key difference in completing the argument as in (b) is that Currying allows us first complete it with the first evidence x and pack the result as an argument definition given by the upper arc arrow; the latter can then be unpacked and completed with the second evidence y. Alternatively, we could begin with Currying w.r.t. the second entry port and form $g^{\lambda'}: B \to A{\Rightarrow}C$, complete it with y, unpack, and finish completion with x thus obtaining $g''(x, y) := x; g''(\_, y) := (g^{\lambda'}(y))_{MP}(x)$ It follows from CCC equations that all three completions specified above are equal,

$$g(x, y) = g'(x, y) = g''(x, y),$$

which can be written in the following suggestive form:

$$g(x, y) = g(x, \_)(y) = g(\_, y)(x) \qquad \text{(Binary Interleaving)}$$

164

i.e., completing a binary argument at once with both arguments as on diagram (a), or consecutively one after the other (with packing in-between) as in diagram (b), or consecutively with the other order of completion, result in the same evidence for the conclusion C denoted by $g(x, y)$.

Suppose now that we have a ternary argument $g \colon A_1 \wedge A_2 \wedge A_3 \to C$. Using associativity of conjunction, $(A_1 \wedge A_2) \wedge A_3 \cong A_1 \wedge (A_2 \wedge A_3)$, we can proceed as above inductively: first consider g as $g_{12} \colon (A_1 \wedge A_2) \wedge A_3 \to C$ and proceed with $g_{12}^{\wedge} \colon A_1 \wedge A_2 \to A_3 \Rightarrow C$ and apply binary interleaving to g_{12} to show $g(x, y, z) = g'_{12}(x, y, z) = g''_{12}(z, x, y)$, and so on. Care should be taken with conjunction's associativity which, in general as a categorical product, holds up to isomorphism. Then to obtain equality in the interleaving equations we need to consider arrows up to equivalence as is typical for managing coherence conditions if we want equalities between argument arrows (1-arrows) rather than 2-arrow isomorphisms between 1-arrows. A precise arrangement will appear elsewhere, but it is clear that with a suitable equivalence relation between arguments, we can connect their entry ports with evidence arrows in any order so that the following equations hold:

$$g(x_1, ..., x_n) = g(\_, x_2, ..., x_n)(x_1) = ... = g(x_1, ..., \_{}_i, ..., x_n)(x_i) = ...$$
$$\text{(Interleaving)}$$

Howard-Curry isomorphism mentioned above for Cartesian categorys holds also for CCC and acquires a richer content. Now it says that logic as a theory of deduction, and typed lambda-calculus as a theory of function's application, are basically isomorphic. Specifically, the so called deduction theorem in logical systems is a counterpart of so called functional completeness of functional systems (e.g., typed lambda calculus), and they both are instances of some abstract algebraic property of CCCs (usually referred to as functional completeness too) —this is discussed in detail in [17].

4.2.1 Building assurance cases via CCC.

We finish this section with an instance of diagram Fig. 4(b), which formally specifies the substitution schema discussed in Section 3.2 (the part of the diagram with thin black and blue dashed arrows); the main schema considered in Section 2 is also shown by thick black arrows. The former actually implements the latter: two lower dashed arc arrows are equal to their thick black counterparts.

In this diagram, node $\mathsf{allChecks}(\mathcal{P}rod^{\boldsymbol{w}})$ denotes the claim $\bigwedge_{\mathbf{A}_i^{\boldsymbol{w}} \in \mathcal{T}heory} \mathcal{P}rod_{w,i} \models \mathbf{A}_i^{\boldsymbol{w}}$, node $\mathsf{allChecks}(\mathit{thisP})$ is claim $\bigwedge_{t \in \mathcal{T}est}$ $\mathsf{Check}(\mathit{thisP}, \mathrm{t})$, and arrow $\overrightarrow{\mathbf{T}(\_, \_)}$ is the closure of the argument/inference tree (see Section 3.2) when all arrows the tree consists of are composed. To complete $\overrightarrow{\mathbf{T}(\_, \_)}$, we can substitute all evidence arrows, i.e., connect them

165

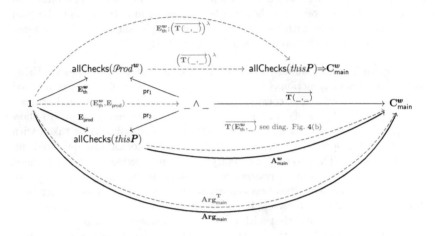

Figure 5. CCC and standardization of assurance

to entry ports, all at once, or consecutively in one or another order. The schema shown in Fig. 5 assumes that first all side assumption evidences were substituted (on the Standard side), the resulting argument is packed as shown by the upper dashed arrow (and shipped to the OEM). Then it is unpacked (on the OEM side) as shown by the dashed blue arrow below $\overrightarrow{\mathbf{T}(\_,\_)}$, and completed with product evidence, which completes the assurance case. An abstract view of the story shown by thick arrows is nothing but the Main schema discussed in Sect. 2 (specifically, Modus Ponens used in the Main Argument on p. 8 is the Meta-MP specified above).

5   Related Work and Conclusions

The triple name, *Claim-Argument-Evidence*, of an assurance framework developed by Adelard [5] is itself an excellent core schema of assurance, which makes it directly amenable to categorical formalization and was impactful for this paper. The idea that an assurance argument can be seen as a fully deductive part supported by (inductive?) evidence had been promoted by John Rushby [22] but more as a conjecture and a goal to be achieved; now we see how it can really be done. The idea of collecting all side assumptions into a side theory is mentioned in the recent manifest [6], but was not elaborated. There are several papers that claim formalization of the argument flow without actually being such and hence are not cited here. I am not aware of argument formalization based on CCC.

Overall, formalization of assurance cases has a bad reputation (perhaps deserved) in some assurance circles. For example, in his brief, clear and elegant online course on assurance [13], in Module 5 called Speculations, Michael Holloway presents two lists of research areas: one ranges them by perceived popularity in the assurance literature, and the other ranges them by practical usefulness; both lists have eight members. Formalization of arguments is placed second in the first list, and is the last in the second list. The present author shares this general scepticism about the usefulness of semi-baked formalizations that can be found in the assurance literature. Creating a formal or wider a mathematical model is a design problem, and as such needs a systematic approach based on appropriate design patters to be realized by people with a suitable background; ad hoc solutions rarely work well for design as has always been emphasized by Tom. On the other hand, several authoritative assurance authors stress the necessity of making assurance more rigorous and formal than it is now: John Rushby in [21], Robin Bloomfield and John Rushby in [6], and Tom Maibaum and his former students, Valentin Cassano and Silvia Grigorova, in [7]; specifically, the latter paper vigorously calls for explicit, precise and well-founded assurance arguments.

Possible practical applications of the framework developed in the present paper can be divided into i) conceptual and methodological, and ii) facilitating AC writing with a suitable tool support. For the former group, the following list of guesses seems reasonable.

a) A clear and simple formal model of connecting evidence to argument (logically and functionally, it is substitution, algebraically – arrow composition) should help to think about assurance in a clear way and surely will be useful educationally. Specifically, this fundamental operation finally obtains its own name (argument completion) and can be referred to explicitly and unambiguously; this should help to write and read the assurance literature.

b) Making side assumptions the first-class citizens of the assurance land, who play a fundamental role in the argument flow, would definitely clarify the argument, and make it far more explicit and rigorous.

c) The CCC framework provides two equivalent and mutually transferable views of the assurance inference: type-theoretical/logical based on the typed lambda calculus (everything is a substitution), and categorical/algebraic (everything is arrow composition). The possibility to switch the glasses depending on the context usually helps to see the subject matter clearer and helps thinking about it. If writing assurance cases needs clear thinking, this CCC-facility may be useful.

d) Staged completion, and new possibilities of assurance standardization it opens, are perhaps the most unexpected consequences of the CCC formalization. The current either-or practice of assurance standardization (an AC is fully built on either the standard side or the OEM side) seems to be too rigid for our time of "daily" appearance of new complex systems that

167

need a trustworthy assurance. The either-or arrangement inevitably lead to the trend of writing AC fully on the OEM side, which is suboptimal if there is an option of sharing AC writing between the OEM and the Standard.

As for the second group ii) of possible applications, any accurate formalization based on an established mathematical framework is potentially useful for creating an effective tool support. However, it may but not necessarily guarantee such, and to avoid speculations, let us postpone this discussion until (and if) some tooling is created. Moreover, papers on WF^+ argue and show that automation of AC writing and maintenance is even necessarily due to the necessity to maintain a huge array of traceability links. It implies that thinking about automation seriously does need considering dataflow as a major actor in AC: assurance reasoning is to be reasoning over data structures and dataflow. This side of the story is so far beyond the framework developed in the paper, and automation thus requires an integration of CCC and WF^+. This is our future work.

Acknowledgement. I am grateful to Tom for several expository and fruitful discussions of safety reasoning several years ago. Despite their emphasis on logic, my own activity in the area went on the process-dataflow side of the subject (known in McSCert circles as Workflow$^+$), and hence special thanks go to Alan Wassyng and Mark Lawford who kept my interest in the safety argument subject alive. Alan had always been stressing the crucial importance of assurance argumentation in making WF^+ a truly foundational framework for assurance, and Mark never hesitated to emphasize the necessity to relate WF^+ to GSN and hence, to safety argumentation if we are serious about practical applications of our theories. I am also indebted to Nick Annable, and Alan again, for several stimulating discussions of argument flow in the WF^+context, and to Valentin Cassano for several early discussions of inductive logic. The last but not the least, I am truly grateful to Editors of this volume for the invitation to write a paper for it, and their endless patience during endless re-engineering of the paper and delays in its submission.

References

[1] Adelard safety case development manual. Technical report, 1998. `http://www.adelard.com/resources/ascad/`.

[2] Nicholas Annable. A model-based approach to formal assurance cases. Master's thesis, McSCert, Dept. of Computing and Software, McMaster Univ., 2020.

[3] Nicholas Annable, Alison Bayzat, Zinovy Diskin, Mark Lawford, Richard Paige, and Alan Wassyng. Model-driven safety of autonomous vehicles. In *proc. of CSER*, 2020.

[4] R. Bloomfield and B. Littlewood. Multi-legged arguments: The impact of diversity upon confidence in dependability arguments. In *International Conference on Dependable*

Systems and Networks (DSN'03), pages 25–34. IEEE, 2003.

[5] Robin Bloomfield and Peter Bishop. Safety and assurance cases: Past, present and possible future – an adelard perspective. In Chris Dale and Tom Anderson, editors, *Making Systems Safer*, pages 51–67. Springer London, 2010.

[6] Robin Bloomfield and John Rushby. Assurance 2.0. *CoRR*, abs/2004.10474, 2020.

[7] Valentín Cassano, Thomas S. E. Maibaum, and Silviya Grigorova. *Towards Making Safety Case Arguments Explicit, Precise, and Well Founded*, pages 227–258. Springer Singapore, Singapore, 2021.

[8] Zinovy Diskin, Nicholas Annable, Alan Wassyng, and Mark Lawford. Assurance via workflow+ modelling and conformance. *CoRR*, abs/1912.09912, 2019.

[9] Zinovy Diskin, Tom Maibaum, Alan Wassyng, Stephen Wynn-Williams, and Mark Lawford. Assurance via model transformations and their hierarchical refinement. In Andrzej Wasowski, Richard F. Paige, and Øystein Haugen, editors, *Proceedings of the 21th ACM/IEEE International Conference on Model Driven Engineering Languages and Systems, MODELS 2018, Copenhagen, Denmark, October 14-19, 2018*, pages 426–436. ACM, 2018.

[10] DO-178C. *Software Considerations in Airborne Systems and Equipment Certification.* Requirements and Technical Concepts for Aviation (RTCA), Washington, DC, 2011.

[11] Barry Goodno and James Gere. *Mechanics of Materials*. Cengage Learning, 9th edition, 2018.

[12] Stefan Gruner, Apurva Kumar, Tom Maibaum, and Markus Roggenbach. *On the Construction of Engineering Handbooks - with an Illustration from the Railway Safety Domain*. Springer Briefs in Computer Science. Springer, 2020.

[13] C. Michael Holloway. Understanding assurance cases. Technical report, NASA Langley Research Center, 2020. https://shemesh.larc.nasa.gov/arg/uac.html.

[14] C. Michael Holloway and Patrick Graydon. Explicate '78: Assurance case applicability to digital systems. Technical Report DOT/FAA/TC-17/67, NASA, 2018.

[15] ISO 26262. *Road vehicles – Functional safety*. Int. Organization for Standardization, Geneva, Switzerland, 2018.

[16] Vladimir A. Kolupaev. *Equivalent Stress Concept for Limit State Analysis*. Advanced Structured Materials. Springer, 2018.

[17] Lambek, J., and Scott, P. *Introduction to Higher-Order Categorical Logic*. CUP, 1986. Revision 2.

[18] Jean Piaget, Gil Henriques, and Edgar Ascher. *Morphisms and categories. Comparing and Transforming*. Lawrence Elbaum Associates, Publishers, 2009.

[19] H. Rasiowa and R. Sikorski. *The Mathematics of Metamathematics*. Monografie matematyczne. Polish Scientific Publ., 1970.

[20] David Rinehart, John Knight, and Jonathan Rowanhill. Current practices in constructing and evaluating assurance cases with applications to aviation. Technical Report NASA/CR–2015-218678, NASA, 2015.

[21] John Rushby. On the interpretation of assurance case arguments. In *New Frontiers in Artificial Intelligence - JSAI-isAI 2015 Workshops, LENLS, JURISIN, AAA, HAT-MASH, TSDAA, ASD-HR, and SKL (Revised Selected Papers)*, volume 10091 of *LNCS*, pages 331–347, 2015.

[22] John Rushby. Understanding and evaluating assurance cases. Technical Report SRI-CSL-15-01, SRI International, 2015.

[23] S. Toulmin. *The Uses of Argument*. Cambridge University Press, 2003.

[24] Turski, W., and Maibaum, T. *The Specification of Computer Programs*. Addison-Wesley, 1987. Revision 2.

[25] Union®, A WireCo® WorldGroup Brand. Wire Rope User's Handbook. Technical report, 2000.

[26] Walter Vincenti. *What Engineers Know and How They Know It: Analytical Studies from Aeronautical History*. Johns Hopkins Studies in the History of Technology, 1993.

[27] Fredrik Warg, Martin Gassilewski, Jörgen Tryggvesson, Viacheslav Izosimov, Anders Werneman, and Rolf Johansson. Defining autonomous functions using iterative hazard analysis and requirements refinement. In Amund Skavhaug, Jérémie Guiochet, Erwin Schoitsch, and Friedemann Bitsch, editors, *Computer Safety, Reliability, and Security -*

SAFECOMP 2016 Workshops, ASSURE, DECSoS, SASSUR, and TIPS, Trondheim, Norway, September 20, 2016, Proceedings, volume 9923 of *Lecture Notes in Computer Science*, pages 286–297. Springer, 2016.

A   Appendix. Example of Assurance: Super-Problem Solving (SPS) with Coffee and Beer

The goal of this section is to develop a simple example illustrating ideas developed in the paper. Creating a good example in the assurance domain is notoriously difficult as the very nature of assurance requires attention to details, and a more or less reasonable AC (assurance case) for even a very simple product is quickly growing into a bulky document, whose writing and reading consumes significant time and effort. Creating an example for the present volume is even more difficult due to an understandable requirement to make it somehow entertaining and interesting yet corresponding to the serious nature of the assurance business. Actually such integration is never easy in any technical domains but, in general, possible as shown Tom's and Wlad Turski's early monograph [24], which presents an encouraging sample of skillful weaving seriousness and entertainment. The monograph is devoted to a fundamental software problem but is written in an easy to grasp and light-weight style combining witty belletristic pieces and deep scientific discussions not outdated even today after more than thirty years after its publication.

Our route for sailing between the Scylla of seriousness and the Charybdis of entertainment will be as follows. We will address assurance of an entertaining dependability claim for a product that is easy to mold to show non-trivial concerns of inductive logic and their management in an AC, but the logic of the domain will be built along the lines of a real assurance domain—assuring structural strength and safety of mechanical systems based on the so called *safety factor (SF)* approach (e.g., see [11]). The parallelism of two assurance logics will be taken very seriously so that it would not be too difficult to translate our AC example in Fig. A.2 into a top general part of a real AC on mechanical strength. We will begin with a primer on the safety factor approach to assuring mechanical strength in Sect. A.1, then translate it into the SPS domain in Sect. A.2, and finish with an AC in Sect. A.3

A.1   Mini-primer on assurance of mechanical strength

Non-functional safety is an established part of the assurance industry, e.g., it is a central notion of a classical engineering branch—mechanical strength of materials. It is much simpler than functional safety as the interaction between the system (a crane, a bridge, or a building) and its environment amounts to the loads (forces and moments) on structural elements of the system, and for the classical (non-probabilistic) strength assurance that does not take material

170

fatigue into account, system's reaction to a load is plainly Boolean: either the system sustains the load or breaks. This simplicity is however much illusory as there are different types of loads (static, dynamic, high-frequency cyclic and low-frequency cyclic) to which system reacts differently, and it is often an issue to find the maximal possible load (e.g., the load caused by winds), and materials typically deteriorate more or less progressively due to corrosion and other environmental factors whose effect is inherently difficult to predict and measure in a numerical way. The result is that the logic of assuring mechanical safety is still a complex issue being studied and debated in mechanics of materials under the name of the *safety factor* approach [11,16]. The principal idea is to build systems intentionally much stronger than it follows from their strain and stress analysis to take into account the inherently approximate nature of such analyses and deterioration of materials' strength mentioned above, and to allow for unexpected and emergent loads.

The scientific side of the story encompasses theoretical and experimental issues of mechanics of materials and structural mechanics. The practical side includes (enormous) national and international standardization activities on material properties and normative documents regulating required strength reserve of constructions. It also includes our subject matter – assurance cases — as to release a mechanical system design for production and use, the engineers must write a safety case showing that the system has sufficient strength for its intended safe use. In parallel to functional safety, non-functional strength assurance is a challenge due to major uncertainties and hence the inductive logic nature of the problem: it is impossible formally prove that a system is mechanically safe, all you can do is to provide more or less convincing evidence that the system can sustain the intended load.

To assure that a product P (a crane, bridge, building, car's body, aircraft's fuselage) has sufficient strength for its safe use in the world w, engineers do the following analyses:

(i) *Load analysis*: analyze the interaction of the product with the environments and specify a set of maximally possible loads $\mathcal{L}^w(P)$,

(ii) *Static analysis and Load decomposition, Strain and Stress Analysis*: For each load $L \in \mathcal{L}^w(P)$, evaluate stresses and strains in P's elements based on their geometrical and physical parameters and the way they are joined together, which results, for each element X of the product, in

   b1) load L_X on the element X, whose sum $\sum_{X \in P} L_X$ balances product's load L,[7],

---

[7] notation $X \in P$ actually means that X is an element of the functional architecture of the product, i.e., $X \in \mathsf{FA}(P)$; we will use such simple notations as abbreviations to shorten formulas

b2) stresses $\sigma_L(x)$ under load L_X for each point $x \in X$, whose sum $\sum_{x \in X} \sigma_L(x)$ balances L_X;[8]

(iii) **Determine realized safety factors**: For each element $X \in P$, find the maximal value $\sigma_L^{maxReal}(X) := \mathrm{Max}_{x \in X} \sigma_L(x)$ and calculate the *realized safety factor*

$$\mathsf{SF}_L^{real}(X) := \sigma^{maxAdm}(X) / \sigma_L^{maxReal}(X) \qquad (\text{A.1})$$

where $\sigma^{maxAdm}(X)$ is the maximal stress admissible by the material of element X (before it yields for ductile materials like steel or breaks for inelastic materials like concrete).

If all the analyses involved into finding the realized safety factor would be extremely precise and dependable, safety could be assured by requiring $\mathsf{SF}_L^{real}(X)$ to be more than 1 for all L and all X. However, there is a whole range of factors (see subsection A.1.1. below) inherited in the analyses above, which make the determined value of $\mathsf{SF}_L^{real}(X)$ a more or less rough approximation of the real strength reserved in the given design of element X. It implies that safety is to be assured by requiring $\mathsf{SF}_L^{real}(X)$ to be much greater than 1, but how much greater? Hence the need in the next analysis.

(iv) **Determine the required safety factor** of element X, $\mathsf{SF}_w^{req}(X)$, based on the type of X (is it a cable, or a bolt, shaft, ...), the entire product type (a crane, a hoist, a bridge, an aircraft, ...) and the type of interaction with the world (e.g., a road heavy-traffic bridge across a river in a northern territory, a heavy lifting hoist, an inter-state aircraft); Fig. A.1 below (taken from an informational resource https://www.engineeringtoolbox.com/) gives the idea. In the notation of Section 3, the required $\mathsf{SF}_w^{req}(X)$ depends on the element's ("local") product type $\mathscr{P}rod_i^w(X)$, the entire product type $\mathscr{P}rod^w(P)$, and their interaction with our world w so that we can write

$$\mathsf{SF}_w^{req}(X, P) = \mathsf{SF}^{req}(\mathscr{P}rod_i^w(X), \mathscr{P}rod^w(P)). \qquad (\text{A.2})$$

(v) **Assure the top claim**: Product P is considered to be safe for its intended use if the inequality
$$\mathsf{SF}_L^{real}(X) > \mathsf{SF}_w^{req}(X, P)$$
holds for each load $L \in \mathscr{L}^w(P)$ and for each element $X \in P$.

A.1.1   A.1.1. Choice of the required safety factor.

Setting a proper value of $\mathsf{SF}_w^{req}(X)$ is a highly non-trivial problem. If it is too low, X's safety is compromised, but making it too big would unnecessarily increase the sizes, the weight and hence the cost of X; moreover, being multiplied

---

[8] again, $x \in X$ means that x is a point in the geometrical solid associated with element X; the latter encapsulates geometrical and physical parameters, and a functional goal

Equipment	SF_w^{req}
Aircraft Component	1.5-2.5
Bolts	8.5
Cast-iron wheels	20
Engine components	6-8
Heavy duty shafting	10-12
Lifting equip./hooks	8-9
Turbine components/static	6-8
Turbine components/rotate	2-3
Spring, large heavy-duty	4.5
Structural steel work/buildings	4-6
Structural steel work/bridges	5-7

Figure A.1. Typical required SFs

by the number of elements in the product, it would significantly increase the sizes, the weight and the cost of the product, and its transportation, installation, maintenance in a cascading way. A reasonable compromise between high safety guarantees and costs is a necessity and challenge of mechanical and civil engineering. Here is a direct quote from the textbook [11]: "The determination of a factor of safety must take into account such matters as the following: probability of accidental overloading of the structure by loads that exceed the design loads; types of loads (static or dynamic); whether the loads are applied once or are repeated; how accurately the loads are known; possibilities for fatigue failure; inaccuracies in construction; variability in the quality of workmanship; variations in properties of materials; deterioration due to corrosion or other environmental effects; accuracy of the methods of analysis; whether failure is gradual (ample warning) or sudden (no warning); consequences of failure (minor damage or major catastrophe); and other such considerations. Because of these complexities and uncertainties, factors of safety must be determined on a probabilistic basis. They usually are established by groups of experienced engineers who write the codes and specifications used by other designers, and sometimes they are even enacted into law. The provisions of codes and specifications are intended to provide reasonable levels of safety without unreasonable costs." (The inset table is taken from an educational and informational resource https://www.engineeringtoolbox.com/)

A.2 Super Problem Solving (SPS) Assurance

A.2.1 A.2.1 The SPS story.

Suppose some research centre is going to create several teams to attack the most challenging technical problems of our time such as design of a flying car or colonizing Mars. To obtain funding, the centre needs to assure the granting agency that the teams to be created, and the way of their management, can indeed provide a high confidence in teams' capabilities to solve such super-problems. In other words, the centre needs to build an assurance case demonstrating that its teams are *Super-Problem Solvers* (SPS). One factor of a team's SPS property is clear: team members are to be super-strong researchers whose joint work is properly organized. However, it is not enough: to attack super-problems, researchers are to be in an active and focused working shape for a long time, and the centre has developed a novel approach to achieve and maintain such a state of a team member. In developing its SPS-knowhow, the centre used structural similarities between how a mechanical system reacts to and sustains its loads, and how a research team reacts to and attacks a super-problem. These similarities are documented in Table A.1 in a self-explained way.

Nevertheless, as it was underlined in the assurance case prepared by the centre, the parallelism described by the table is not more than an analogy and SPS-assurance has its own logic and process.

A.2.2 A.2.2 SPS-Assurance: Notation

Notation for ACs deserves a special discussion. As a typical AC involves quite a number of claims (logical statements) of rather different semantic meaning, we have a problem. On the one hand, the essence of AC is manipulation with multiple claims but with an explicit record of what goes where; to ease this traceability, claims should be given short names that ease their identification in different places of AC, e.g., C_1, C_2 etc. for claims of one type, and B_1, B_2 etc. for claims of another type as is typical for mathematics (as an art of pushing symbols). On the other hand, classification of claims in a typicla AC may be rather challenging, and even if it is done somehow, the number of claim types would be so big that the only way to ease the recovery of claims' meaning seems to be giving them long meaningful names. The author is not aware of whether this problem is addressed in the assurance literature in a systematic way (if at all), but it needs to be solved somehow for our AC, which is although simple but still involves 20 claims. An additional requirement to make the case compact enough to fit in one page of the paper amplifies the problem even more. Without any pretension to universality and applicability beyond the present paper, the notational discipline used for the case is as follows.

There are two special variables: T for a generic research team the case is about and X for T's members so that we will omit explicit mentioning $X \in \mathsf{members}(T)$. Variables T' and X' will refer to any team of type $\mathcal{T}^{\boldsymbol{w}}$ and any researcher of type $\mathcal{X}^{\boldsymbol{w}}$ resp., where $\boldsymbol{w}$ is a constant referring to our world as before. All claims are instances of the following general formal:

$$[\mathsf{ClaimType}]^{[\mathsf{ClaimName}]}_{[\mathsf{ClaimQualifier}]}(var1, var2, ...) : \quad \begin{array}{l} \text{Definition of the claim by a short tex-} \\ \text{tual description or a formula} \end{array}$$

(Claim Format)

There are three instances of [ClaimType]: claims about teams, for which [ClaimType] is denoted by $\mathbf{C}$, claims about researchers denoted by C, and side assumptions, either about the world or the centre, denoted by $\mathbf{A}$. For example, formula $\mathbf{C}^{\mathsf{SPS}}_{\mathsf{team}}(T, \boldsymbol{w})$ is to be read as a statement about a team (namely, T), which claims that T has SPS property formulated for teams (note the qualifier team), while formula $C^{\mathsf{SPS}}_{\mathsf{person}}(X, \boldsymbol{w})$ is to be read as a statement about a researcher (namely, X), which claims that X has the researcher-oriented version of the SPS-property (note the qualifier person). There is some redundancye.g., both the qualifier team and the variable T point to the same type but it may be useful for type-checking (think of AC with hundreds of claims), and allows for omitting variables if needed. Note also that both claims are indexed by constant $\boldsymbol{w}$; in fact all claims depend on $\boldsymbol{w}$ and the latter could thus be omitted and assumed by default, but perhaps it makes sense to keep it for clarity and as a reminder about the inductive nature of the assurance business.

A.2.3   A.2.3 SPS-Assurance: The Argument and its completion.

The argument is specified in Fig. A.2 as a CAE-hierarchy: claims are specified in dog-eared rectangles (as representatives of the UML constraints), and argument steps are enumerated (AS_i, $i = 1, 2, ...$) and placed into parallelograms as is usual for CAE/GSN. As explained at the beginning of Section 3, pink claims are constraints for a generic team T that for a concrete team instance $thisT$ can turn into valid statements and become green or fail and become red. Side assumptions about the world are all assumed trustworthy upfront and thus coloured green. Their "greeness" is supported by evidence not shown in Fig. A.2 to save space, but in a correct AC, colouring a leaf/port claim green means the existence of evidence supporting the claim. In Section 3 we have also used suggestive checkmark symbols $\checkmark$, which are omitted here. Note thin grey frames of side assumptions that point to the their inductive nature. Two side assumptions for step AS_5, A5' and A5", are statements about the Centre and their greeness is also supported by the evidence not shown in the figure. If there are precise specifications of the parameters determining the trustworthiness of the claims (e.g., "variability of coffee types and flavours", etc) and their qualities ("sufficient") in measurable terms, these claims can be considered mechanically verifiable; hence their thick blue frames.

Now let us consider the argument flow and begin with step AS1. This step derives a strong inductive claim about team T from two weaker claims. Is it a

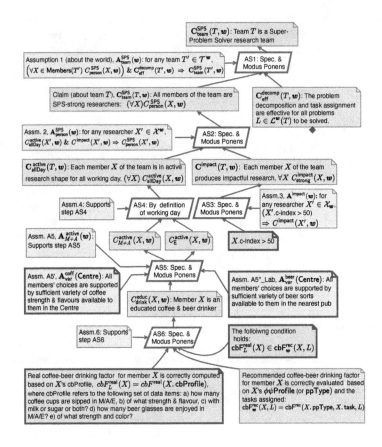

Figure A.2. Argument assuring a generic team T is SPS

justifiable step? It seems reasonable but we may miss an important premise, e.g., the availability of funding. If there is a team, say, *thisT*, satisfying the two premises but failing to be an SPS team (as demonstrated by its failure to solve some super-problem), then *thisT* would be a defeater for step AS1. If a further investigation would find that *thisT* did not have enough finding, then we would add to step AS1 the third premise claiming funding as a necessary factor and fix the issue. Another potential problem with step AS1 is how to assure the effectiveness of problem decomposition: this claim is excluded from further consideration in the case (note the diamond symbol below it playing the role of a stub), and we also excluded an important claim that the set $\mathcal{L}^{\boldsymbol{w}}(T)$ of problems is complete. There are several possibilities the step AS1 can fail in the sense that the premises are trustworthy while the conclusion is not—this is the nature of inductive logic. However, we encapsulate the strength and the weakness of the step in its side assumption: the step is always syntactically correct as being based on a valid inference rule Modus Ponens, and a semantic failure of the step means a corresponding failure of the side assumption. An advantage of this approach is uniformity and clarity: we always know what should be fixed. Other steps besides AS4 work in a similar way, and we can even omit the description of their side assumptions: they can be routinely derived from the premises and the conclusion. Step AS4 is just a little bit more complex: "by definition" means that we deal with a bidirectional equivalence rather than unidirectional implication in that the quality of being active all working day is merely defined as being active in the morning, afternoon and in the evening so the conclusion is logically equivalent to the conjunction of the two premises. This equivalence is based on the side assumption that states Day=M+A+E while night is not included irrespective to whatever challenging problem is being solved by the team. Thus, the logic as such, i.e., inference, of the AC is trivial—each step is based on Modus Ponens or equivalence. What makes a step non-trivial is finding its underlying decomposition structure and evidence supporting the side assumption justifying such decomposition.

Note also the overall flow of the case from "very inductive" top claims about the team towards claims about members of the team in the middle (where we omitted the universal quantification over them) towards more verifiable claims in the bottom. The final distinction between the realized factor $\mathsf{cbF}_L^{real}(X)$ factor shown as mechanically verifiable and the recommended (required) factor cbF_w^{rec} shown inductive is typical for the safety case approach. However complex are strain and stress analyses for complex structures like, say, a car's body or an aircraft's fuselage, powerful numeric methods like FEA allows to do them with sufficient accuracy, r at least properly estimate the degree of inaccuracy. Although making them really verifiable would need further going down in the tree, perhaps sufficiently far down, it is clear how to do decomposition and finally arrive at verifiability (which typically includes the team competence in the analyses performed, e.g., FEA, and certification of software used for those analyses). In contrast, required (recommended) safety factor summarizes a whole set of hardly measurable, uncertain and fuzzy factors, and thus inherently resists mechanical verifiability. Reduction of such claims to evidence is more problematic but is typically achieved be referring to the previous experience, established trustworthy patterns, careful standardization and other means from this (non-analytical) compartment of the engineering toolbox. The trustworthiness of this way of assuring the conclusion is to be based on the corresponding side assumptions. In this way, the argument tree finally reaches the (considered to be) verifiable set of leaves, for which an appropriate evidence can be presented. This would make the leaves green, and hence all the tree green by completing the argument steps as explained in the paper.

Mechanical strength	Research power
System/product P is *Safe*, if it is capable to sustain all most hazardous loads L from set $\mathcal{L}^{\boldsymbol{w}}(P)$.	Research team T is a *Super-Problem Solver* (SPS) if it is capable to solve all most difficult research problems L in set $\mathcal{L}^{\boldsymbol{w}}(T)$ of such problems assigned to the team.
Load decomposition: A product oad L is decomposed into element's loads L_X for each element X of product P.	*Problem decomposition*: Given team's goal — super-problem L, each team member X is assigned with her own set of tasks $\mathsf{Task}_L(X)$ such that if each team member fulfils all his tasks, the problem is solved. (Think of a set of tasks $\mathsf{Task}_L(X)$ as a distribution of load L_X.)
Product P is Safe under load L if each element X is safe under its part of the load L_X.	Team T is SPS if all its members are SPS, i.e., each member X is capable to solve all tasks $\mathsf{Task}_L(X)$ assigned to her. To simplify presentation, a crucial factor of a properly organized teamwork is omitted.
Element X's load L_X strains and deforms it, which creates an internal stress distribution $\sigma_L^{\text{real}}(x)$, $x \in X$, computed with elasticity theory methods, e.g., FEA (Finite Element Analysis). The internal stress balances the load L_X unless its value exceeds the element's material limits. Hence, the level of element's strength is measured by its *realized Safety Factor*, $\mathsf{SF}_L^{\text{real}}(X) = \sigma^{\text{maxAdm}}(X)/\sigma_L^{\text{maxReal}}(X)$ which is to be more than 1.	Member's task set $\mathsf{Task}_L(X)$ increases coffee consumption during the day time, which is complemented with a reasonable beer consumption in the evening.[a] This allows the member to be intellectually active all the day, which along with the member's high research capabilities measured by his/her citation index, c-index(X), ensures the task completion. The level of coffee-beer consumption of a member X solving problem L is measured by his *coffee-beer Factor*, $\mathsf{cbF}_L^{\text{real}}(X)$, computed by a special algorithm (a specialization of FEA to the coffee-beer consumption problem), which inputs data from X's coffee-beer consumption profile and returns $\mathsf{cbF}_L^{\text{real}}(X)$. However, to keep the member active and productive all day, factor $\mathsf{cbF}_L^{\text{real}}(X)$ is to be kept within certain limits. [a] According to trustworthy scientific research, the human brain continues to attack a challenging problem subconsciously when the human being is relaxed. Moreover, a properly organized interleaving of the active-passive stages is key to brain's effectiveness.
To assure element's safety, its safety factor is required to be substantially more than 1 and satisfy the condition: $\mathsf{SF}_L^{\text{real}}(X) > \mathsf{SF}_{\boldsymbol{w}}^{\text{req}}(X, P)$ where element's *required safety factor* $\mathsf{SF}_{\boldsymbol{w}}^{\text{req}}(X, P)$ is to be computed based on X's and product's types and usage $\mathsf{SF}_{\boldsymbol{w}}^{\text{req}}(X, P) = \mathsf{SF}^{\text{req}}(X.\text{type}, P.\text{type}, \boldsymbol{w})$	To assure member's productivity, his cbF-factor is recommended to be within a certain interval $\mathsf{cbF}_L^{\text{real}}(X) \in \mathsf{cbF}_{\boldsymbol{w}}^{\text{rec}}(X, L)$ called *recommended cfFactor*. This interval $\mathsf{cbF}_{\boldsymbol{w}}^{\text{rec}}(X)$ is computed based on X's physiological and psychological type, $X.\phi\psi\text{type}$, the type of tasks to perform (e.g., machine learning, control theory, etc.), and the goal problem L (e.g., autonomous driving, space travelling, etc.), $\mathsf{cbF}_{\boldsymbol{w}}^{\text{rec}}(X, L) = \mathsf{cbF}^{\text{rec}}(X.\phi\psi\text{type}, X.\text{tasks.type}, L)$. The third argument is included to compensate possible inaccuracies in the problem decomposition into tasks as additional tasks or difficulties in performing the original tasks can be revealed during the course of the project.

Table A.1

Comparison of the two assurance domains

Effectiveness and Programmability

In Defense of a Relational Notion of Computation

Javier Blanco

Universidad Nacional de Córdoba, Argentina
javier.blanco@unc.edu.ar

Pío García

Universidad Nacional de Córdoba, Argentina
pio.garcia@unc.edu.ar

Abstract

We focus on the distinction between effectiveness and programmability. We propose that effectiveness can be understood in terms of a mechanistic account which may also assume an axiomatic approach. Programmability can be, in turn, analyzed as the characteristic feature of a relational account of computation. A system will be called *computational* if it is both effective and programmable and, furthermore, being computational will turn out to be a gradual concept that depends on the degree of programmability of a system. We show that many fundamental questions in philosophy of computing can be better addressed from this perspective.

1 Introduction

In order to solve the Entscheidungsproblem, Turing had to accurately characterize the notion of effectiveness. He addressed this problem by defining what a computable function is, and identified effectively calculable with computable functions [17]. The computable functions were defined by reducing the calculation procedures to a small set of elementary steps to be carried out by a human computer. Although his main interest was this analysis of computation, he also presented, in the same article in 1936/37, the construction of a universal machine, i.e. a machine whose behavior will be determined as part of the input, a machine that can imitate the input-output behavior of any other machine.

During the decade of 1930 many researchers were looking for a characterization of effectiveness, and there were some alternative definitions. Turing's became the most convincing one, although there is still some ongoing debate concerning the reasons of the almost unanimous acceptance [3]. Besides his analysis of human computation based on the limitations of human perception and memory, his construction of a universal machine was also unique, it did not appear in other works of that time. Whether or not it had some role in convincing the community of the correctness of his approach, it established the basis of

179

what would later became the programmable computers. Our claim here is that both notions, effectiveness and programmability should be analyzed separately in order to properly understand the interplay between mechanisms, programs and computations.

There have been also some well-known challenges to the notion of computation. Inspired by Hilary Putnam, John Searle has defended that any complex enough system can be seen as computing any function [15]. In this account, computation became only a way of interpreting a system. This trivializes the idea of computation and computer, and would "solve" the issue of whether a brain is a computer: it can be consider a computer because anything complex enough, for example a pail of water in the sun, would satisfy this criterium. We will show how the relational account of computation can be used to contest those challenges.

There were some attempts to distinguish effectiveness from computability. As Shapiro [16] remarks, effectiveness is an intensional concept, it expresses a property that applies to the definition of a function, to the way in which it is defined. On the contrary, the notion of computability is extensional. A function f is computable if there is an algorithm, or mechanical procedure, that computes f. This existencial presentation is ipso facto extensional. We claim that being computational can be considered as an intensional property as well, which implies that there can be two different systems which exhibit equivalent observable behaviors and that one may be considered computational and the other not. This could help also to clarify, among other things, the meaning of computer simulations. The simulation will be, according to this definition, a computational process, whereas the simulated system may not be so.

Furthermore, being computational will be for us a gradual notion, we will consider systems that are more or less computational. The degree of computationality of a system will be given by how programmable it is. This agrees with many considerations about the specific character of computers and computer science, with the history of the field and with current practices.

In summary, in the present article we will present an intensional account of computation. First, we will distinguish between effectiveness and programmability, as two essential aspects of computing. Then, we will suggest a way of characterizing the notions of effectiveness and programmability, and quickly survey some axiomatizations of their relevant properties which appeared in the literature. This very brief account is aimed at showing that the distinction we propose has been at work for a long time in the fields of logic and theoretical computer science. We believe that this kind of analysis has some advantages to address different problems in the philosophy of computing, in particular understanding what is computation and having precise criteria to determine when does a system, physical or abstract, compute. This may provide, also, a different key to understand or review many debates in fields related to philosophy of computing, like cognitive science or philosophy of technology.

2 Effectiveness and programmability

The hypothesis we suggest here is to consider two different concepts, which are applied in different domains, and whose conjunction gives rise to the idea of effective computing: on the one hand, the idea of effectiveness which seems to be, in principle, linked to mechanisms, on the other hand, a relational idea of computing, specified in terms of programmability. From this perspective "to compute" involves a constitutive relation between a codification or program and its behavior. This relation can take different forms according to the different systems, concrete or abstract, that implement computation. Both notions usually appeared intertwined, since many approaches are based either on a characterization of effectiveness defined in terms of a human following rules - being then in an implicit programming relation-, or they are based on a preset relation between indices and functions, and some properties of the operations on the indices are sought in order to achieve Turing-completeness. It makes sense to have non-programmable effective mechanisms and also sub-recursive sets of programs and even, perhaps, hyper-recursive ones. In these last cases, the properties of the relationship between indices and behaviors should be restated [1].

One can raise this question by considering that there is an intuitive notion of effectiveness associated with machines - from the functional structure of the machines - and a notion of effectiveness associated with procedures - in the tradition of calculation. Turing seems to exploit the confluence of those intuitions, but machine effectiveness was not analyzed until later. Another way to raise the question is by pointing out the difference between an extensional notion - computation- and an intensional concept -effectiveness-. As we said above, according to Shapiro, the issue about effectiveness is how to define or present, in this context, a function. In this sense effectiveness is an informal, "epistemic" and "pragmatic" notion. The intuitive character of effectiveness can be traced back to the strategy carried by Turing in 1936. Turing loosely links mathematical calculation with machines. In order to do this, he considers the procedures that a human being carries out to solve a calculation problem. He also qualifies this procedures as "mechanical". According to Kennedy [12], Gödel's view about the absoluteness of Turing's proposal was associated with their "intuitive" and non-circular character. It can be said that much of the strength about the intuition came from the images evoked by machines. A way to elucidate the relationship between effectiveness and a relational notion of computation is through the analysis of Copeland. In the context of the assessment of the scope of the Church-Turing thesis, Copeland propose the thesis M:

(M) Whatever can be calculated by a machine (working on finite released in accordance with a finite program of instructions) is Turing-machine-computable [4].

---

[1] In the next section we will develop this idea.

181

Following Copeland, there are two possible interpretations of the thesis M, depending on the type of machine considered. In a first interpretation, only physical restrictions are considered – those restrictions that conform to the known laws of the world. In a second interpretation of the thesis M, if we only take into account a notional machine, abstract restrictions are relevant. The believers in hyper-computation would claim that, under the first interpretation, the Church-Turing thesis may be false. An elucidation in terms of the type of restrictions imposed by kinds of machines is related to a "relative" notion of computing [5]. The scope of what is computable depends on the resources available. This is the reason why they distinguish between a computation that can be performed by a human being and a computation performed by a machine. An analysis of effectiveness and computation in terms of kinds of machines could be useful in some contexts, but it does not have the degree of generality required. A better approach can be established by changing the perspective and the categories of the problem. For the first task - changing the perspective- we can use Webb's analysis. For the second task we can use our distinction between effectiveness and programmability. Effectiveness can be elucidated in terms of mechanists restrictions, whether they are due to humans or machines. We may consider here what Webb calls Turing's thesis T:

(T) A procedure (function) is 'effective' just in case it can be simulated (computed) by a Turing machine [18].

In our approach, thesis T tells when a given procedure is effective, but does not necessarily mean that it is a computation. What is "computed" is what the Turing machine does thanks to a human computer following the instructions of its transition table. Clearly, there is plenty of examples of non-computational procedures that can be simulated by a Turing machine, or a computer. If they can be simulated, they can be considered effective, they can be described as mechanisms, at least in the sense that [10] gives to the word, but not necessarily as computational -programmable- mechanisms. An account of effective calculability describes a human computer performing elementary steps prescribed in a transition table. This presuppose a different nature or role for the instructions, the description of the algorithm, and the data upon which the computer operates. But the universal machine shows that in a precise sense both, programs and data, can coexist in a common domain. Computer science rests, in many respects, on this coexistence.

If a human or mechanical computer could execute only a very limited set of programs, if they do not understand all the instructions or they have external limits, we consider them to be less than computers, even if they can show at particular times some behavior equivalent to that of a full-fledged computer. Kleene's fixed point theorem shows that for any program p there is at least one input data (seen itself as another program) q for which it will behave exactly as the universal machine, it will interpret this program. This does not make p universal, this does not by itself make p a computational system.

Our proposal depends on how to characterize a relational account of computation. In earlier work, we have proposed the centrality of the concept of programmability to understand computational systems by means of a characterization of what we have called "interpreter", which is a slight generalization of the usual notion in computer science. The central idea is that an interpreter produces behaviors from a codification that accepts as input. The relations between such input, which we call program, and the prescribing behavior, can be characterized by a function of interpretation, i.e. the standard semantics of an interpreter. We present the main ideas in a very general an abstract way.

The notions of interpretation function and program are relational and inter-defined, i.e. an interpretation function is such when it prescribes behaviors from a given set of programs, it is an interpretation function for such a set; a program is such when there is an interpretation function for it. There is nothing intrinsic in being a program (Gödel numbers, for example, allows us to consider numbers as programs), it is only such in relation with the interpretation function. Hence, conceptually, interpretation function, program and also programming language are inter-definable. An interpretation function prescribes a behavior from some input, usually called program, that codifies it. More precisely, given a set B of possible behaviors and a set P of syntactic elements, an interpretation function is a surjective function $i : P \to B$ that assigns to a program $p \in P$ a behavior $b \in B$. When syntactic elements of P are constructed using some "language", we call it programming language. When B is a set of input-output behaviors, i is generally written down in its "uncurried" version as $i(p)(x) = d$.

The property of "being an interpreter" for given sets of programs and behaviors can be satisfied by different systems. The implementation relation can be realized in very different ways, not only by a computer with a von Neumann architecture. For instance, a DNA computer or a quantum computer which may have no structural resemblance with a traditional computer, or Babbage's analytical engine. Conversely, the same system can implement different interpretation functions. However not every system is a candidate to be considered an interpreter. At least its input subsystem must be modifiable to allow the reception of the program (and its input data) and the output subsystem should have enough different states in order to be able to recognize that a computation has been performed. The proofs or justifications of the concrete correspondence between the prescription and the performance of the system may require different methods, both mathematical and empirical, depending on the chosen implementation technology.

Our notion of interpreter generalizes its usual definition in the area of compiler and language theory where an interpreter is a program (for a digital computer). This generalized idea is implicit in some classic texts of computability, for example, in the book by Neil Jones, who speaks of a machine code interpreter (which obviously would not be a program but the mechanism of the hardware of a machine performing the normal execution cycle of instructions). The following quotation is from the book [11]:

"The "computing agent" then interprets the algorithm; it can be a piece of hardware, or it can be software: an interpreter program written in a lower-level programming language. Operationally, an interpreter maintains a pointer to the current instruction within the algorithm's instruction set, together with a representation of that algorithm's current storage state. Larger algorithms correspond to larger interpreted programs, but the interpreter itself remains fixed, either as a machine or as a program."

Given an (surjective) interpretation function $i : P \to B$, the degree of programmability of the system will be B, i.e. the set of possible behaviors for that codification. In most cases, B will be an infinite countable set, then the cardinality will not say much about it. Set inclusion can be used as an interesting (partial) order between computational systems. If we disregard hyper-computers, the order will have an equivalence class of top elements: the Turing-complete systems. Another partial order (interpreters compose) which sometimes coincides with set inclusion, but which is conceptually relevant, is considering a system A more programmable than B if there is an element in A which is an interpreter for B.

One can analyze different properties of codifications and behaviors, but it seems like a fertile starting point. In the next section, we mention some works that tried to found a theory of algorithms on this grounds. As Andrei Ershov stated it [7], any rigorous theory of algorithms should start by taking some elements of the domain as data and some operations on the objects to represent them as programs. Then we will need a single "superalgorithm" (an interpreter) which is uniformly applied to every program. He then identified effectiveness with certain "finiteness" conditions for this interpreter. We fully agree with this approach, and we believe it can have a wider scope than just recursive or computable functions.

The relational way of presenting computation supposes a usually accepted consequence, that there are procedures that have the relational structure of the computation but go beyond the computable - hypercomputation. But they also have another controversial consequence: that we could have effectiveness beyond computable relational procedures.

3   On axiomatizations

An old idea, stemming from Gödel in the early thirties, is to have axioms that capture the essence of effective computation and from them "demonstrate" the Church-Turing thesis. There have been two different ways to assess this challenge and to search for the right axioms. Building on works of computability theory, mainly Kleene's enumeration theorem, the first historical approach to axioms for effective computation are the Uniformly Reflective Structures developed by Wagner in the late sixties and continued in the works of Strong and Friedman, and with some different flavors Moschovakis and Fenstad [8]. In one way or another, all these works are concerned with the relation between codifications or indices and functions, and with finding operations on indices that can uniformly capture the main properties of recursive functions. The basic judgements in which all these theories rest is the relation

$$\{a\}(b) \simeq c$$

Where a is a code or index for a function, b and c are input and output data of the same type of a, and $\simeq$ is equality when the function is defined. It turned out that having a universal function, or enumeration, is strong enough to get all recursive functions if also the presence of composition of programs or indices is given. This means that in order to get axiomatization for weaker computational systems, for example for primitive recursive functions, the universal function cannot have a code in the structure, and this may imply a different presentation of the formal system. It is also possible to generalize the axiomatization to include other behaviors besides input-output. An interesting endeavor could be a development of axiomatic systems for other notions of behavior, or even some abstract version with the main characteristics that hold in any of them. This illustrates the usefulness of a relational notion of a computational system.

There is another tradition within the axiomatization effective computability, one that emphasized the notion of effectiveness, trying to characterize, in very general terms, what are the principles of mechanisms. After the pioneering work by Robin Gandy [10], there have been reformulations, generalizations and refinements of these axioms which mainly try to establish restrictions on systems in order to be considered mechanical or effective. These restrictions, based on physical and mechanical limitations, are used to prove that the transition functions that describe the system behavior will be Turing computable. It is debatable whether these restrictions on mechanisms are reasonable, and is not our objective here to discuss them, but rather to indicate that these principles do not apply only to computational systems. The fact that one can say that a non-computational system "computes" a given function seems to be a careless use of the extensional property of computability: a system S computes f in the sense that f is a computable function, not that S is a computational system. This linguistic use should not hide the essential differences.

Apparently, Hilbert's challenge entailed focusing on a characterization of effectiveness and the idea of program or algorithm remained only implicit as a means for it. Assuming the set of effectively calculable functions coincide with the computable ones, the programmability did not have any relevance in solving the Entscheidungsproblem. Furthermore, in current computer science, one of the main techniques of analysis and verification of computer programs is the generation of a model of the executions of the programs, for example its execution graph, and then working only with this model. The program disappears. This approach is also used in some foundational works, like the axiomatization of abstract effectiveness from Dershowitz and Gurevich [6], which can be included in this tradition.

4   Problems in philosophy of computation

A well-known and profusely assessed problem in the philosophy of computing is to determine whether a given system computes, sometimes formulated as what is computation, or how to distinguish between a "merely" causal behavior and a computational one. We claim that the analytical separation we presented between mechanical and computational properties illuminates what is distinctive for computational systems: its programmability, the constitutive relation between codings and behaviors. This answer seemed to be implicit in many different approaches. In the article *What is computation?*[2], Copeland tries to determine when does a system computes. He correctly distinguishes two main components, which he called algorithm and architecture. They seem to coincide respectively with our program and interpreter. As Fresco and Wolf [9] claimed, Copeland's algorithm is actually a program; we disagree, however, with his consideration of computation as the execution of algorithms rather than programs. Algorithms, in Roland Backhouse words [1],have been used for millennia, but it is only since the "computer age" that they are considered in themselves, not only as media to get something done. One of the main characteristics of their current mode of existence is that they are also just ordinary data. To understand when a system computes, Copeland uses one of the main tools in mathematical modelling, first-order logic. Given an algorithm (or program) and an architecture, he constructs a family of first-order predicates -called SPEC- which models the intended execution of this program within the architecture. Then, some particular models (not all of them) of SPEC will be considered as computations. Inspired perhaps by Gandy's characterization of mechanisms, the models of SPEC will be generated by a labelled finite system. The actions, axiomatized from the coupling of the chosen architecture and the program, are mapped into relations between the states of this labelled system. However, some more requirements should be imposed on these models in order to avoid trivializations, like Putnam's or Searle's, of the notion of computation (any model with enough different states would model the execution of any program). Copeland asks for the labelling not to be constructed *ex-post-facto* and that the model is standard, i.e. that the actions axiomatized in SPEC are interpreted as actions in the model. These conditions, however, are very difficult to enforce and it is not clear which is their status in first-order models. Moreover, the "models" proposed by Putnam and Searle, are quite standard with respect to this last requirement: action predicates are modeled as actions, only not the type of actions one would like, not actions prescribed by the program. Also, adding *ad-hoc* restrictions on models weakens the usefulness of axiomatizations which cannot express them [2].

This first-order logical approach can be pursued in a different way, in fact, it has been already used. One may exploit the fact that programs are part of data (perhaps after a codification), and instead of having a specification for the execution of one program for a given architecture, we can axiomatize the behavior of any program. For example, in the book of Neil Jones Computability and Complexity a first-order logic is defined in order to model the possible behaviors of the language *WHILE*, an imperative language that operates on

---

[2] These models are generated by a finite labelled system, but the models themselves are not necessarily finite. For divergent behaviors, in particular, they cannot be finite.

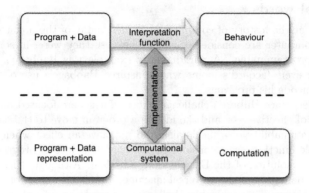

Fig. 1. Interpreter

LISP-like lists, used as a vehicle to define computability concepts. By induction on the constructions of the language, an infinite family of predicates is defined (see chapter 12 of the book for the details), one for each program. Given a program d, the predicates $G_d(e, f)$ will be true if when starting the execution of d with initial state e the program eventually terminates and the final state is f. Given this family of predicates, a new predicate $R(d, e, f)$ can be defined, which would take the role of Copeland's action predicate, in the following way

$$R(d, e, f) = Prog(d) \wedge G_d(e, f)$$

where predicate $Prog(d)$ would indicate that d is a correct *WHILE* program (it can easily be defined like a parser).

Now, a model of R can be constructed following the same idea, but this ternary predicate should be defined for any program d, i.e. in the model there will be an association of an input-output behavior for every program d. There is no need of counterfactuals or restrictions on the models, since the association established for any possible realized program will be enough to avoid trivial interpretations. This is similar to some operational semantics definitions in computer science. This one is codified in first order logic in order to use the same notion of model. The main point is to have programs and data in the same universe, both should be in the domain of the model, disregardless of its nature, whether it is a concrete or abstract system.

This way of realizing programs in computational systems is illustrated in figure 1, as a relation of relations. In most definitions of program realization the left-bottom corner is missing.

In this specification, a model will not be a computation, but rather the set of all possible computations, what is a computation should be defined as certain sequence of actions in the model. This is what is usually done in computer science, although the inclusion of the program itself as part of the model is not always explicitly done.

187

5 Final words

If we look at the history of computer machines, many of the precursors of the modern computer are considered as such because they were, in some way or another, programmable. A paradigmatic example was Babbage's analytical engine, or even Jacqard's looms which inspired Babbage's use of perforated cards to encode his programs.

However, since Hilbert's challenge, most efforts were focused on a characterization of effectiveness, and the idea of a program move to the background. The programmability of a mechanism did not have an effect when the set of computable functions were considered, and hence the idea of program was not central for a solution of the Entscheidungsproblem. Although Turing's article included a definition of the universal machine, its existence was not a necessary condition to prove it unsolvable. Following instructions as a characterization of effectiveness was an easy way to define it but, as Gandy showed in 1980, not necessary. In any case, the notion of a human following instructions allow for these instructions to belong to a completely different kind than data. Fresco and Wolf [9] assume an ontological difference between instructions and data, which is possible[3] but, we believe, it is contrary to the development of computer science. A relational account of computation, as we propose here, do not need an ontological distinction. However, as long as the system is specified, the distinction between program and data is assured by their relational nature.

The Church-Turing thesis was the main conceptual tool for the consolidation of an extensional notion of computability. The set of computable functions became then stable and it could be considered as the set generated by human computation, machine computation or mechanical behavior. In this paper we have defended the distinction between effectiveness and programmability. We also propose that effectiveness can be understood in terms of a mechanistic account through an axiomatic approach. Programmability can be, in turn, analyzed as the characteristic feature of a relational account of computation. In this sense, computability is the intersection of effectiveness and computability, and computation is a gradual concept that depends on the degree of programmability of a system.

Webb [18] mentions Turing thesis for mechanisms as "A procedure (function) is 'effective' just in case it can be simulated (computed) by a Turing machine." The fact that Turing formalism is paradigmatic as a characterization of computation, may have been the reason to identify computation with a simulation by a Turing machine, which rather quickly leads to the trivializations of the concept of computation. What makes the process achieved by the human computer a computation is the fact that he is an interpreter for all possible transitions tables of Turing machine's descriptions, and this in no way means that an equivalent behavior produced in a different way will also be a

---

[3] Actually, even von Neumann advocated for a distinction between instructions and data. He even suggested to reserve one bit in every memory word to indicate whether it was or not part of the program.

computation.

We already compared our approach with Copeland's. In order to avoid trivialization arguments, Copeland requires "honest" models, where honest means that the logical relations are interpreted in the intended way. But this last claim carries the same problems he started with (how can we characterize that some model represents the intended meaning of computation?). Furthermore, this honesty of models is not a property that can be predicated by the logic itself. He also required that the labeling of the system (used to construct a logical model from a concrete system) cannot be done *ex post facto*, what may be a good methodological constraint but it is not easy to predicate that about a given system. Our interpreters satisfy by construction both properties.

An interesting approach is the mechanistic account of Piccinini [13,14], with which we believe a fertile dialogue can be established. His main thesis is that a computer is a special type of mechanism (i.e., a system subject to mechanistic explanation) whose function is to generate output strings from input strings and (possibly) internal states according to a general rule that describes the behavior of the computer in question. Besides, being subject to mechanical explanation, the reliability of the computational mechanism is captured, in this case, by the fact that one can recognize certain lawful temporal and spatial configurations of certain primitive physical entities or states of the system (the digits) which correspond to the operations of concatenation among the formal symbols found in the abstract descriptions of computational systems. Based on his characterization, Piccinini proposes a taxonomy of various different types of computers [14] according to their components and the interactions between these components (their "architecture"). We fully agree that computational states should not be individuated semantically, and consider that his mechanistic description of computers is correct and provides good insights into what makes certain systems computational.

Although Piccinini's account of computers established a well organized taxonomy for different realizations of computational systems, and, furthermore, provides an explanation of computers without resorting to any semantical characterization, he does not provide a clear demarcation criterion. On the one hand, his characterization is too narrow, since the structural characterization seems to work fine for current computer technology, but not necessarily for older ones (for example Babbage's analytical engine) or for non-conventional ones (DNA-computers, quantum-computers, or many different computers that may come). The mere fact that these devices can be considered as computers calls for a demarcation criteria that is not so dependent of a particular class of realizations. On the other hand, it is too wide, or at least not sharp enough, since it classify as equally computational systems that are clearly different from a computational point of view (for example Hollerith tabulating machines and a full-fledged current computer). This last problem seems to be only solvable by a characterization in terms of degrees; any binary classification will have the same problem. We believe that the relational idea of interpreter (and the derived hierarchy of computational systems) establishes a general and well defined criterion for demarcation of how computational a system is. Piccinini's work may be understood, provided we agree with this criterion, in part as showing that there is a family of devices with certain architectures satisfies it. His requirements that vehicles manipulated by computational systems are medium-independent and that the rules are sensitive to certain vehicle properties, seem to be necessary conditions for our interpreters to be realizable.

Finally, many interesting relations can be established with Fresco and Wolf's instruction information processing account, and it may be the case that our explanation and theirs are compatible. There are, however, at least two important differences: First, whereas their definition of when a system computes is also gradual, the different degrees, or kinds, proposed seem rather /emph ad hoc, and only distinguish between very elementary (called trivial in their work) systems and full-fledged computers. Our definition, instead, considers as possible degrees any set of behaviors and codifications, which includes all interesting computational notions (for example primitive recursive functions, higher-order primitive recursion, etc.). As a counterpart, we do not establish a clear distinction between computational and non-computational systems. Second, as we already mentioned, in their approach instructions and processes are different kinds of entities, whereas one of the main points in our approach is that programs and data belong to the same domain.

References

[1] Roland Backhouse. *Algorithmic Problem Solving*. Wiley Publishing, 1st edition, 2011.

[2] B. Jack Copeland. What is computation? *Synthese*, 108(3):335–59, 1996.

[3] B Jack Copeland. *The essential turing*. Clarendon Press, 2004.

[4] B. Jack Copeland. The church-turing thesis. In Edward N. Zalta, editor, *The Stanford Encyclopedia of Philosophy*. Metaphysics Research Lab, Stanford University, summer 2015 edition, 2015.

[5] B. Jack Copeland and Richard Sylvan. Beyond the universal turing machine. *Australasian Journal of Philosophy*, 77(1):46–66, 1999.

[6] Nachum Dershowitz and Yuri Gurevich. A natural axiomatization of computability and proof of church's thesis. *Bull. Symbolic Logic*, 14(3):299–350, 09 2008.

[7] Andrei P. Ershov. Abstract computability on algebraic structures. In Andrei P. Ershov and Donald E. Knuth, editors, *Algorithms in Modern Mathematics and Computer Science, Proceedings, Urgench, Uzbek SSR, USSR, September 16-22, 1979*, volume 122 of *Lecture Notes in Computer Science*, pages 397–420. Springer, 1979.

[8] Jens E. Fenstad. *General recursion theory : an axiomatic approach*. Perspectives in Mathematical Logic. Springer Verlag, Berlin, New York, Paris, 1980.

[9] Nir Fresco and Marty J. Wolf. The instructional information processing account of digital computation. *Synthese*, 191(7):1469–1492, 2014.

[10] R. Gandy. Church's thesis and principles for mechanisms. In K. J. Barwise, H. J. Keisler, and K. Kunen, editors, *The Kleene Symposium*, volume 101, pages 123–148, 1978.

[11] Neil D. Jones. *Computability and complexity: from a programming perspective*. MIT Press, Cambridge, MA, USA, 1997.

[12] J. Kennedy. *Interpreting Godel: Critical Essays*. Cambridge University Press, 2014.

[13] Gualtiero Piccinini. Computing mechanisms. *Philosophy of Science*, 74(4), 2007.

[14] Gualtiero Piccinini. Computers. *Pacific Philosophical Quarterly*, 89(1):32–73, 2008.

[15] John R Searle. Is the brain's mind a computer program? *Scientific American*, 262(1):25–31, 1990.

[16] Stewart Shapiro. Effectiveness. In Johan van Benthem, Gerhard Heinzman, M. Rebushi, and H. Visser, editors, *The Age of Alternative Logics*, pages 37–49. Springer, 2006.

[17] Alan Mathison Turing. On computable numbers, with an application to the entscheidungsproblem. *Proceedings of the London mathematical society*, 2(1):230–265, 1937.

[18] J. Webb. *Mechanism, Mentalism and Metamathematics: An Essay on Finitism.* Synthese Library. Springer Netherlands, 1980.